Q'sapi

A History of Okanagan People
as Told by Okanagan Families

Theytus Books

Q'sapi

A History of Okanagan People

as Told by Okanagan Families

written, edited and transcribed by

Shirley Louis

Theytus Books
Penticton, BC

Library and Archives Canada Cataloguing in Publication

Louis, Shirley, 1946-
Q'sapi : a history of Okanagan people as told by Okanagan
families / written, edited and transcribed by Shirley Louis. -- Rev.

Includes bibliographical references.
ISBN 978-1-894778-64-0

1. Okanagan Indian Band--Biography. 2. Okanagan Indian Band--
History. 3. Elders (Native peoples)--British Columbia--Okanagan Valley
(Region)--Interviews. 4. Okanagan Indians--Biography. 5. Okanagan
Indians--History. 6. Okanagan Indians--Genealogy. 7. Okanagan Valley
(B.C.: Region)--Biography. 8. Okanagan Valley (B.C. : Region)--History.
9. Okanagan Valley (B.C. : Region)--Genealogy. I. Title.

E99.O35Q82 2008   971.1'500497943   C2008-902757-4

Editorial: Greg Young-Ing
Design & Layout: Florene Belmore
Proofing: Chick Gabriel, Anna Lizotte
Okanagan Language Consultants: Delphine Derrickson, Jeannette Armstrong
Special Thanks: Linda Armstrong

Printed in Canada

Mixed Sources
Product group from well-managed
forests, and other controlled sources
www.fsc.org Cert no. SGS-COC-003563
© 1996 Forest Stewardship Council

Printed on Ancient Forest Friendly 100% post consumer fibre paper.

www.theytus.com

In Canada:
Theytus Books
Green Mountain Rd., Lot 45
RR#2, Site 50, Comp. 8
Penticton, BC V2A 6J7
Tel: 250-493-7181

In the USA:
Theytus Books
P.O. Box 2890
Oroville, Washington
98844

*Theytus Books acknowledges the support of the following:
We acknowledge the financial support of the Government of
Canada through the Book Publishing Industry Development
Program (BPIDP) for our publishing activities. We acknowledge the support of the Canada Council for the Arts which
last year invested $20.1 million in writing and publishing
throughout Canada. Nous remercions de son soutien le Conseil
des Arts du Canada, qui a investi 20,1 millions de dollars l'an
dernier dans les lettres et l'édition à travers le Canada. We
acknowledge the support of the Province of British Columbia
through the British Columbia Arts Council.*

BRITISH COLUMBIA
ARTS COUNCIL
Supported by the Province of British Columbia

Canada Council   Conseil des Arts
for the Arts   du Canada

Patrimoine   Canadian
canadien   Heritage

TABLE OF CONTENTS

ACKNOWLEDGEMENTS

This project was made possible with the financial support from Canada Council for the Arts, the BC Heritage Trust Fund, the Department of Canadian Heritage, The British Columbia Arts Council and First Peoples' Cultural Foundation of British Columbia.

I also extend my appreciation to the many parties and individuals who assisted in the completion of Q'sapi. First of all, I would like to thank all the Okanagan Band members who graciously gave of their time to convey their memories of kinship and family ties, related stories family photographs and journals of births, marriages and deaths. Special thanks is extended to Hilda Belanger and Isaac Parker.

I also express a debt of gratitude to the many individuals and local organizations for assistance in attaining documents and photographs. First of all I would like to thank Peg Barone, archivist of the Roman Catholic Church records, for her friendly support and speedy response to my requests: Ken Mather, curator of the historic O'Keefe Ranch, for the use of the dark room, camera, photograph collection, documents, photograph development advice and overall support, especially in the early stages, in getting this work to the completion stage: to the staff and volunteers of the Greater Vernon Museum and Archives who gave their utmost to assist with the vital information. Of special note are Patrica Bayliss and Ken Ellison for the clippings from the Vernon News; archivist Linda Wills for accommodating my constant requests and assistance with copy editing: to Sheila Miller for believing that this work is important; and to all who submitted the many articles over the years to the Okanagan Historical Society Reports. These reports assisted in the compilation of the family trees and history of early settlers who leave descendants at the Head of the Lake.

I would also like to extend my appreciation to the staff and employees of the En'owkin Centre and Theytus Books who have assisted in locating the pertinent information and putting up with my late rewrites. I would like especially to thank Jeannette Armstrong and Delphine Derickson for the translation of the Okanagan names, as well as to Chick Gabriel, Anna Lizotte and Linda Armstrong for their assistance during the course of this work, and Greg Young-Ing and Florene Belmore of Theytus Books for giving me the opportunity for hands-on experience in publishing.

And last, but definitely not least, I would like to extend my gratitude to my family for allowing me the time to complete this book. And to my sister Barbara P. Marchand for the use of her technical equipment and lodging on my visits to Penticton. I also extend my sincere thanks to my mother Alice Miller, for her constant faith in me and to my mother-in-law Rose Louis for her fearless faith that Q'sapi will make a difference in our lives and in the lives of our children.

INTRODUCTION

Q'sapi is a phrase in the Okanagan language that means "long time ago." It is an expression often heard among the Okanagan people to introduce a story. In this respect, I find it a fitting title in regard to the time frame and stories told here by Okanagan Elders and families.

Q'sapi was conceived through my own search for my Aboriginal roots in the First Nations communities in the Okanagan Valley. Although no marriage record can be found of the marriage between my Aboriginal great great grandmother, Melie, and her Hudson's Bay spouse, John McDougall, their sons sacramental records list Melie and John as their parents. Melie and John were among the first settlers of present day Kelowna. John pre-empted at Kelowna in 1860s. In 1859 the Oblate missionaries arrived and proceeded to administer the sacraments to the Aboriginal and settler families. In doing so, they entered vital information in record books and journals. Today this information, even with its exclusions and errors, is important to family research. The records provide the link between Melie and John and the McDougall sons and their Okanagan Aboriginal wives.

Most of the scenes and stories recorded here take place in the northern Okanagan Valley at the Head of the Lake Indian Reserve near Vernon, British Columbia. In all, the Okanagan Indian Band No.1 is made up of seven locations. These were given numbers after the Royal Commission visit in 1913. Together they are presently known as the Okanagan Indian Band No.1 and are included here.

There are several reasons why Q'sapi is written. First, it is an effort to provide a record of family kinship lines and identity for the younger generations. Second, it seeks to promote dialogue within the family and community. Third, Q'sapi serves to pay tribute to our ancestors and fourth, it provides the means whereby the Okanagan people at the head of Okanagan Lake and Duck Lake can remember their history through stories and photographs. Last, but not least, Q'sapi was written as a means to preserve traditional Okanagan names.

The names are important as they often serve to describe the individual's character as well as creating the link between the family, their individual skills, land, forefathers and mothers and their Nation. Given the importance of names, it is no wonder that after the missionaries and government agents arrived and mingled with the Okanagan, kinship lines became fragmented and personal and community identity was nearly lost. For this reason, I have collected as many traditional names as possible and have written them here in their most simple form of expression.

Some of the dates on the family trees are taken from sacramental records that date back to 1860, while others are taken from census records dating back to 1877. However, in order as not to leave a birth year open, I subtracted ages at death and entered an approximate birth year. This must be taken into consideration when reading the family trees. Another consideration must be given to my narratives that include my search of family surnames. For instance, the Jacko name seems to first appear in the area with the fur trade. Mary Balf, former curator of the Kamloops Museum and Archives, includes the name as part of her documentation of place names. Since she suggests that Jacko owned land at Kamloops and may have been a part of the Jacco Finlay family, I researched other sources and include them here. Doing this serves to lay a foundation, if sometimes only based on assumption, for future study.

Other names, not originally included as part of the Okanagan people were brought to Okanagan territory with men of the fur trade, miners, cattlemen and settlers. Some men settled in the Okanagan and mixed with the Aboriginal people. Others married into Okanagan families. Consequently, as time went by, some men were allowed to stay on reserve while others were allowed entrance by Indian Agents. In most cases the name carried on through the descendants and are now present among the various families. In the same time frame traditional names were exchanged with English Christian names causing many of the original Okanagan families to be known by names such as Joe, Jack, Pierre and Abel. Today we find roots that stretch into the Westbank, Penticton, Oliver, Similkameen and Nicola Band as well as into the Okanagan-Colville Tribe in Washington State. Others married into the surrounding tribes of Shuswap, Thompson and Lillooet Nations families. All of these family names are included in Q'sapi, but since the English surnames are more prominent in the North Okanagan community today and a good number identify themselves by their European surnames, I am using the paternal system as a base for the family trees.

* * * *

Arnie Louie was a gifted young Okanagan man with roots in the Inkameep Band at Osoyoos. He was a credible writer of First Nation's poetry, prose and journalism. He wrote both professionally and for his own enjoyment. Through his writing he made a difference in First Nation's affairs. Still, while Arnie interests lay in the political field, he was also identified with the individual. Accordingly, when he asked to come on board as co-writer for Q'sapi I appreciated his sincerity and talent and immediately accepted his offer. As it happened, Arnie passed away shortly after we received financial support from Canada Council, but not before he penned out what he saw were the hopes and dreams of Okanagan Elders. The following was written by Arnie as part of our joint effort to record the family histories. I was told later, this mission statement was one of Arnie's most favourite achievements.

ARNIE LOUIE

"The richest place in the world is the graveyard for there you'll find stories that were never told, ideas that were never expressed and visions that never lived"

My memories are not so much of things as they are of words that gave shape and substance to my being and form to the world around me. Born into two different cultures the spoken word held me in the mystical and intimate ways it has touched others who come from similar societies and whose primary literature is oral.

In such cultures the spoken word is revered and to it are attributed certain qualities. One quality is akin to magic, or enchantment, because mystery of language and speech and the processes of their development, as well as their origin, can never be fully explained. For the same reason, the spoken word is believed to be power that can create or destroy.

Members of non-literate societies spend their lifetime reaffirming that the spoken word lives of its own indescribable power and energy, floating apart and separate from individual human voices who utter it. Yet, paradoxically, we are also shown that it is through the power of speech and the larger unified voice of oral tradition that we exist as we do.

There are many individual voices, male and female, old and young, scattered about me. These voices expressed themselves in two languages. Okanagan and English. Okanagan was unwritten for the most part. But more often than not, as if by some magnetic pull of oral tradition, the individual tribal voices unconsciously blended together with the English voice, like braided strands of thread, into one voice, story, song and prayer. That thread stretched unbroken to the pre-time and origin that still lived in the mystery and power of the Okanagan language; their spoken word even translated into English as it had been for well over decades before I was born. The echo of that tribal voice, in Okanagan and English, never disappears or fades from my ear, not even in the longest silences of the people or in my absences from them.

Q'sapi, meaning "long time ago," is a book about capturing that language, by those who remember it, by going back in time and linking memories through a family tree. Q'sapi is also a book about renewal. It is the re-birth of a First Nation's community's identity. It is about making right a wrong that has plagued this country ever since colonization. It is an exercise of re-uniting families. It is an education of a people's history and the stories associated with that history. More importantly, it is about how the printed word can come alive and demonstrate the memories of Elders, and the usage of language and how language and culture changed. Lastly, it is a book about photographs and how pictures, inter-connected with words, become alive and real to be absorbed and to be remembered.

Arnie Louie, 1998

Before contact the Okanagan people existed as one in a number of matrilineal groups of Salish speaking people of the Western Plateau. Most are recognized as groups of hunters, fishermen and gatherers with a total dependence on resources specific to their land base. And although each Nation speaks their own language, embodied within their language are their particular histories, customs, traditions, values and beliefs. These stories have survived through the practice of oral tradition whereby myths and legends were passed down from generation to generation. Okanagan legends speak of a time long before the First People.[1] It was a time when there were beings who were neither human nor animals. It was also a dangerous time for the new People who would be inheriting the land. Therefore, when the Creator saw this he chose Coyote, or Sen'klip, to pave the way for the coming People. Sen'klip had the special task of protecting and teaching the People to live on the land. And even when he fell into folly, through human vices, his antics were used in stories told by the People to teach their history, beliefs, and often morals. The People were still actively practicing their customs and telling these stories when the first significant group of European men came to the Okanagan Valley.

The original homeland of the Okanagan People was comprised of approximately 43,000 square miles of mixed desert and fertile land.[2] Historically their territories were bordered closely on the north by the Shuswap Nation, to the west by the coastal Nations, to the south by the Spokane and to the east by the Kootenay and Blackfoot Nations. The political system was guided by sub-chiefs strategically located at prime food gathering places. But it was the Tribal Chief who carried out the will of the People. He took responsibility for the safety of the People, the protection of the territories, and among other duties, regulated trade with other Nations.[3] Given that each Nation had their own food gathering territories, peace in trade made it possible to share surplus items. On the other hand, when territories and lives were threatened, wars occasionally occurred. For instance, hereditary Chief N'Kwala went to war with the Lillooet[4] in an act to avenge his father's death and again with the Shuswap over territories. This latter war resulted in the Shuswap being pushed north across the Shuswap River.[5] After the fur trade established itself in the area, hereditary Chief N'Kwala, became highly involved with the traders, not only for trade purposes, but also with horticulture and stock farming. Eye witnesses saw him growing a small crop of potatoes at Kamloops, and at another time, in possession of a primitive plow at the Head of the Lake.[6] According to his great granddaughter, Maria Houghton Brent, he cultivated such things as corn and tobacco under the direction of the Hudson's Bay Company "...at his home by the lake, eight miles down from the head of Okanogan Lake."[7] After the implementation of the Indian Act of 1876, chiefs were appointed by the Department of Indian Affairs. After that time all Indian political action became illegal and trade with other Nations discouraged by limiting the Interior tribes to their own particular reserves.

Family life is still central to the preservation of Okanagan culture. The People established a well structured existence of matrilineal family life that included immediate and extended family, distant relatives and close associations. These ties to one another, and to their Nation, created a strong sense of family and community identity. And being that the family usually resided with the mother's family, their children experienced strong maternal ties. According to history, Okanagan women were kind, strong individuals who worked along with their male counterparts. They were not coddled or weak willed. They were venerated for their gift of life.[8] Some married for the reasons of wealth and status, but the average marriage resulted in a long lasting relationship. There was some protocol for marriage, but rules were not written in stone. According to South Okanagan woman, Mourning Dove, marriages were sometimes arranged by family Elders, but "Usually the girl had the final right to approve or reject a marriage."[9] All children thereafter were raised within the family network. Being that harvest was an immediate necessity, the younger children were often left to the care and tutelage of older family Elders. Mourning Dove wrote that, "Children were encouraged to develop strict discipline and a high regard for sharing. Grandparents were always kind and indulgent, teaching morality through stories and example."[10] The family unit became fragile when the English took over from the French and the paternal system came into use. Children were then sent to residential schools and the adults confined to reserves.

In 1812, the Northwest Fur Company established a trading post at Fort Kamloops and operated under a license to trade with the Indians.[11] In their bid for economic success, the North West Company, and the succeeding Hudson's Bay Company, encouraged trade on the age-old Native trail on the west side of Okanagan lake. Eventually the trail became known as the Hudson's Bay Brigade Trail. The route began at Fort Okanagan, at the confluence of the Okanagan and Columbia River, and wound its way north to the Thompson River post at Kamloops, and into the Cariboo.[12] Early historian Frank Buckland noted that "...as many as 300 horses made up one brigade" and after a day's travel of about seven hours, the brigades stopped at such places as "...the head of Osoyoos Lake, the crossing at Shingle Creek, Westbank, the head of Okanagan Lake, and Grand Prairie...",[13] which is now Westwold. These locations, however, were not only places for the traders to water and feed their horses, but places where they formed socio-economic relations with the Okanagan. As there were few fur bearing animals in the Okanagan, they traded services such as guiding and packing, and trade items such as traps, guns, tobacco, yard goods, beads, medicines, potatoes and horses. Early fur trade explorer and trader Alexander Ross noted the skill of the Okanagan horse and rider when he wrote "...where the rabbit can pass, and where a horse can pass, the savage, who sticks to his back like a crab, passes over hill and dale, rock and ravine, at full speed..."[14] Ross also married Sally, a southern Okanagan woman, and had several children. Therefore, when taking into account the numbers of men traveling the trail and the number of Okanagan people in residence in the Valley, it is no great mystery that they would strike up relationships. Some surnames of the traders still remain on Okanagan soil.

The miners, freighters and settlers that followed in 1858 and 1859 in the wake of the fur trader were a very different set of people. When gold was discovered in Kamloops, the Brigade Trail was flooded once again with hordes of unruly, fevered men who pilfered and destroyed Indian food supplies, rampaged village sites, dug up the streams and murdered without conscience.[15] In retaliation the Okanagan threatened war which made the Colonial government take notice of their condition. To make matters worse, settlers began to encroach on traditional lands and take up valuable grazing ranges. Finally, in 1861 the Okanagan, in defense of their rights against the miners and encroachment, threatened war, forcing the Colonial government to take responsibility for the protection of the people and their right to continue traditional activities. Thus, a large tract of land for the exclusive use of the Okanagan was reserved in 1864, and noted Thomson, included good bottom land, village sites, fishery locations, garden sites and winter stock ranges.[16] However, one year later due to settler interests in ranching, the former reserve was drastically reduced, leaving the Okanagan confined to meagre plots of land. Discontented with their condition and treatment by the authorities, Native people of the Interior gathered and threatened war. To stave off inevitable conflict, the federal and provincial government formed a three man Indian Reserve Commission in 1877 to investigate Indian complaints. It wasn't until the last decade of the 1800s, and after the implementation of the Indian Act in 1876, that the reserve was enlarged to include approximately 25,000 acres for exclusive use by the Okanagan and an added 25,000 acres to be used in common for Okanagan and settler stock grazing land. On the other hand, as more settlers arrived more land was needed for settlement and under settler demands in 1893, the 25,000 acre commonage was cut off and opened for preemption. A further Indian Reserve Commission cut off other valuable resource territories between 1912 and 1916.[17] The issues of boundaries and land use among the Okanagan at Head of the Lake have never been rectified. From the Colonial period forward the people saw their lands, language, culture and traditions undermined for the sake of settlement. But, Dr. Jean Barman argues, even though,

"Indigenous people were easily shunted aside... perceived as nuisances, particularly in their persistent demands to retain land... they were never completely stripped of their dignity. They were able to retain elements of their earlier ways of life while adjusting to the new social and economic order."[18]

In so far as the question of lands and culture changed over the years, the social and family life of the Okanagan also changed. Scrolled within the annals of history are some of the ways the Anglo men infiltrated the Okanagan communities and built relationships with the Okanagan. In order to have access to Indian lands the men in collaboration with Okanagan women produced the first generations of mixed blood children. Among them were Colonel Houghton and Sophie, Charles Forbes Vernon and Katherine, Cornelius O'Keefe and Rosie, Thomas Greenhow and Marianne, Francis Xavier Richter and Lucie, John Carmichael Haynes and Edward J. Tronson and Nancy, and Charles Brewer and Jenny. All of these families are included in the family history section. They too have their own stories but are relatively distinct from the Okanagan family histories. Before turning to the other relative subjects and family histories, Okanagan Band members have offered a special view of how relationships, both within the Aboriginal community and on the fringes, cause some today to be confused about their identity. Ned Louis also gives us a closer look at the Brigade, or Native, Trail on the west side of Okanagan Lake.

Jenny Marchand: *Long time ago there was no border. The people could live anywhere. Some people tried to have other people kicked off the Reserve because they said they were Americans. But look at Pierre Louis. His father was from Oliver and his mother was from here [Vernon]. They were not Americans 'cause long time ago there was no border. And some people try to say, "Oh, those people are from Enderby. They're Shuswap!" But I remember when Narcisse Duteau and his family were living right here behind my dad's house.*

When his daughters were in the teenage years he sold that property to my dad and he went to Enderby and stayed there because that is where his sister, ol' Millie Brewer, was. And ol' Millie belonged here. She was ol' Billie Brewer's wife. The Kings are from the Duteau family and from Billy Brewer. And they say that the Kings at Westwold and Duteaus were Indians from somewhere else. Millie married another man from Enderby after Billy died in the war. Altogether in the Duteau family, that I can remember, was Narcisse, little Paul and Millie.

Edward Fred: *A lot of our Elders moved to Enderby. One of our chiefs was Pachise Nicholas. When he was no longer a Chief here he moved to Enderby and lived and died over there. Ol' Francis Thomas's great grandfather was Okanagan and he moved over there. Enderby is on the border and they speak Siw-um-pum. More Siw-um-pum than Okanagan. A lot of them people over there should be listed as Okanagan not Shuswap because they are right on the border.*

Ned Louis: *Yeah, the Thomas' at Salmon River and Enderby are my mother's relations from Oliver. They're Okanagan Indians. A lot of our Okanagan people first lived at Salmon River, Okanagan territory, then later moved over there to Enderby and as far as Salmon Arm. You look at the people too who lived at Westwold before they cut off that land. We were all Okanagan and when that cut off happened some moved to Fish Lake and stayed Okanagan. The others moved over to Neskonlith and are listed as Shuswap. Tommy Gregoire's family comes from Neskonlith and now lives here. He is listed as an Okanagan because he is!*

John Marchand: *When the Irish Creek was cut off from the main Reserve back in history, white men moved on this place. It was like a refuge for them. Those guys married Okanagan women and when the Reserve was given back those men were allowed to stay because they had Okanagan wives and kids. That's why you see men like Bessette here at Irish Creek. Ol' Peter Bessette was from a French family out at Lumby. He got married out here and stayed.*

The following mental map is given through Ned Louis. The map takes in particular areas on the Native Trail. It can be compared, in part, to Buckland's map in the Second Report of the Okanagan Historical Society Report.

Ned Louis: *The history of our people and the names of the places need to be written for our kids. It's just like the white people call the road on the west side, the Hudson's Bay Brigade Trail and claim that all the names for the places from here to Kamloops were given names by the whites, but, actually, these places had Native names long before the whiteman came here. Our ancestors lived at these places. Even today, you ask an ol' person the name for a place and they will tell you. It's like the mountains around here, they had Okanagan names, 'cause that was the traditional huntin' and berry pickin' grounds used by the people. The Penticton people still talk their Okanagan language all the time, so they still know and use the names for all the mountains and trails. The Okanagan travelled a long way over on those Native trails and they know the shortest and the fastest way to get to where they were going.*

From the east, the Okanagan came from Nespelem, Washington, over Beaver Dell through the old road on the other side of Woods Lake to Oyama. The Kettle railroad track is on the trail now and that's how they came up here to the hop yards at Coldstream and that's where a lot of people met one another. That's why you find some of our people being born over at Needles and farther over into the States, on the Columbia and Kettle Rivers. They knew the shortest route and the fastest way to get where they were going. Black Mountain and Big White are on those trails.

Black Mountain is called Sn-skal-ten, that means "to make their ammunition." The trail went into the ski resort at Big White and that was their main hunting grounds. Mom and them used the Native's names and told me when she was just a little girl, they went back and forth there on top the mountain all through the fall time and got back to Penticton just before Christmas. Most of the time they were at the Kettle Valley or on top the mountain at the Kettle River. They went there for berries too, but mostly they were there in the late fall drying meat. The men hunted and the women dried the meat. Mom used to say when the hunting is all over, the ol' fellas would pack every horse with dried meat and take it back to Penticton and the women folks stayed in the camp fixing more meat. Sometimes they said it would get pretty scary. The ol' grizzlies were all around there. The men would come back from Penticton and when they were all done the men would get a couple of fresh deer and they'd all go home together.

From here at Six-Mile to Westwold was a lot shorter distance than going on the highway like they do now. Back then they cut over the hill here and went through Pinaus Lake. They'd hunt all through there and chase horses and stuff like that.

Going south they'd go over the hill and when they got to the creek on the other side of Westbank, where the highway raises hell, they'd go straight over to Trout Creek, then to Sheep Creek then on till they hit Green Valley Road and that's the shortest way between Twin Lakes to Oliver. Ben was the only one that I know of that rode through there. He and Johnny Oppenheimer came from Inkameep to Westbank, leading wild horses, in just a day. They just cut across through Fairview and between Twin Lakes and hit the Green Valley Road then Shingle Creek and Trout Creek and said it was just a short ways to Westbank.

All the places that have Okanagan names are Okanagan territory. Even right here on the west side of the lake the white people teach our kids that it is the Hudson's Bay Brigade Trail. Actually, it's the old Native Trail and should be remembered that way.

All along, back then, you would find little villages of Okanagan people and the places that people stopped and camped. Like further south there is a Native trail on the east side of Okanagan Lake that the people from the Similkameen and Penticton travelled to get to the Mission at Kelowna. One person was ol' Kruger from Penticton. Back in the thirties and forties, ol' Kruger used that main trail to bring his horses to the valley for the horse races.

Aks-klukem is the Indian name for Winfield. That is where there was a village of Okanagan people. It is still part of our Reserve. Long time ago the people went there to fish in Woods Lake in the late fall, at Oyama, or what we call, Axts-lu-chus. Above where that amusement park was, between Axts-lu-chus and Winfield, is the place the people used to call Indian Point. Above there are the flats, and that is where the people camped and dried the fish. I remember when ol' Allen Edwards and some of the other people used to go down there with horses and camp together with the people from Westbank and them guys would fish and pack it up that hill to the camp. Back in the 1930s the game warden tried to kick them guys out of there, but that was part of our Reserve.

There is a place at Oyama where Harry Robinson was born, that is called Siwash Point. They were coming to the hop yards when his mother had to stop and camp. The point before you reach Oyama, there was an old Native road that went down to the beach. Now, there's a camp ground there. At that time there was a lot of feed for horses, so that's the reason the people stopped there. Mom told me that. She is a close relative to Harry Robinson, on the Qualtier side.

That peninsula that goes between the lakes at Oyama was all part of our Reserve. It is called Axts-lu-chus. It means "the peninsula going across." There's a graveyard on the knoll there. Dad told me that when he was in his teenage years he spent winters in there cougar hunting with ol' Smitken. In fact, that's how I got to know about ol' Smitken. They used to stay there off and on at that Island and hunt cougars on the side of that mountain. Then around in November they'd come on this side to hunt because the ol' people were getting hungry for groundhog.

Already, in late summer, early fall, the groundhogs are already denned up, but ol' Smitken can call them out of their dens. They get only what they want and go on hunting all evening then go back down to their camp. Dad said ol' Smitken would just take his mouth and give it a little twist with his hands and make that noise and the ground hog would come out and they'd shoot them with a forty-four rifle. Yep, Dad said them were the only guys that could call a groundhog out. At certain times of the year, they called the does out too, by getting a leaf and folding it up in some way or another, and blow on it, and call out the does. Then you talk about the wolverine.

One time, it was on top of the mountain behind Oyama, Dad and the Smitkens, they were trackin' down a cougar and they seen a buck. Ol' Smitken was a good shot, but somehow that time he boobooed and they went back the next day and were trackin' him. They caught up to it and I guess it died and the bears were eatin' on it. It was in a gully, with just a few bushes around it, and all of a sudden ol' Smitken said stop! He seen the two bears eatin' at the carcass. At the same time, out of the corners of his eyes, he seen the wolverine sneakin' around the draw, coming up to the carcass. They did stop and they watched and watched and watched. The wolverine came into range and he sneeeaked and all of a sudden his hair stood up and he looked really, really big. But, in fact, he is only that big! Dad said the wolverine run and jumped on the back of one of the bears, bit him and started clawing him. Well, that bear took off and he started on the other one. That one took off, and they came back after, then took off again and never came back. Dad said that wolverine gorged himself and after he got his fill he put his scent on all of it. Dad said they never shot it, they just wanted to watch and see what he would do.

At Okanagan Landing that place was called Sucker Creek, or Nka-kul-kem. Now they call it Vernon Creek. Just below the airport this way is a graveyard. The mainstay of the people lived there and they just come over here [west side] at a certain time of the year. I used to stay at the Landing over night at Jack Bonneau's place there and come up to the rodeo at Polson Park. That way I wouldn't have to come back here. The Bonneau's stayed there, and across the lake, at different times of the year. The bulk of the people lived there and came over here just now and again until TB wiped a lot of them out. That's why there's an old graveyard there and you find most of the people live here, now. Back then, if a disease hit in a village the people left that place and went somewhere else. They would only move back after a few years passed.

Back in the early days all of South Vernon was Native holdings and some of the people lived in Vernon, too. The Kalamalka Hotel is built right where Billy Swalwell's uncle's teepee was. So that's why ol' Billy Swalwell would say, "take me to my uncle's teepee!"

When I was just a young fella there was just hundreds of horses. Actually, every big rancher in the Valley never had their own ranges. In the spring they come past the cattle guard at Head of the Lake and they turn their cows loose and the cows come through here and go down to the lake and up the hill. The BX ranch was one of the bigger ranches at the time. Their cows went up here and into Pinaus Lake. The country is all open. Well, when I was a teenager those old trails were real deep and wide. They were well used. Ben and I used to chase a lot of horses on the ol' trails through here. That's all we ever did. We run on them trails. It's just in the last few years everything got fenced off and the logging and the skidding and the roads ruined all those trails. If you know the country you can still see them.

Getting back to the west side, at Nahun you look back and can see the whole valley. That's why that place is called Nahun. It was a stopping and camping place that the people used on their way south. Then you keep coming north and you will get to Shorts Creek which the whites named after Captain Shorts, but we know that place as Sna-weeo-weeo-wtn. One story them guys used to tell was one of the local guy's slave gals got away. They were trailin' her down here and that's where they got a hold of her and brought her back. There are other stories about that place too, but I don't think anyone knows for sure. Above there is Sugar Loaf Mountain which the people call Tq-waq-wa-qantn. Tq-waq-wa-qantn is the people's hunting grounds. Long time ago the people used dogs to chase the deer around on that mountain. Back down here, on the old trail, is what the whiteman calls Whiteman's Creek and that's the first place coming north that you will find a village. To the Okanagan it is known as N-klee-num, which means Birch Creek, because at one time that place used to be just white with birch trees, all the way up from the lake.

Then you come along north to Emery Robins' place, where that little rock pile is. That is Puq-pesaken. It means "white rock." Near there are some Indian paintings. Next you get to the mud hole, where the kids swim and on the left hand side of the road there is a patch of fir trees. That *is Nkaklapeenak. All the rest is pine trees, but that place is all straight fir. Then at Timmy Alexis', you call that place Spuk-lemees which means "the end of the bush."*

After that is Siwash Creek. They call it that because one time when Tommy B. Struthers lived up on the Six-Mile flat he was gone for quite a while. When he got back up the flat his neighbour, Dave Cameron asked him where he was for such a long time. Tommy B said, "I was visiting at Siwash Creek." After that, the name stuck, but to the Okanagan it is Nas-qweetak or Cedar Creek.

Then after that is Six-Mile, which is really called Sn-kla-hootan. Down here, near the lake, there was an encampment of old people that got slaughtered by a grizzly bear. From the stories from away back, the old people used to say if you see a grizzly with silver tips, there will be only one. But you take the mother grizzly she has two, maybe three, small cubs with her, and the jersey colored grizzlies come in sixes and eights. They said, them are the dangerous ones. When one comes after you, they all come. Anyway, that's what might have happened down there. Anyway, it wasn't till them guys cut their dogs loose, and they got him up on the Six-Mile flats. So that's why they call this place Sn-kla-hootan.

From here at Alex's place now, to where the teepees are, there used to be a ditch going there. It looked like a chicken's foot. And right from the road there was all these bushes growin' and that was all a Chinese village, all the way up to here. At the foot of the hill there used to be a garbage dump at the ol' Chinese campground. That dump stayed there for years. And all the canneries were workin'.

Later in years, there were two English men who acted as straw bosses. One was named Filler and one was Beesman. They didn't get along, so one built his cabin down there on the lake below Terry Jack's, and the other built his house below Pete's place, on the mouth of the creek. Ol' Filler used to come every evening to Dad's to get his milk. We ran milk cows then.

The old trail went down below the ol' St. Theresa's church at Six-Mile Creek and crossed, then went back down below Pete Marchand's place. From there it went clean around to the old spring down by the lake. That is where you'll find holes that the people made long time ago for their lodges. You can still find those holes right there in that thick bush. Then the trail made its way over to the Ko-mas-ket place, or what the people nowadays call Blacktown. Ol' Tommy B Struthers named that place. He called it that because of the black smoke that filled the air when those people there burned pitch wood. Really, though, that place had the name hahyt, or Holy Thorns, the ones with the red berries.

The Chinese tent town was a regular village. It had boards on the floors and on the sides. The tents made the roofs. There was a big tent town up on the flats [Six-Mile Creek] where the hydraulic mines are. They had a store up there, too. The Chinese didn't work in the mines. They panned for gold in the creeks. That disappeared years later then ol' Alec Clark, a black man, moved up there. Ol' Alex was from the south. He used to come to Dad's every Sunday. I guess he was a bachelor and he'd come for a home cooked meal and to visit. That is when we found out that he was dead scared of cougars. He got his first big scare on his way up here. First, he lived above Irish Creek, but a cougar scared him out of there, and he came over here on the flats and built a cabin in the open, along the creek up there, along the bench. He was there till he died in the late 1920s.

The trail then made its way over to Bradley Creek, or what we call N-sis-oolahw, where that old mission was on the bay there below Mary Abel's. The old Native Trail went from there up to that deep gully called Neehoot or Deep Creek. Up the hill from there to the top of the ridge is called tqult-kan then after that is Speep-cn or Rope Ranch. Rope Ranch is where there is hemp, or what the people call Speep-cn.

I don't know where the whites got the name Irish Creek, but the people call that place Nskapelks. That means, the bush or swamp and creek at the end of the lake. Then you follow the road and go over to where the rodeo grounds are now. Back then, it was more mud than solid ground, because of the level of the lake. They call that Nkukukalalahw which means mud hole. You go about one quarter or a one half mile further and they call that Sku-kn-kilap, which means thorns. That is over at Tommy Gregoire's place.

Then across the lake is Goose Lake range. Three of them lakes get their names from the people, like Bonneau Lake is named after Jack Bonneau who fenced off that place and boarded rodeo horses there in the early days for a stock contractor from Calgary. Then you get Antoine Lake and Jimmy Steele Lake. Jimmy had a cabin and barn there and you can still see piles of rocks that he cleared to grow oats and potatoes and turnips and stuff like that. Blue Lake is called that because it's the only lake up there that you can drink. Mule Lake gets that name because, from a distance, it is shaped like a mule's head. There's a place up there, too, that is called Sn-marcel-tn which means where Jimmy Marcel lived.

From there you swing around and go back north to Dirty Lake. They sure named that right! It's called N-kak-sitak which means dirty lake. You keepa goin' north and they call St. Ann's hill, Sn-kalt-kan. Then you come to that hollow where Round Lake Treatment Center is now and they call that Sn-lah-hoola.

Salmon River was called scuwin which means bony fish. When the spring salmon used to come up they call it n-tee-teew which means they are fat, but by the time they get here to Salmon River they are just bones. That's why they call it scuwin.

Then you go on to Falkland where the main trail cuts over to Chase and on to Westwold which is called Sookin was where a lot of our people lived. When the government made that place a cut off the people split and some went to live at Fish Lake, or Ak-look-meena, while the others went to Neskonlith. Like the Smitken girls, they lived at Westwold and then went to live at Douglas Lake and Fish Lake which is still Okanagan territory. The same thing with the Similkameen people. Charlie Allison's sisters all moved up in there too and now have relatives up there. Neskonlith is now in Shuswap territory.

Of the trail on Westside Road the Vernon News said in September 1916:

"What a thankful people the Indians appear to be. A most interesting episode took place at Nahun last Friday when two different tribes of Indians met to celebrate the completion of the road from Ewing's Landing to Nahun. The two chiefs met, shook hands and gave a speech in their native tongue, thanking the men who had been working on the road and saying how glad they were it was made thus enabling the two tribes to meet more often."

Among others to arrive to the valley over the Native trails were the Oblate Missionaries of the Order of Mary Immaculate. However, they were not the first Roman Catholic Order to establish a mission among the Okanagan. The Jesuit missionaries of the Order of the Society of Jesus were the first to establish a mission in 1846 "... at the end of Lac Ocangan, by the Indians of the Grand Chief Nolcolas who wished to cede this very fine property."[1] The mission survived for approximately one year and the only physical evidence left behind, says Buckland, was seen later through an Okanagan man who was "... wearing the priest's cassock, and another who thought the Church vestments were suitable material for making leggings."[2] While the Jesuit's presence proved to be temporary the Oblates established a more permanent foundation. Two Oblates are prominent individuals whose pioneer spirit, faith and achievements are still discussed to this day.

First of all, Father Pandosy (1824-1891) arrived in the Okanagan in 1859 in flight from the Indian wars in Oregon territory. Accompanying him was an entourage of faithful companions including the niece of Chief Francois of Penticton. After reaching Penticton, Theresa, the Flathead wife of Cyprian Lawrence, found it necessary to plead with her uncle to allow the priests to settle. After further consideration, Chief Francois relented and guided them to the south end of Duck Lake, where they spent the first winter living off the land.[3]

Finding the land to be of excellent quality for crop growing and the Aboriginal people to be potentially good for the advancement of Catholicism, the Oblates pre-empted a parcel of land and established Immaculate Conception Mission. As events would have it, their pre-emption was near a prime fishing station of the Okanagan, a place traditionally known as "N'Wha-quisten" meaning "a stone found there for shaping weapons of the chase and of war."[4] It was also a place described by Ned Louis as "a place where late in the summer, around September and October, the fish used to run in Mission and Mill Creek at Kelowna. Those creeks around there were just red with fish. The people used to camp there, and later, around November they fished at Woods Lake."[5]

Working from Okanagan Mission headquarters, which incidentally was moved to Kamloops in 1879,[6] the Oblates sought to civilize and convert[7] the Okanagan, learn their language and supervise their would-be flock until they became loyal and devout Christians. Since the area was vast they created sub-missions at Penticton, Head of the Lake and Kamloops. Father Pandosy spent six months of every year at Penticton while the accompanying priests attended to the mission at Kelowna.[8] While at Penticton, Father Pandosy chose first to baptize the grandparents of Penticton's Chief Edward. In doing so, as told by Kowrach, he changed their traditional names of So-remt and Qual-ulkh to Adam and Eve.[9] The Okanagan Garden of Eden, however, was not without obstacles. The language proved difficult and the missionaries became frustrated over the seeming lack of sincere interest the Okanagan had for Christian teachings.

Other obstacles included the long distance between seasonal camps and the competition offered by medicine people or Shamans which was, in their view, adverse to Oblate teachings. The missonaries considered the Aboriginal people to be "weak willed"[10] and prone to revert to the vices of dancing, gambling, and the practice of shamanism, if not carefully monitored. A further discouragement was the seasonal absence of many families from the main village. For out of sight they could not be saturated in Christian doctrines. Therefore, in an effort to centralize their would-be flock, the missionaries employed the Durieu system created by Father Chirouse and "...formalized by Father Paul Durieu.... The system was... aimed not only at religious conversion but also at the economic and social transformation of Indian life."[11]

Centralization of the people, however, could not have occurred without the chief's approval. Therefore, to gain the confidence of the tribe, the priests had to start at the top by working with the present chiefs. Said Thomson, "They counseled the chiefs closely and exhorted them to behave according to church precepts and to enforce compliance with Oblate-inspired regulations..."[12] When the chief was not compliant or indifferent, a church chief was chosen. Once the chiefs were in place the chief and the Oblates chose the hierarchy of captain, watchmen, policemen, catechists and sexton, as well as other minor leaders, to impose and maintain Oblate policy for full conversion.[13]

By 1872 with the help of present Chief Moise or the French, *Cinq-Coeur,* or the English, Five Hearts, the Oblates succeeded in convincing the Indians to gather in one location at the head of Okanagan Lake. Soon after the people began to adjust to a regimented controlled climate regulated by the sounding of the church bell. To his delight Father Baudre reported that at the head of Okanagan Lake the Indians "... in very large numbers had decided to gather around the church and build comfortable homes. Four years later he reported a large and beautiful church with a large house for the priest..."[14]

FATHER LE JEUNE, OMI

Approximately seven years later, in 1879, another much younger Oblate missionary arrived in British Columbia and by 1882, succeeded in finding a method to solve the communications problem. Cronin expands upon the many talents of Father Le Jeune and the history of his successful efforts.

"Gifted with a lively intelligence, a prodigious memory and an extraordinary aptitude for languages, Father Le Jeune soon picked up all the different languages and was thus able to converse with the Indians in their own tongue as well as in the Chinook jargon.... For the next eight years he traveled among the Indian bands of central BC, advancing civilization among them through the comprehension of their own tongue. He tried to teach them English, but failed in every instance. Only when every possible means of communication and learning had been exhausted... he was struck with a brilliant idea. Why not devise a system of shorthand by which even the most simple mind might be taught to read and write?"[15]

"Into a merchant's store one day walked a diminutive missionary priest and a young Indian boy.... As the trader waited on the priest he cast a contemptuous look at the native boy who he knew didn't understand a word of English.... 'You can never teach a young boy like him anything,' he sneered. 'Why do you bother with these Indians?' The priest only smiled. Then he took a piece of wrapping paper from the counter and with a pencil wrote some weird-looking hieroglyphic on it. Turning to the boy he spoke to him in the lad's native tongue. 'Read it,' he commanded.... With perfect enunciation, and in English, the boy read: 'You should not doubt the ability of others. I can speak English as well as you. Furthermore, I did not have to go to school for years and years to learn how to do it.'"[16]

Father Le Jeune not only developed this successful means for wider communication, but expanded his talent to develop the "Kamloops Wawa"[17] It was a newspaper that could be developed into a means of instruction while the missionaries were away from the villages. He began publishing in 1891 and in 1904 folded the Wawa due to the opening of the residential schools, where the English language was enforced. Special editions were published until 1917.[18] In all, Father Le Jeune worked for close to forty years out of Kamloops and died in 1930.

Ned Louis: *That's right. The ol' people used to talk about him a lot. They said it was amazing how he could speak so many Native languages. And another thing, you see, back in them days we were lucky if the priest came even once a month. Before that, he maybe came around every four years or so. So you see some of the kids didn't get baptized until they were older and some of our people were buried without a priest. But even without the priest, the people still went to prayers and benediction. You knew when the prayers were going to start because someone would blow that old buffalo horn and it didn't matter where you were down this way, you could hear that horn sound. Back then it seemed like everyone went to church for prayers during the week and on Sundays.*

Millie Steele: *Mom knew Father Le Jeune and told me that if you had a baby girl that you wanted to get baptized and you didn't have a name for her, Father Le Jeune would name them Mary. That's why there are so many Mary and Mary Anne's and Ann's on the Reserve. Yeah, she said he was great for that! He used to write to her too in English and Chinook and he'd send those little religious cards too. They were pictures of Jesus and Mary and some saints, I think. And they had little prayers and stuff on the other side of the cards.*

In the same year of the birth of the Wawa, the Vernon News included the announcement that "A one-toned church bell arrived for the Indians at Head of the Lake."[19] Then in 1894, a second church was "... being erected on the Indian reserve at Head of the Lake..."[20] However, as noted by early historians, construction of many of the early Indian village churches was often supervised and constructed by "... inexpert designers and carpenters..."[21] In the case of the Head of the Lake Church the carpenter was an inept but conscientious engineer, leading one to wonder, "... how those carpenters built that old church. The steeple was built separate and nailed to the building after. It didn't take long for it to start separating."[22] Although this church is not included in the book *Early Indian Village Churches*,[23] a photograph was discovered in Mary Abel's collection and is used on the cover of this book.

ST. BENEDICT'S PRE 1950

This church survived for fifty-four years until 1950 when the present one was built under the supervision of Father Wilfred Scott, O.M.I. While present band members have clear memories of this early church building they also remember the gatherings, celebrations and services held there in the early days. Ned Louis begins by speaking of the Roman Catholic feast days of Corpus Christi that were held in June of every year. Others build upon his memories.

Ned Louis: *We had the Corpus Christi every year. Sometimes the priest comes to the Head of the Lake, maybe Enderby, Salmon Arm and other times to Penticton and Westbank. We always knew where it was gonna be a year before 'cause the priest announced it at the last Corpus Christi. At Head of the Lake, I seen when I was just a teenage, tents all the way from the church to the highway and back down below the graveyard, all the way to the creek. The priest stayed about a week and as long as the priest was there the people stayed too. Later on in years, I was just a little fella then, them guys' horses, of course, wanted to go back to their home range, so early in the mornin' them young guys is trackin' their horses sometimes to Salmon River, before they catch up to them. They'd still be hobbled. Finally, the ol' people talked about that problem at the Corpus Christi and they went ahead and fenced it.*

Jenny Marchand: *In the winter we would go to Chief Michel's house at the Head of the Lake for a get-together after church. You should hear the singing in church. Gee it sounded nice. It seems like everybody come to church then and we have lots of fun playing ball and visiting. People knew one another then, but now, I don't know anybody's kids or even half of the parents of the kids. The people got far away from one another. It's not like it was long time ago. The priest come only about once a month, or so. Now there's mass every Sunday.*

My dad and ol' Bessette used to fix that old church before Christmas. They put little boards across and down those old rounded windows and stuck candles in every one. And they put candles all over and around the altar and when they light those candles for Christmas prayers, you could look from over here that way, and the light was just as bright as could be. Annie Swalwell, Mary Ann Marchand, Joe Abel, and other ones that I can't remember now, used to sing. I couldn't believe how they could sing! When those ol' people sing, you can just see how much they enjoy it. And at Easter, you should hear ol' Pierre Michel's wife, Buckskin Susan, sing. She knew all those hymns and her voice sounded so nice.

Johnny Pants and Mary Ann Marchand led the prayers. They took turns or helped one another. For the longest time, nobody went to the church at Six-Mile, they all came here to Head of the Lake. On Sundays, some come from Enderby, Salmon River, Salmon Arm, Westbank and Penticton. But at Corpus Christi, you should see the people! They come from Enderby, Salmon Arm, Douglas Lake, Westbank, Penticton, Oliver, Chase, Squilx and even from the States. All around the church at Head of the Lake was just packed with horses, people and buggies. And you should see when the people go around in a circle. Some people was just getting back to the church and people were still in a line leaving the church. That's how many people there was in that procession. And talk about flowers; they were everywhere along that same path. The same with the celebration for the Blessed Virgin and Easter Sunday. All those years people used to do those things.

Marguerite Marchand: *I remember at Christmas time at the ol' church. My dad [George Bessette] and ol' man Brewer used to decorate there and they'd put Christmas trees in two rows in the front entrance. The people used to go between the trees after Mass and go around and shake hands with each other.*

Lavina Lum: *That was a good way. They don't do that today. That was very interesting and touching. And at New Year's the young people would fire up the firecrackers and I don't know how old I was, but I do remember I was dead scared of firecrackers. Even today, I don't like the sound of thunder and lightnin'. Anyway, they started that and I took off runnin' and I run into the cemetery and hid between the two graves, you know, and by then I was cryin'. My mom and my dad was lookin' for me. They said, "we're lookin' for a little girl." They followed my footsteps in the snow to the cemetery. I was cryin' and they found me there.*

Ned Louis: *Them guys used to drive their buggies close to the church and it made a rut there. In the spring time the water run from one side to the other, under the church. Sometimes that water under there was really deep. That bell tower was built separate from the church. It was real tall and it started leanin' to one side. They sent Jimmy Antoine up into that tower to take the bell off. It was real tricky, but he was the only one around with a tractor, and he finally got it down and moved it to one side and let that whole thing just fall down. Not too long ago, you could still see the big rocks that made the foundation to that ol' church.*

Pete Marchand: *The steeple that held that bell was coming loose from the building and that's why they tore it down. It was real dangerous to go in there to ring the bell. I was in there at the time and I heard a noise an' all of a sudden, a two by four fell down. It scared the heck outa me.*

Jenny Marchand: *My dad was chief when they built that new church. They had to get the logs and take them to the sawmill and trade it for lumber. Indian Affairs wouldn't pay for a thing. The people never got paid for them logs. They had to work for the lumber. From what I remember, my dad, George Bessette and, I think, Tommy Gregoire from this end, worked a lot on that church.*

Rose Louis: *The church is built on the same spot where the old church was, but the doors to that old church were facing the lake. My mother [Emma Gottfriedson] went around the Reserve and collected money to buy the doors for that church. At the time the people were given logging permits. Ben and Johnny Bonneau logged and gave half the lumber to build that church. Other people did the same and people volunteered and it got built. I remember Violet Marchand cooked for all them guys that were working there.*

ST. BENEDICT'S 1950

Edward Fred: *I remember that day when Father Scott was building the new church. He had the spot measured out. We were all at Head of the Lake playing ball and he came over and asked for volunteers to help build the church. Two guys volunteered and after that ol' Brewer got a hold of me and commanded me to go way up on the steeple and repair the crack in the cross. You didn't disobey ol' Brewer. You did what he tol' you to do. He was big and one of his hands was as big as two of mine put together.*

Art Marchand: *I can't remember who else worked there, but me and Pat Wilson worked with the wheelbarrow and hauled cement for the foundation.*

Rose Louis: *Jimmy Swite used to come to the Head of the Lake for ball games. He had a candy wagon and he'd sell candy there. There was always kids hanging around him. He was their best friend. Sometimes in the warm months the people gathered there for baseball, horse races, and foot races and sometimes they'd put on a wrestling match. They really had a thing going for quite awhile and it was really something to see Alex Louie wrestle with Henry Wilson. Alex was blind but he could still do lots of things you wouldn't think he could do. No one really won, but it was something to see.*

Louie Jim built a second church at Six-Mile around the time that he was chief. Some claim that he built the church for the people and not for the priests. The newspapers, however, claimed he was a pagan and the present priest, Father Marchal, agreed with the Indian agents refusal to grant Louie Jim the chief's seat as he was overly traditional and opposed the presence of the church in the community.

Saint Theresa, The Little Flower of Jesus, withstood the opposition and remains at Six-Mile Creek as a landmark and symbol of the times when the church and DIA imposed their ideals and regulations. Sometime after Louie Jim's time the church was opened to the Oblates in which they proceeded to conduct the sacraments of the church. Mary Ann Marchand, the niece of Louie Jim, and import Johnny Andrew, also known as Johnny Pants, can be seen as remnants of the Durieu system. They helped the Oblates and were keen prayer leaders in the community.

Of Mary Ann, descendants often say that Gramma Marchand was really holy; they didn't dare talk or laugh or move around too much in church when she was there. If they did she'd use her cane on them. And if she caught the young guys gambling or not going to church she'd use her cane on them and chase them into the church. She was holy but she was strict too. When Johnny Pants led the prayers they said they would have to kneel for hours on that hard floor and pray and pray and pray. It seemed like he didn't know when to quit. They didn't like to go to benediction when Johnny Pants was leading.

ST. THERESA'S – SIX-MILE CREEK

David Parker and Ned Louis reflect back on their experience at Six-Mile and their association with Saint Theresa's Church:

Dave Parker: *I never knew who Spe-pa-cheen's family was. He used to come to Whiteman's Creek to Semo and Susette's place and we used to come up here to Six-Mile to visit Johnny Pants on Sunday. We were there one day and pretty soon I heard this sound. It sounded like pooow, pooow. Then everybody started to get ready. They put their coats and things on and told me to come with them, they were going to church. As I was goin' along there, I seen this man come out of the church and he made that sound again. Pooow, pooow. It was that man, ol' Spe-pa-cheen, blowin' on a horn. It looked like a bullhorn. I often wondered if that's why they call him Spe-pa-cheen. The name sounds like the sound of the horn!*

Ned Louis: *That horn was actually a buffalo horn, or n-pook-men, and was kept there at the old church. Somehow later on it went missing. They did get a bell but it got stolen later. In the 1930s some of the people got together at the old church and covered the logs with board siding. The roof got shingled and Willie Williams built the belfry. It was only lately that they put a new floor in there. Of course, we don't use that ol' church anymore!*

ST. THERESA'S 1970s

FUNERAL - HEAD OF THE LAKE

MILLIE GREGOIRE FUNERAL - HEAD OF THE LAKE

GATHERING - SIX-MILE CHURCH

GATHERING - SIX-MILE CHURCH

Duck Lake Congregation

Corpus Christi

Five years after establishing the Mission at Kelowna, the Oblates attempted to furnish an education to Okanagan boys of the area. Thomson's thesis is again important here as he presents a time table, origin numbers of students, their duties, and reasons for the Mission school's eventual closure in 1868.

Five students of Shuswap origin were enrolled in 1865 and 1866, and it was not until the autumn of 1866 that Okanagan parents agreed to send twelve boys. Only seven were accepted two sons of Chief Moise or Cinq Coeur and the others from families who could afford to provide maintenance for their sons.[1] While the Oblates endeavored to provide the rudimentary elements needed for a meagre education they also concentrated heavily upon the needs of the Mission. Thus the students were expected to follow a closely monitored routine of educational studies and agricultural duties of planting and harvesting, brick making and construction, and temporal duties of food preparation and meals.[2] Enrollment increased in September of 1868 to twenty boys, but by Christmas the Oblates were experiencing difficulty with the language and overcrowding. Some deaths occurred and disease became difficult to control. Parents, too, blamed their children's unhappiness, sickness and death, on being forced to live in the severely regimented environment.[3] Finally a frustrated Father Richard threw his hands in the air and declared, "The Okanagan who love their insolent children so much can keep them at home."[4] Thus, at Christmas the school was closed and the Okanagan were without educational opportunities, says Thomson, for approximately fifty years.[5]

In 1880, on the recommendation of Indian Agent MacKay, plans to establish a residential school at Kamloops were put into motion. In 1887 a school site was selected and secular staff chosen and financed by the government. Again only Shuswap children attended this school. Public opinion, at the time, was that the "... children besides being taught the three R's will be taught farming and trades" and return as "... the best civilizing agents the Government can possibly have."[6] Fifty-three Shuswap students were enrolled in 1901 and were unconditionally forced to attend for six straight years without release until later when the death rate became critical and students were released at age thirteen.[7]

Thomson notes that the Okanagan were probably spared the early residential school experiences until after World War II. On the other hand, oral history interviewees remember four students of Okanagan, Shuswap and mixed-blood descent attending this early school. Julia Tonasket, nee Duprett, and Ella Alexis, nee Cameron, were taught the basics of English, cooking, sewing, embroidery, knitting, crocheting and personal care. Julia went on to marry Johnny, the son of Chief Tonasket, and Ella married Johnny Alexis. Jimmy Antoine and Alphonse Louie were also taught basic academics as well as planting, harvesting and cultivating and some carpentry and mechanics. Alphonse stayed on at the school working for room and board and after returning home utilized his skills to assist others in their agricultural pursuits and language interpretation. Jimmy, on the other hand, used his education to promote his own ideas on the social, economic and political front until his death in 1970. However, in the early years, refusals by parents to send their children to residential school brought reprisals and threats of being jailed.

KAMLOOPS INDIAN RESIDENTIAL SCHOOL 1929 - 1930

Elders, Lavina Lum and Rose Louis, speak of their experiences at Kamloops Residential School, while others of the younger generations describe both their residential, day and public school experiences:

Lavina Lum: *The Indian Agent and the police came to our house to make me go to school. My dad tol' them that we had a school here. He said when my daughter gets old enough then we'll send her to school. But they wanted me to go to Kamloops School and were gonna put my mom and dad in jail if they didn't send me there.*

LAVINA, THERESA & DORA

That picture is when they took me away from my mom and dad. We were sittin' down eatin' when the police and the Indian Agent come. See how long my hair is? My mom [Annie] braids my hair all the time and in that picture my hair is loose and I didn't like it. My mom [Annie] always dressed me in my own clothes. In this picture that's not my dress. I was mad 'cause they put that dress on me and undone my hair. I was really mad. You can see that! After the Indian Agent and my mom [Theresa] took I and Dora to Vernon, they had all those clothes and made me wear it for that picture. The only thing Mom didn't change was my shoes and stockings. You see my sister, she was happy 'cause I was there. Then later that day, they put us on a train for Kamloops and I cried just about all the way 'cause they took me away from my mom and dad. Then it got real dark and Dora was tryin' to console me 'cause I thought I'll never see Mom and Dad again! When we got there them nuns cut my hair and that really, really hurt me.

KAMLOOPS INDIAN RESIDENTIAL SCHOOL 1929 - 1930

I turned eleven in school at Kamloops. I went to Grade Five. You know, after I went there I was so willing to learn. I didn't really like it there, but I thought while I'm here, I'm gonna learn. They taught us the ABC's and, of course, I spoke Okanagan and English, so it wasn't hard for me. I remember when Jenny and Hannah Brewer went they couldn't speak English so I talked Okanagan to them. I got my ass beat a lot of times, but they didn't beat it out of me, 'cause when I got home I still continued to speak my language. My mom and my dad, weren't on speakin' terms for a long time over that move!

Rose Louis: *When I was at Kamloops School, I had no trouble with the way the nuns treated me. A lot depended on what grade you were in. On Mondays you went down to the laundry room. Then after lunch you were sent to bed until suppertime. On other days you went to the sewing room, if you could sew. We would patch clothes and darn socks and stuff like that. In the afternoon, you had to go to school. If you were a kitchen girl then you went to the kitchen around four-thirty. Then there was some girls who were servers. They had to go and serve the food on the table. All these jobs were given to you. If you were too young, you didn't have to do anything except maybe dusting and learn how to darn socks and sew and things like that. Some times the little girls looked like a bunch of old ladies, sitting there darning socks.*

I couldn't see anything wrong with the way we were taught. To me it was a good thing. We learned how to sew and cook and things like that. We learned how to be clean and we couldn't answer anyone back. It sure isn't like it is now days. The kids sass you back. We were taught to respect the older people. I can remember only being hungry once or twice and have to admit that I stole some food because I was hungry! It never turned into a habit though. I did it because I was hungry!

In school we learned arithmetic, language, spelling, drawing, geography, reading and how to write stories. At the time I was there so were Jenny Marchand and her sister Hannah Brewer, Florence, Isabelle and Wilbur Harris. Florence has always been my good friend. I liked the younger nuns like Sister Rosalie Ida, Mary Clarissa and Mary Bridget. They played with us and we had lots of fun with them. The only time we mixed with the boys is when there was a picnic or something like that or like when the first snow fall happened we could get together with the boys for a snowball fight.

Appeals made by parents to Indian Affairs for on-reserve day school, were not realized until after World War I in 1920. The local press noted that "... an Indian Training school was to be started at Six-Mile Creek to accommodate about 30 children..."[8] Elder Ned Louis describes the event leading up to the opening of the school in 1923:

SIX-MILE CREEK SCHOOL - 1923

Ned Louis: *Dad [Pierre Louis] didn't want us kids to leave home, so he pushed to have the day school built here at Six-Mile. He went to St. Mary's Mission at Omak from the time he was young to when he was a teenage and didn't want us kids goin' to one of those schools. Julia Tonasket backed him and moved from Irish creek down here to Six-Mile Creek so her kids Martin and Casimir could go to school. The first group that went to school here were older teenagers of band members and non-status people. Some that I remember are Charlie and Victoria Marchand, Tommy Struthers, Gus and George Gottfriedson, Willie Marchand, Ida Abel and Ella Cameron. In the second group was Bobby Cameron, the Tronson teenagers and other people their age. I went there for one year in 1924.*

The opening of the Day School did not provide for the educational needs of the whole community. The reason, said Pete Marchand, was, "even though we had the school here some of the kids still went to the residential schools. If you didn't live at Six-Mile and there was no one to board you here, then you went to Kamloops."

Tim Alexis, now in his mid-sixties, compares the teaching staff at Kamloops School and Six-Mile Creek Day School.

Tim Alexis: *You know I went to school here at Six-Mile when Sister Patricia was here. She couldn't sing at all, but you know she had a really good choir. Not only that, she could tell real good stories that made you believe in yourself. She'd always point out to us that we were just as good as anyone else. That must have stuck with us 'cause you look at the kids that went there, they all believed in themselves and went on to be business people. There was, of course, Leonard*

CLIFFORD MARCHAND, TIM ALEXIS, BANKER ALEXIS, MR.CHAPIN, MURRAY ALEXIS, BETTY NEAVE (O'KEEFE)
SUSAN ALEXIS, BERTHA WILLIAMS, LEONARD MARCHAND, CHRISTINE MARCHAND, UNIDENTIFIED, UNIDENTIFIED
SHIRLEY MARCHAND, WALTER LOUIS, JEFFREY LAWRENCE, RAYMOND WILLIAMS, UNIDENTIFIED

Marchand, Bertha Phelan, Rita Clark, Vera and Jimmy Cameron and a lot more. They are all good at what they do. This is what made me mad when I went to Kamloops School. They had talent nights every once in while, but they never encouraged us to keep playing music or to believe in our own talent.

Pete Marchand: *My grampa went to school at the Mission in Omak, but he run away from there. Well, you know, in them days they were treated pretty rotten. They don't give you the proper food. They were seein' maggots in their food. That was good enough for my grampa and he run away.*

I talked Okanagan ever since I was old enough to talk. My grampa got by with my gramma and could talk it pretty good. Well, his mother was Indian from Colville, you know, and the language was a little different, but not much. I could understand it. But I wasn't allowed to talk Indian at school. A lot of my friends at school couldn't talk Indian. In them days they said don't teach your kids to talk Indian, teach them English. Now only a few can talk Okanagan.

When I was nine years old Mr. Walsh came over here and told my grampa to send me to school. I went to school with Johnny Bonneau, Hank Alexis, Joe, Sadie and Mary Parker, Elsie, Sally and Mary Jane Louis and Lilly and George Bonneau. We all went to school here. From here at Six-Mile that way, they all went to Kamloops School.

SIX-MILE CREEK SCHOOL, CLASS OF 1920s

Tommy and Mary Gregoire they come and asked Grampa if they can build a house down over there so their kids can go to school. It was then that their kids went to school here at Six-Mile for awhile. That house burned down after awhile. One night I woke up and I seen a bright light over there. Grampa and them were upstairs. I hollered at Grampa that the house is on fire over there! He came down and we went over there. Someone set fire to it.

I went to school over here at Six-Mile, only to sixth grade, that's all. But I did a lot of reading and I looked at dictionaries and I learned more from there. My first teacher was Mr. Walsh. Then the sisters came. Then I had a fight with that last teacher. My knee went out of joint when we were playing football and I was limping around there when he slapped me across the face and said, "Don't you wanna play." So that's as far as I went. I was sixteen years old then, so I left and came home. Grampa asked me what's the matter and I told him I had a fight with the teacher. Well, he went right up there and give him heck.

Eva Lawrence: *I must have went to school when I was ten or eleven and just went to Grade Three. Then Granny got a stroke and I had to quit and look after her. But I guess if I went to Kamloops School I'd be on a different path than the way I was. When I went to school there was Mary and Joe Parker, Elsie Louis and Edward Fred and his two sisters, Elizabeth and Lena Fred. Miss McDonald and Miss Hepworth were my teachers. They were good to me and I guess I wormed my way into being a pet at school. I remember Miss Hepworth used to have a police boyfriend. She'd always keep me after school. And he'd come and she'd take me along on a car ride. Either we went that way to Whiteman's Creek or up the hill above Six-Mile. I thought that was the greatest.*

MISS HEPWORTH

You know I couldn't speak one word of English when I started school. I had to have interpreters for a whole year. They were Edward Fred, his two sisters, Elizabeth and Lena, and Elsie Louis. I remember one time my teacher told me to take the cat litter to the woodshed. I guess, at that time, she thought she could tell me even though I had an interpreter 'cause I'm picking up the words. I thought she said shit house not woodshed! She saves her litter, it was hard times then, and I took it and I dumped it down the toilet and left the thing there. She asked me to go get it, so after school, I went and got it. I came back and she was so shocked. Then my interpreter came in and asked me in Indian, what did I do with it. And I told her, in Indian, what I thought the toilet meant. I told her, that's what I thought she said! That was so embarrassing!

34

My dad, Johnny Oppenheimer, never speaks English and when I got kids my dad speaks English to them instead of talking Indian to them. He would not say one English word to me when I was growing up. My two brothers Ernest and Angus went to Kamloops School and they learned. They didn't know English either when they went. Anyway, I picked up pretty fast in school because my teacher promoted me to Grade Five and I barely started that, when my granny had a stroke. So I bought a big dictionary, and the books that I needed to learn at home. Dan Logan helped me then and when Angus and Ernest came back from Kamloops School they tutored me too and that really helped me to learn. Chista Logan's wife Annie went to Grade Eight down the States and she helped me too. I remember she tried to get me to say Rumpelstiltskin. She made me say it over and over again. I told her I just can't get my tongue to say it. Somehow I said it and she kept helping me. I liked her, she was real kind and smart.

TOP ROW: UNIDENTIFIED
BOTTOM ROW: EVA OPPENHEIMER, LENA FRED, UNIDENTIFIED, WILLIE LAWRENCE

Edward Fred: *I came with my grandparents to Six-Mile when I was nine years old. I started Grade One in 1930 at Six-Mile School and finished Grade Eight, all in seven years. I couldn't speak one word of English when I started, so my cousins, Mary Jane, Elsie and Sally Louis were my interpreters. A lot of times we didn't have recess because we had to work in our gardens. We had garden plots out here between the school and the creek. We got our water from the irrigation ditch that was built by Pierre Louis and a crew of men from here. Sometimes we flooded our gardens and had to start all over again. We had pretty good gardens in the end though.*

JOSEPHINE ARMSTRONG, WILLIE WILLIAMS, LAURA MARCHAND, UNIDENTIFIED, IRENE MCDOUGALL, FRONT 2ND RIGHT: DANNY LOGAN

Riley Brewer: *I got my early education at Kamloops Indian Residential School and for another year after that I stayed with ol' Mary Ann at Six-Mile and went to school from her place. Mr. Walsh was my teacher. I went to school with Hughie Lawrence, Joseph Parker, Dan Logan, Robert, Florence and Betty Cameron, and Sally and Mary Jane Louis. That's where I got my degree!*

SIX-MILE CREEK SCHOOL GARDENS

Victor Antoine: *In September of 1949 they loaded us up to go to Kamloops School. That time they had to have the kids ready to be loaded onto the truck, over there by that little pond across from Spallumcheen golf course, by O'Keefe Ranch. The truck started off in Oliver to pick up kids and by the time they got here they were full. I remember that day because Archie and my Aunt Madeline brought their three kids to our place early that morning. And by one or two o'clock the folks drove us over there to O'Keefe Ranch.*

We didn't know what was happening, nobody told us. Anyway, the truck was too full, so they stuck two of the kids onto the truck and our folks drove me and Aunt Madeline's kids up to Kamloops. When we got there we were playing around together outside and the folks, I guess, went into Father O'Grady's office. We didn't know what was going on. They came out of the school and waved to us and said, "Be good!" and "See you!" A whole bunch of kids were crying and screaming from being left. I thought why did they leave me, what did we do wrong. Then I heard some older boys like Earl and Ernie Lezard and Bobby Joe talking Indian in another part of the dorm. I ran after them and they said, "Don't get caught talking Indian. They'll whip you!" Well, I got caught and was sent to Father Shea's office. He was the priest who dispensed punishment. You had to drop your pants and hold your ankles. He had a stick about two inches wide and three quarters of an inch thick. He whipped me and all you had to do was get whipped once and you learned never to talk Indian again.

I didn't realize until later that the priests singled you out if they knew no one was watching over you. They knew I was being watched because I got packages from home and some spending money. The priests were in charge of your money and packages and doled a little out to you on Sundays to spend at the little store they had there. Same with the packages you only got a little at a time. Anyway, I had a protector, an older boy, Bobby Joe. He knew we were related but I didn't and he became my protector and I paid him to protect me by sharing my packages and candy. He protected other younger kids too. The other kids had their own protectors as well. Those older boys settled things if we were getting picked on by other kids. They'd settle things either by scrapping or by talking it over, but more by scrapping.

One time Bobby Joe and this kid from Duncan got in a fight in the wood-working shop. If I remember right, it was over marbles, because marbles were a big thing then. There was blood all over and us little kids scattered and hide under the tables. At one point in the fight Bobby knocked the other kid down and the other kid lost grip of a steel bar that he had tucked in his fist. Bobby seen that and then they really went at it and it ended into a free for all, by the time the staff got there. But even then they had a riot on their hands and had a real hard time separating Bobby and that kid.

If kids showed that they were smart or musically inclined or good athletes they were favoured. These people sat at separate tables and ate better than the others. They got to put on school uniforms and go out to track meets and baseball games and compete in other sports. My protector Bobby Joe was a real good tumbler. Even after he got home we'd go to dances at Head of the Lake and Bobby would dance and flip right over on the dance floor. He was real good at it.

Raymond Williams: *I first went to Kamloops School in 1941. I stayed there until 1943 coming home only for the summer. I was then six years old. I went there by train through Salmon Arm. At first I thought it was pretty good because I got to ride on the train and see all the soldiers. My* dad, *Willie Williams*, took me and my brother *Dickie*. When we got there, and to the dormitory, they split us up. *Dickie* was on one side and I was on the other. Some of the guys I had to stay with were way bigger than I was. I found out later that we had some cousins there the same time. They were Okanagans, but I didn't know what an Okanagan was. I didn't even know what a Shuswap was. I was too small to know there was a difference. I remember *Scotty Brewer* was there, he was older than me. He was the one who watched over me.

Then we came back here on cattle trucks and they let us off by the corral over at O'Keefe Ranch. *Mom* and *Johnny Bonneau* were living up Salmon River by then on that place that my mom got from her brother *George Gottfriedsen*. They took me over there and I stayed with them. From there I went to Salmon River school for one year and it was there that I learned phonics and learned to read. When I came to Six-Mile School they skipped me ahead to Grade Three.

I went to Kamloops for two years, but I don't remember any crayons or reading or anything like that. So when I left after those two years I was still trying to get into Grade One. So I don't know what they did with me for those two years. I do remember we had to sing. I found out that the parents were going to be there. So when they were going out to sing I took off and sat with the other kids to watch. The next day they gave me the strap and pound and pound the shit out of me. We stayed there for Christmas holidays. Most of the kids did. But we came back for the summer. Some of the kids stayed though. They were worse off than us.

Then the following five years I went to Six-Mile School up until Grade Seven. I remember only two teachers and those were *Mrs. Olsen* and *Sister Patricia*. The year following, I went back to Kamloops School where I started Grade Nine. They never assessed me or anything, they just put me in Grade Nine. I came home again and tried to attend Grade Ten in town.

At that time the band had a little bus and they picked up *Bertha*, *Vera*, *Leonard Marchand* and *Lloyd Wilson* and I. But I couldn't go that way. Kamloops was so different. I fell behind and I quit. Speaking for myself, I found public school was hard. I didn't know how to ask questions. Kamloops was so structured. We just did our work. Later, I thought about it and thought we should have stayed in public school until we graduated and then maybe we would have gone on from there and knew what we wanted out of school. Anyway, I quit after about six months and was going to follow *Lloyd Wilson* down the States because he quit at the same time. But I ended up in Vancouver somewhere. Then I came back and went back to Kamloops.

I liked sports and gymnastics and playing ball when I was at Kamloops before. But I really liked gymnastics. We had won four out of five championships at Burnaby while I attended at Kamloops. But all I wanted to do was graduate. I didn't try to get good marks. I wanted only to get by and pass on into the next grade. That's why I got only average marks on that report card. When I graduated from Kamloops School I didn't have a clue of what I wanted to do or what I wanted to be. Then in 1957, until 1960, I worked in construction. After working for three years I talked to those guys in Vancouver because I wanted to be an electrician, maybe even engineering, but they advised me to try university and go in for a physical education teacher and maybe go back to Kamloops to teach P.E. So I did and attended UBC for one year.

At first, I thought I don't have a hope in hell of getting along in there. But I went along anyway, at the same time with Vera and Leonard Marchand. I signed up for classes and took chemistry, physiology, math, English and French. Why I chose those electives I don't know but I bombed on chemistry.

At UBC I got to play all kinds of sports such as gymnastics, swimming, boxing, track and field, and even some football. I was only one hundred and thirty-two pounds then and a lot of them guys were a heck of a lot bigger than I was. But I couldn't get organized, or know how to study, and was on my own for the first time. I wasn't used to that, especially after being in residential school where you always know what was going happen next. Anyway, after that one year at UBC, even though I still wanted to become an electrician, I ended up taking electronics at King Edward Vocational School in Vancouver. There I took up radio telecommunications and after two years graduated with an international certificate of proficiency in radio. Then went to Ottawa for six months to take up meteorology for radio operator for the Ministry of Transport. After that I went to Alaska and worked there for quite a few years and came home after that.

Peggy Green, now a band member through her marriage to William Brewer was the last instructor to teach at the local day school at Six-Mile Creek. Rather than include her story in the family history section, it is better included here, as her story illustrates the closing of an era of education at Okanagan Indian Day School:

Peggy Brewer: *In 1950 I was working in Jasper, Alberta. That was the year that the C.N.R. strike came. At that time, most of the guests came by train to Jasper, but because of the strike most of them couldn't get in there so by the end of the season we didn't have much money. We were only being paid minimum wage and we relied mainly on tips. I wanted to go to school for social work and was worried that I couldn't pay my tuition. My brother wrote me and said why don't I write to Indian Affairs to see if I could teach on one of the reserves. So I did, and a few days later got a phone call to go to Edmonton for an interview. At the interview they said there was a job in the Okanagan, but they needed two teachers. The girl that was with me at Jasper, Marion McPhee, had taught school before and was older than me. So she agreed to come with me to teach. We didn't get here until the middle of September 1950. We went to the Indian office in Vernon and they said they would give us a ride out here.*

We went to get some groceries first and we came out. Of course, the road was just gravel then and it didn't cut through the L & A Ranch then either. And neither was O'Keefe Hill like it is now. It was steeper, but we kept driving farther and farther into the bush to get here. Finally, we got to Six-Mile and went into the school. It was real dirty, because they hadn't had classes for a year. So our first job was to clean it up and we scrubbed that bare board floor. Chief Pierre Louis came over and we told him that school would open in a few days after we got it cleaned up. When we did, Marion taught Grade One to Three in the morning and I taught Grade Four to Seven in the afternoon. We only had scribblers, pencils and rulers when we started. We didn't have teacher's aids or not even a teacher's guide, just the basics.

We stayed right there in the living quarters. Marion was dead scared at night. She used to tell me there was people outside looking in. I thought she was nuts. I found out after that that those boys used to ride horses and they used to come around at night and look in at us. I guess they were curious. Then Father Scott helped us quite a bit. He offered us his car, but neither of us could drive. He was good to us too in other ways and helped us to manage to survive.

I hadn't worked with Native people before coming here but had gone to college with some in Prince Edward Island. They were active in sports and that's where I got to know them. Actually, they used to come from Lennox Island across to Prince Edward Island and go around to different communities and sell their baskets. They'd set up camp in my cousin's place, that we called The Woods. They used to come to our place and my mother used to give them things. The only difference between those people and us here, is that they were a lot more Indian. They had a school on Lennox Island that was run by the sisters.

The first Saturday here came round and we needed groceries. Being from Prince Edward Island we were used of a store being close around so we started walking. We got to the Ko-mas-ket place and there were some people fencing there. I don't know if it was Charlie Lezard and maybe Eddie Wilson, but they were older men. We asked them how far it was to Vernon and they laughed and laughed because we were starting to walk. Then somehow we got Joe Lawrence to give us a ride to town. He used to have a vegetable garden and went to town sometimes. Then the old mailman, Mr. Goldie from Ewing's Landing, would take us, but could only take one of us. So we alternated every Saturday.

Bertha, Timmy and Pat Wilson were my Grade Seven students. And of course, all the other kids from Six-Mile were in the lower grades. I remember going over to see Eddie Wilson to see if he would send Martin and Percy Wilson to school and he wouldn't. I remember he was chopping wood, and Martin told me later that he was so glad because he thought the old man would let him go to school but he wouldn't. In fact I went a couple of times to see them. They lived in the old house then where Percy's house is now.

They had those big long desks in the school at that time and you really had to teach because it was so crowded. We didn't have any problem in the classroom with discipline, but did have some problems on the playground. All in all though, I found that the children wanted to learn. The classes were quite large so sometimes it was hard to teach but they behaved really well. Like I told Dora Alexis yesterday, the kids I had in Grade Seven, like Bertha, Timmy and Pat, they went on in school. Bertha went on to finish school in town and graduated. Timmy went on the graduate at Kamloops School and Pat stayed home to work because his dad, Henry Wilson, was in hospital with tuberculosis. They had enough of a basic education at Six-Mile to continue in their grades elsewhere. They said it was kind of difficult at first because they were away from their families, but they got on well after they adjusted.

I'll never forget Evelyn Paul [nee Louis] at one of the Christmas concerts. We tried to have a newspaper and Evelyn picked up things from the community, you know, about different people, and she would pretend to read the news in front of the class at the Christmas concert. It was hilarious. They were supposed to be a bunch of women sitting around talking and reading about social events. All the older girls together created this newspaper skit as the play of the night. It was lots of fun for everyone.

I met William through one of the dances we held at the school. Some of the boys used to come to the school in the evening to play crib. As a matter of fact, Ed Wilson taught me to be a good crib player. He was always trying to beat me so I had to pay attention. They used to come to play cards and the Alexis' used to come and play music and tell stories. It was at one of those dances that these same older boys dared me to go ask William to dance. And I did. Then right after that he left. That was the first time I really saw him.

Then later Father Scott brought William and Raymond Simla down to the school and they had supper with us. After that they said let's go down to Johnny Lawrence's and play some music. That was the first time I really met William. Then I started going out with him during that summer and we got married in June. It was when I married William that Indian Affairs told me that they no longer needed my services as a teacher and gave me a job as school councillor for DIA. At the time the teaching position wasn't refilled. Their reason was because my aunt, who lived in Victoria, wrote a complaint to them. She resented the fact that I was marrying an Indian. However, in 1961 they couldn't get another teacher, so Mr. Hett, the Indian Agent, asked me to go back to teaching. I taught until 1967 and after that the kids were forced to go to school in town.

I've been told by some of my former students that going to school out here was the best years of their lives. That they missed being close to home and the social activity that once went along with having a school here. Once the school closed the community spirit that went along with having a nearby school also faded. It saddens me to think that the public schools at the time didn't realize the potential of the Native students or try to promote their talents.

To date the children of Okanagan Band attend public school in Vernon while others further their studies at post secondary colleges and universities. It is to their credit that the band has produced many trained people. Primary education is offered at the pre-school and day care centre at Blacktown.

NEW SCHOOL BUILT AT
SIX-MILE CREEK 1950

IRISH CREEK SCHOOL
BUILT AT HEAD OF THE LAKE
1950

As World War I approached, the Okanagan people were undergoing many changes. It was the era when Chief Baptiste Logan was replaced by Chief Pierre Michel. The Spanish Flu epidemic confined people to their homes. Yet whether it was from the Armed Forces ads, or the anticipation of journeying abroad, the Okanagan of the valley and the neighbouring Shuswap enlisted for active duty. Two local men did not return from WW I. Johnny Harris, a family man, and husband to Harriet Maloney, joined the Infantry at Ewing's Landing and died from head wounds while in combat, August 15, 1918. Billy Brewer, also a family man and the husband of Amelia Duteau, was also killed in France in 1918. He left three children. Others known to have joined in the war effort were Charlie Parker, Harry Parker, Manuel Bercie from Enderby, Harry Tronson, William Lawrence, Charlie Edwards, George McLean, Charlie Simpson, Tommy Armstrong and five Tronson boys.

Between 1939 and 1945 while Pierre Louis was Chief several more Okanagan men and women enlisted for service. At home, the political atmosphere was still strained. For some it appears these were the lean years, given the era followed the great depression. On the other hand some still maintain that they fared better than most as their homegrown gardens produced needed supplies. Socially the people enjoyed gatherings such as dances, rodeos, horse racing and baseball. Since the army camp was located in Vernon the people considered themselves fortunate to meet soldiers from neighbouring reserves. John Marchand expands on these most interesting times in the following section of wartime experiences.

Friends and family have proudly submitted the following names and photographs for the purpose of preserving the Okanagan's effort in World War II: Albert Saddleman Sr., Edward Fred, John Marchand, Willie Williams, David Parker, Richard Parker, Angus Oppenheimer, Art Brewer, Stan Mitchell, sisters Winifred and Florence Harris, Riley Brewer, Johnny Shuttleworth, Gilbert Antoine, Wilbur Harris, Thomas Struthers Jr., Bobby Cameron, William Steele, Norman Steele, Joseph Fraser, and the six Simpson sons from Duck Lake – Clarence, Harvey, Ernest, Percy, Tom and Bert. Willie Lawrence re-enlisted and served as guard at Vernon. Other would-be service men enlisted but were denied due to recent contact with tuberculosis and related health problems. Others were refused because they had large families. Three out of these twenty-six soldiers did not return home. Albert Saddleman was killed in Riccione, Italy, 1944. Joseph Fraser joined the US Marine Corps and was killed in 1944 in Germany. Clarence Simpson was killed in France in 1944. The following stories were collected from Okanagan veterans.

David Parker: *I joined the first Special Service Force in 1942. That means we were a group of highly specialized people such as mountain climbers, amphibious divers, skiers and paratroopers. All throughout the war I didn't shoot at anybody and nobody shot at me. I was on night patrol, wandering around in No Man's Land, seeing what the enemy was doing and things like that.*

You know that story about "A Bridge Too Far?" I was there, but not to the bridge. I thought we already sank that bridge, but it was a different one that we sank. That was a great big one that goes across the Rhine River. When I finally got there that bridge was down in the drink. We had Bailey bridges; one goes and one comes across. [mimicking Owen Bradley] We thought "we were goin' into Berlin with heavy loads and tanks and we were gonna chase them dog-gone Germans and we were gonna come down hard on 'em!"

I was in England after the war and went around bivouacing – camping out in tents. When I was there I got word to go for an audition. So I went and picked up my guitar and went to Army Show Headquarters. I sang a couple of songs for the sergeant major. After the audition, I saw him write "Better than average. Personality pleasant." So I take it they liked my personality and talent. Anyway, he then told me that they didn't have a western show in progress right then. I thought, well, I just as well go back and play around the bivouacing! But before I left, I was told to go have lunch. So I did and after visiting a while, I went down where the huts were and saw the show people practicing their dances and they were all singing and yodelling. Well, to me, that was heaven! I thought to myself, "Dog-gone, I'd like to be here." After a while of watching on, I picked up my guitar and went toward the highway to get a ride out of there. Then all of sudden here come the sergeant major and a corporal. He said the corporal here would like to hear you play your guitar and sing. So I went to where the show was just getting organized. The name of it was Hill-billy Blues. A special show for hospitals.

They asked me if I knew anything with a hillbilly lilt to it, you know, hillbilly sound. I said how about this one, "Love don't mean a thing in my life, somewhere, somehow, I'll live..." So that is what I did after that. We would stay at the hospital and entertain the soldiers that were taking treatment from their war wounds. And I guess that is where I played and sang for Edward Fred. It wasn't until I came home that he told me about this. Then I knew who he was.

Edward Fred: *I didn't volunteer for the services, I was lured in when I was in Vancouver looking for a job at the shipyards. I heard about the logging in Scotland and joined up. Anyway, they put me through Driver Mechanics training and I went overseas with the Third Division Infantry. I never touched a vehicle while I was in the army but was driving one for a friend when we had a wreck. I ended up in the Horsham General Hospital in a body cast when I seen Dave Parker. But I saw his grandfather first.*

I was in Vancouver for Basic Training when I was walking down the street and heard someone calling my name. He was yelling to me, saying, "Hey! Edward Fred!" I looked around and didn't recognize anyone, then saw this red-headed man with a red coloured mustache standing on the corner across the street. It was Charlie Parker, Dave Parker's father. Yep, all them Parkers had red hair and blue eyes.

Dave and his hillbilly band came in there when I was in that hospital in a cast. He sat on the foot of my bed, picked up his guitar and sang a song for me. At that time I was thinking to myself "that good lookin' blue-eyed whiteman sure can sing."

I didn't recognize him and he didn't recognize me. It was three or four years after the war that we were having New Year's dinner at my home that I saw Dave again. He came to my home with my logging partner George Parker and his family. He seen my guitar, picked it up, tuned it a little and be dog-gone if he didn't sing that same song. I asked him if he was ever in the Sixteenth Canadian General Hospital in England. He said, you know how he talks, "Well, yeah, I coulda been." It was then I officially met him. Yep, all them Parker's had red hair and blue eyes.

John Marchand: *Billy Cohen got a logging contract at Copper Mountain, above Princeton, in the late summer of 1940. Billy, Stanley Mitchell and I worked there until the snow got too deep in late November. We then came down and stayed at the Princeton Hotel and that's where we heard* *about logging in Scotland for the war effort. Anyway, we enrolled and because we did, the army picked up the bill at the hotel and paid for our rooms and meals. A few days later they sent us uniforms. We were then bussed to Penticton for the rest of our army tests then on to the Vernon army barracks, and then on to Vancouver for Basic Training. It was then that we found out that we had to be forty years old or older to go to Scotland. So then we had to choose between the infantry or the artillery. We chose artillery because Willie Lawrence told us that the infantry had to walk everywhere and we didn't want to do that.*

First we were in training at Vernon, then went to Borden, Manitoba, for advanced training. Then we were sent overseas in July of 1942, and were supposed to be stationed at Borden England, but because that was over full we went to Bramshott Light Anti-aircraft Training Base. Once there we spent three weeks training as re-enforcements to units already out in the field. That was when Stan and I were separated. They divided us into two divisions and our numbers were on the dividing line. We tried to stay together but you can't break the rules.

In the summer of 1942, Stan and I were sent back to the Vernon Army Camp from Vancouver for six weeks training before we went overseas and on weekends were allowed to go home. At the time the Indians from out here used to go either to Mings or the Commodore Cafe. So we knew we could get a ride out to the Reserve. On Friday nights we'd all walk down to Mings and, of course, some of the other Indians couldn't go back to their reserves, so they'd come out with us. One time, I remember, we caught a ride out with Joe Lawrence. He was farming then and about thirty of us soldiers hopped in the back of his truck and rode out as far as Six-Mile. That's what we would do. We'd ask different people if we could have a dance at their house or if we could gamble. Ol' Bessette, Uncle Pierre Louis, my dad, Johnny Alexis and sometimes Harry Parker would let us have dances at their houses. Johnny Alexis' house, though, had the best place for dances and he was easiest to deal with. Bessette let us gamble as much as we wanted. But the best place to gamble was at Six-Mile.

Narcisse Jack was a good gambler. He gambled a lot and knew the soldiers had money. So we'd get off at Six-Mile and go down to a place near the bridge where it was all tramped down from people fishing there. We'd make a fire and gamble all night with Narcisse. Then when there was no more wood around there we moved up to the playground. There was a road there that went between the ball field and your house and Harriet's place. It went to the range through Ben Louis's place. At that time there were lots of stumps in there, so we'd gather boughs and sticks and put them on the stump and light it. That way we could have a fire all night. Usually around three o'clock in the morning we'd shut it down and come back the next night. And that's probably why that picture is taken on the Six-Mile Bridge. Those soldiers probably came out with one of us and were together there. I remember most of the soldiers were from Cache Creek, Deadman's Creek and Merritt. Some, we got to know, were even from Williams Lake. I remember a guy named Minnie. He was probably part of the Minniberriet family from Cache Creek.

During the war I went to Germany, France, Belgium, Holland, Italy and the Mediterranean as a gunner in the Anti-aircraft Artillery. We had a few close calls overseas, but mainly I spent my time as a gunner, shooting at German planes and on reconnaissance duty, walking around the German side to see what they were doing. One of our last jobs was to clear the Friesland Islands in Holland of any explosives. They gave us a Dutch skipper, a tugboat and three barges to do the job. There were two Canadian soldiers and three German prisoners. The skipper told the prisoners what to do and we just stood around with tommy guns and watched them do it. Then in the fall we moved a hospital from Haarlem to Willmshaven. All we did there too, was sit up on the platform of the boat and watch the Germans load and unload.

Cigarettes were like gold overseas. While I was over there, one half my pay went to my mother and the other half she made a deal with the Hudson's Bay store to send me cigarettes, fruit cake and stuff like that. We were supposed to get it once a month, but because we were on the front lines we'd get it only once in awhile. While we were moving the hospital, me and the other Canadian soldier named Bernside and those three Germans would get off the boat and trade cigarettes for fresh vegetables. They tasted like a million dollars after all that time of eating only bully beef, powdered vegetables and powdered milk.

I only saw Allan Manuel from Kamloops while I was overseas and, of course, Edward Fred from here. I saw him at Aldershot standing across on the street corner as we were waiting to be sent home.

I arrived home on the sixteenth of December 1945 with a kit full of cameras, rings, brooches and wristwatches. Mom was staying in Tuma's [Lena Lawrence] log house, down below George Bonneau's place then. The house burned and all those things burned too. I don't know where my medals were. Anyway, they got saved.

When I got home I saw Joe Lawrence was farming so with my veteran's pay of fifteen hundred dollars I bought a tractor and a cultivator and went to work for Joe. That didn't last too long though. And I often wonder about the money I got from the army.

Robert Struthers: [speaking for his father, Thomas Struthers] When my dad was in the army he was picked on because he was an Indian. He was just a little guy compared to some other soldiers. He said it was the French Canadian soldiers that stood up for him. When them other guys would threaten him those big French Canadians would stand between them and after that they left my dad alone.

He said he was in a crowded bar overseas somewhere and went up to the bar to get a round of beer for him and his buddies. He heard someone call his name and he said he didn't pay attention to it because Tommy is such a common name. Anyway, the second time he heard it, someone called his full name, Tommy Struthers! He said he looked back and saw it was Albert Saddleman Senior. So that night they partied together all night long and the next day they were sent out. He said he was the last one he thought that saw Albert alive. Albert was killed in Italy.

Norman Steele: I joined the US Navy in 1943. After I quit work at the Graham and Willis Ranch in Keremeos, Ernie Simpson came and he and I started chasing around together. We decided to join the army. I signed up in Vernon when I was sixteen. I would have never got caught but this sergeant knew my Dad. He said, "What is Willie Steele to you?" Like a dummy, I said, "My dad." I could have said my brother! Anyway, they phoned the agency and found out my true age and said, "Don't call us, we'll call you." From Vernon I phoned Bill Derrickson down here in the States and he said I could baby-sit for him. While I was there I got a job as a baker and short order cook. Then Bill signed for me to join the Navy. I didn't have the schooling to join the Air Force. I should have told them I had Grade Nine because in Canada the education is way above *the education in the States. I joined when I was sixteen. I wrote to my dad, he was in Scotland, but he wanted me to join the Cadets. I was a baker. We were stationed in the South Pacific and were at war with the Japanese. I was discharged in 1946 and came home. The older guys with families were sent home first, then us younger guys went home last.*

My dad, Bill, served in the Canadian Forces in Scotland at the same time. Even though he had only one kidney from an accident with a horse and buggy he was still allowed in the Service. He was in the Searchlight and Artillery. When he got hurt they transferred him to logging in Scotland. He got hurt there and they sent him to Vancouver for an operation. And his friend, a red-headed soldier, told me that they didn't strap him into his bed and he fell out and died. I got a bus ticket and went to stay with Lottie, my stepmother. Only Lottie, Aunt Mary and I and some soldiers were at his funeral.

Tom Tronson: *There were five Tronsons in the first World War. Four of my uncles joined in on the second war. My grandmother was so worried that they'd never come back. They said she died of a broken heart and worry four months before the war ended. But all her sons came back. It took a long time to get Dad's pension straightened out 'cause he lied about his age to get into the army. He was only fourteen. He was kept back though 'cause he was so young and when a lot of guys got killed he was sent to the front lines.*

Riley Brewer: *I was sent to England as a replacement in the Artillery. But I never saw action. Instead I got sick with the mumps and spent the entire time in the hospital. They sent me back and I came home by train in 1945 when the war ended. The only people I saw over there was Lorenzeto and Cohen, and Tommy Dennis from the Similkameen, and Al Manuel from Kamloops.*

GROUP OF SOLDIERS

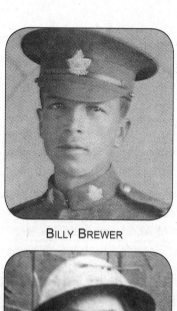

BILLY BREWER

CHARLIE EDWARDS

JOHNNY HARRIS

MANUEL BERCIE

GEORGE McLEAN

CHARLIE PARKER

HARRY PARKER

CHARLIE SIMPSON

JAMES TRONSON

HARRY TRONSON

ALBERT SADDLEMAN

ANGUS OPPENHEIMER

RILEY BREWER

EDWARD FRED

ERNEST SIMPSON

JOE FRASER

WILBUR HARRIS

FLORENCE HARRIS

JOHNNY SHUTTLEWORTH

JOHN MARCHAND

NORMAN STEELE

BILL STEELE

RICHARD PARKER

DAVID PARKER

HARVEY SIMPSON

BERT SIMPSON

CLARENCE SIMPSON

TOMMY STRUTHERS

STANLEY MITCHELL

WILLIE WILLIAMS

TOM SIMPSON

WILLIE BESSETTE, PAT WILSON, UNIDENTIFIED, ANGUS OPPENHIEMER, UNIDENTIFIED, ERNEST OPPENHIEMER
EDWARD BONNEAU, CASIMIR TONASKET, HENRY WILSON

PHOTO COURTESY MARY ABEL COLLECTION

ISAAC HARRIS

PHOTO COURTESY EDNA GREGOIRE

BACK ROW: UNIDENTIFIED, JOHNNY JONES, JOHNNY BONNEAU,
WILFRED BONNEAU, MIKE LOUIS, ALFRED BONNEAU, DICKIE WILLIAMS
FRONT ROW: UNIDENTIFIED, JOHN MARCHAND, FRED LOUIS,
WILLIE WILLIAMS, TIM ALEXIS, PAT WILSON

PHOTO COURTESY BERTHA PHELAN

BACK ROW: ALFRED BONNEAU, GRADEN ALEXIS, MURRAY ALEXIS, TIM ALEXIS

MIDDLE ROW: GEORGE BONNEAU, UNIDENTIFIED

FRONT ROW: ARTHUR MARCHAND, STEVE MARCHAND, JOHNNY ALEXIS, JOHNNY BONNEAU

BACK ROW: TIM ALEXIS, UNIDENTIFIED, WILFRED BONNEAU, ALFRED BONNEAU, GRADEN ALEXIS

FRONT ROW: GEORGE BONNEAU, MURRAY ALEXIS, STEVE MARCHAND

PHOTOS COURTESY BERTHA PHELAN

BOXING CLUB

BACK ROW: WALLY LOUIS, LAWRENCE LACROIX, GEORGE LOUIS, WILLIAM WILSON, MIKE LOUIS, LLOYD WILSON

FRONT ROW: MARTIN WILSON, FRED LOUIS

FARMING ON GOOSE LAKE RANGE   COURTESY MARY ABEL COLLECTION

FRANCOIS GREGOIRE ACTING AS GUIDE   PHOTO CREDIT GREATER VERNON MUSEUM AND ARCHIVES

OKANAGAN FAMILIES

PELKAMULOX / N'KWALA

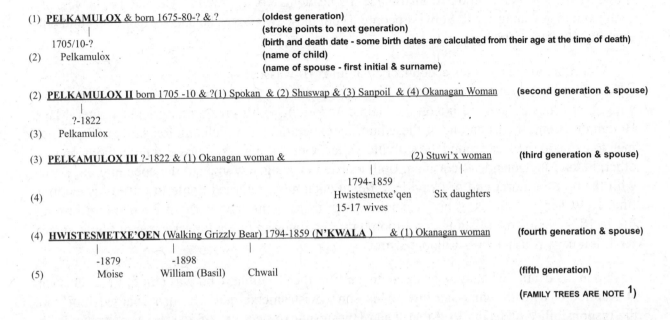

(family head)

(1) **PELKAMULOX** & born 1675-80-? & ? — (oldest generation)
(stroke points to next generation)
(birth and death date - some birth dates are calculated from their age at the time of death)
1705/10-? (name of child)
(2) Pelkamulox (name of spouse - first initial & surname)

(2) **PELKAMULOX II** born 1705 -10 & ?(1) Spokan & (2) Shuswap & (3) Sanpoil & (4) Okanagan Woman — (second generation & spouse)
?-1822
(3) Pelkamulox

(3) **PELKAMULOX III** ?-1822 & (1) Okanagan woman & (2) Stuwi'x woman — (third generation & spouse)
1794-1859
(4) Hwistesmetxe'qen   Six daughters
15-17 wives

(4) **HWISTESMETXE'QEN** (Walking Grizzly Bear) 1794-1859 (**N'KWALA**) & (1) Okanagan woman — (fourth generation & spouse)
-1879   -1898
(5) Moise   William (Basil)   Chwail — (fifth generation)

(FAMILY TREES ARE NOTE [1])

There were three Pelkamulox's in the line of hereditary chiefs before Hwistesmetxe'qen was born in about 1794. The role of chief and the name Pelkamulox was inherited, and prevailed until Hwistesmetxe'qen succeeded his father, Chief Pelkamulox III, in about 1822. The hereditary line of chiefs lasted until 1876 when governmental regulations were put into place and chiefs were appointed under the conditions of the Indian Act.

There is not much documented about the line of chiefs with the name Pelkamulox until the time of Pelkamulox III. However, enough evidence remains to provide the framework to compile a family tree. Fourth generation Hwistesmetxe'qen became known as N'Kwala by the people and given the name Nicholas by the fur traders. Shortly after N'Kwala died, while his son Moise was in power, the process of leadership changed to the degree whereby traditional hereditary chiefs were accepted mainly by the chief's cooperation with the Roman Catholic missionaries and the various governments. As for N'Kwala, some voice the opinion that he sold out the people to maintain his relationship with the officials of the fur companies, while others see him as the last of the great and powerful chiefs in the Pelkamulox line.

According to James Teit and his informants, the first Pelkamulox, or "Rolls over the Earth," was born about 1675 to 1680. He was a Grand Chief and made his headquarters with the Spokane e people. Pelkamulox II was born between 1705 and 1710 and took the former chief's position. Pelkamulox III was the successor to Pelkamulox II and it is with him that more detailed information emerges.

It has been said that Pelkamulox II was chief of the Spokane and according to Teit's sources served as chief of the same people but left his own tribe at Spokane and lived chiefly among the Sanpoil, Shuswap and Okanagan people. He made his headquarters near where Oroville, Washington is today at the junction of the Similkameen and Okanagan Rivers that was called Stuwi'x for its fortress of heaped up stones. Pelkamulox had four wives, one each from the

Spokane, Shuswap, Sanpoil and Okanagan. The fourth wife was the daughter of a head man at Stuwi'x. His son Pelkamulox III also made his headquarters at Stuwi'x. He had two wives, one each from the Okanagan and Stuwi'x people. From these two wives he had six daughters and only one son, Hwistesmetxe'qen.

According to most written accounts Pelkamulox III was a great leader of wars and expeditions. He traveled both near and far making friends and allies with other tribes. He travelled together with other tribes to hunt buffalo on the plains. According to his great great granddaughter, Maria Houghton Brent, it was on one of these hunting expeditions that Pelkamulox saw the first white men to come to the area around the Colville Valley. One was named Legace, a Frenchman and the other, Finan MacDonald, a Scotsman. Both married Okanagan women. After spending the winter with them at the north end of Colville Valley, Pelkamulox returned home to tell of his exciting find. However, his stories of his association with these white men without women cost him his life in 1822. While on a fishing expedition with the Shuswap to the Fraser River at Fountain and Pavillion he was killed by a Lillooet arrow.

Upon his death Pelkamulox charged his half-brother Kwolila, who was chief of the Shuswap at Kamloops with the guardianship of his son Hwistesmetxe'qen. He also charged him with the responsibility of seeing to it that when Hwistesmetxe'qen was of age, he avenge his death. Around the 1830s Kwolila reminded his nephew of the pact he made with their father. Many people of other tribes in the interior joined the expedition and made war on the Lillooet. N'Kwala and his people were victorious over the Lillooet and thereafter he became known as the great Chief N'Kwala. Apparently Chief N'Kwala was so taken with the white men that when the North West Company and later Hudson's Bay Company established the trading post at Fort Kamloops in 1811 Chief N'Kwala welcomed them. Thereafter they lived together in a business and social capacity. He even married some of his daughters to Company officials.

It has been said that N'Kwala had from fifteen to seventeen wives and close to fifty children who are scattered among the tribes throughout the territory. He had two sons from his union with an Okanagan woman and upon his death in about 1859 made his young son, also named N'Kwala, his successor. However he was killed by his jealous brother and another family member became chief.

Chief N'Kwala died in about 1859 and was temporarily buried at Fort Kamloops until springtime. His body was then exhumed and taken by the Indians to be re-buried at his winter headquarters at the head of Okanagan Lake. A monument now stands there in honour of a great chief. Thereafter, the Okanagan went without a chief until one of N'Kwala's sons, Moise Chilkposmen took the seat in 1865 and served until 1879. After his death his brother William or Pasil/Basil Wohollesicle became chief and served from 1879 to 1898. Another brother Chwail, apparently with a south Okanagan mother, served as chief from 1902 to 1908.

The fur companies encouraged unions between their employees and Native women of significant families. Given the fact that status was an important issue among the people, it is easy to see why N'Kwala would marry his daughters to these white men. Teit notes some of these relationships while sacramental records reveal further relationships in later times. Most of the names of families included in the following family histories reveal the point at which European

LOGAN MEMORIAL

MARY TERESE

ANDREW AUGUST
KO-MAS-KET

MADELINE TONASKET

JOE, DONALD, MARY & MARIETTE

MARY

PETE

ABEL / KO-MAS-KET

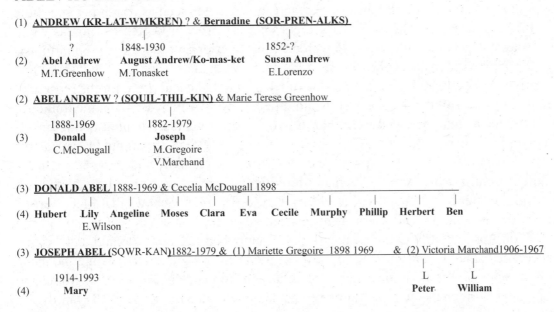

(1) **ANDREW (KR-LAT-WMKREN) ? & Bernadine (SOR-PREN-ALKS)**
?	1848-1930	1852-?
(2) **Abel Andrew**	**August Andrew/Ko-mas-ket**	**Susan Andrew**
M.T.Greenhow	M.Tonasket	E.Lorenzo

(2) **ABEL ANDREW ? (SQUIL-THIL-KIN)** & Marie Terese Greenhow
1888-1969	1882-1979
(3) **Donald**	**Joseph**
C.McDougall	M.Gregoire
	V.Marchand

(3) **DONALD ABEL** 1888-1969 & Cecelia McDougall 1898
(4) **Hubert**	**Lily**	**Angeline**	**Moses**	**Clara**	**Eva**	**Cecile**	**Murphy**	**Phillip**	**Herbert**	**Ben**
	E.Wilson									

(3) **JOSEPH ABEL (**SQWR-KAN)1882-1979 & (1) Mariette Gregoire 1898 1969 & (2) Victoria Marchand1906-1967
1914-1993		
	L	L
(4) **Mary**	**Peter**	**William**

The surname Abel is a primary name at Okanagan No.1 that goes back possibly over one hundred years. Oral history, passed down from previous generations, concludes that Pierre Qway-um-qin, the father of Blind Narcisse, Ko-mas-ket or August Andrew, and Squil-telks or Abel Andrew, were brothers. From the record, their sister Susan married Emmanuel Lorenzo, now known as Lawrence. With the exception of Ko-mas-ket all leave descendants. Today the Qway-um-qin family are known as Pierre and the descendants of Squil-telks are known as Abel and possibly extend to the Williams' family. Rightly, the Pierre and Lawrence families should be included here, but both leave descendants and have their own story. Ned Louis explains the Abel ancestral line.

Ned Louis: *It's hard to explain how things are. I keep telling these guys here that there is one big family. Like ol' Ko-mas-ket is one brother, and Donald and Joe Abel's dad, [Abel Andrew], that's the second brother, and then the other, ol' Blind Narcisse's dad, Qway-um-qin, that's the other brother. From them they all spread out and that's even where the Alexis's and Lawrence's started out. On their grandmother's side, Marriane, she was the daughter of Qway-um-qin and a sister to Blind Narcisse. Of course, they are now the Pierre family.*

Some confusion lies within the identity of Squil-telks' father who is referred to by four different names. The Oblates write his name as "Kr-lat-wmkren"[2] and oral history notes him as Squil-telks,[3] and also Old William, and Doctor William. All written sources attest to Old William's residence at Whiteman's Creek in 1908. He was living there when the Royal Commission held hearings at Head of the Lake in 1913.[4] If he is indeed the same person then the death journal kept by Joe and Mary Abel indicates he died October 26, 1916. In any case, as there is still confusion over the name we will continue with the history of the Abel family as gleaned from further records and oral history.

Dating back to the settlement era, we find that among those who pre-empted land at the head of Okanagan Lake was Thomas Greenhow. Similar business interests such as freighting and cattle raising, saw Greenhow closely associated with settlers such as Cornelius O'Keefe, Thomas Wood and Captain Houghton.[5] Gold had been discovered in the Interior and these early opportunists joined forces to supply vital goods to the miners to the north. With the exception of the Aboriginal people, the Native or brigade trail, on the west side of Okanagan Lake had been, for the most part, unused since the fur trade. With the advent of the gold rush the traffic increased and the trail once again became the main route of travel to the north. Noting the valuable ranching conditions of the northern end of the Okanagan Valley, Greenhow, O'Keefe and Wood pre-empted large parcels of land. In 1871, Wood sold his pre-emption at Irish Creek to Greenhow and moved to what is now Winfield.[6] As oral history has it, Greenhow hired an Okanagan woman, Mary Anne, as a housekeeper and she later bore him a daughter, Mary Terese. The record shows that Mary Terese, daughter of Thomas Greenhow and Mary Ann, married Abel, the son of "Kr-lat-wmkren" and "Sorprenalkrs," on April 28, 1890.[7] Subsequently, the couple had two sons Donald and Joseph. In this instance, the name "Kr-lat-wmkren" appears as the brother's grandfather while the name Sorprenalks reappears as the traditional name of a current descendant. Rosie Abel Marchand named her daughter Sorprenalks without knowing the name was already in use in the family.

Rosie Marchand: *Grampa said his step-father taught him to write. He said he got the Joe right but when it came to writing Andrew it was too much of a challenge so he wrote Abel. Both him and Donald wrote their last name as Abel after that. Mom and Grampa kept a journal of all the deaths on the Reserve. I remember writing in that journal. Grampa would always get us to sign in that book. When he heard of someone passing away it became automatic. Mom would tell one of us to get the book and we would write all the deaths in that book right away.*

Edward Fred: *Squil-telks was one of the last Indian doctors of our tribe. He lived at Whiteman's Creek by Harry Parker's. That's where Joe Abel lived when he was a little fella. Squil-telks is Joe's grandfather and kind of raised Joe and that is why Joe knows so much about what kind of medicines to use. He travelled all over with his grampa and talked about meeting many people.*

Louis Fred: *My pop [Joe Abel] said his grandfather, William, was a powerful Medicine Man. If the people couldn't get cured from the doctors in town they'd send them out here for treatment. It was then that they started calling him Doctor William. There were other medicine people out here at that time and they had their own sumix [animal spirit], but they were all jealous of each other and sometimes they used it on one another.*

Pop told me that long time ago the Nez Perce used to come up this way on Westside to go to the hop yards at Coldstream. William would be at his house at Whiteman's Creek and with his spirit powers he could already tell the Nez Perce were coming. They would stop farther down on Westside and send a few men up to tell him they were coming, but like Pop said, he already knew. They'd bring him gifts because he was such a powerful man. In previous time, in the spirit world, they fought and killed one another. After that happened, to make sure they had peace with each other, they'd send some one ahead to get permission from Doctor William to pass through.

My grampa said that when he did his ceremonies he'd lay a blanket on the floor and put all his symbols of power on the blanket as a sign of all his possessions such as stuffed animals, feathers and stuff like that. It had its own powers and from what I come to understand, from what my Pop told me, the very nature of these things overpowered the man. Like he had the nature of a grizzly bear. They are loners and don't socialize. There were lots of Medicine People along here in them days and my grandfather, Abel Andrew, died young because of the jealousies among the people. Pop told me that his father Abel and his grandfather Doctor William went to sleep on the floor, on the hides. My great grandfather woke up and didn't even have time to see what was going on, but it was too late. He saw he couldn't save him. So that's when Pop's dad knew he was going to die. He could feel it in his chest. He was just a young man.

Rosie Marchand: *Grampa told me that one time old man William was working on a bunch of people at the same time. One man was his good friend, and among the others, was a woman from Siwash Creek. Doctor William told my grandfather to get a block of wood and some nails, and he said, "pound all the people in and give them names." Grampa said he did, and there was no way the nails weren't pounded in really good. Anyway, they put the lights out and began to pray and sing. Then Grampa said the old man started to cry. He then turned the lights back on and he said we lost him. He meant his friend. Sure enough, the nail was out of the wood and laying there. So, the old man told him we'll try again, we'll pound it in again, but stronger this time. They turned out the lights and the old man started to cry again. So he said, "We lost him. There's no reason to try again. It's for the best – I guess. I did everything I could." Sure enough a few days later the friend died.*

Grampa's father died before Grampa was born. He was raised by old William, his grandfather. He said he learned a lot from his grampa. When Abel Andrew died Mary Terese married a Nickelson from Colville, Washington. Grampa called Maria Williams his first cousin. So was Rosie Mitchell. In the Indian way they would have been called his sisters. So was Rosie Barnes; she was Grampa's first cousin. Blind Narcisse was Grampa's first cousin, too. His dad was Qway-um-qin. When you look at it in that way, then Maria's children Albert, Willie, Walter and Harold were my grandfather's nephews. That's what Grampa called them. I was called Rosie after my dad, Charlie Bessette's mother. My grandfather George Bessette paid my mom twenty-five cents to name me Rosie. They said the money then was paper. So maybe it was like a coupon, or something like that.

At first, my grampa lived at Francis Smith's place, but Francis wanted to move to Siwash Creek. So I believe Grampa traded for a team of horses, a wagon and a load of potatoes. He had to give a little money too, I believe, because Francis's place at Blacktown was bigger than Grampa's at Siwash Creek. Grampa owned one of the first automobiles seen on the Reserve, and during the 1950's, I believe, served on Council.

Grampa always carried the cross at funerals. Not only that but he would clean and dress the people after they died when nobody else wanted to. I remember this one old lady had been sick for a long time. In them days you know, they didn't have water in their houses and because she had been sick for so long, she needed to be cleaned up before her funeral. Nobody wanted to do it so Grampa said, he told her in Indian, "It's okay, don't be ashamed, I'm your relation and I'll take care of you."

My grandfather was real generous to all of us kids and my mom was one of the best hide tanners on the Reserve. I used to stay up late at night watching her make gloves. She'd sell them at Pound's and the Hudson's Bay store and to private customers. When Edward was with Mom he used to make her those little sticks that they needed to turn the gloves inside out. One stick had a little groove in it and the other was pointed. My mother showed me how to use them. Mom would do the sewing and Edward would put the little strings on the cuff and turn them inside out for my mother. He would also cut out the pattern of little strips that they use to put between the fingers. When I grew up she'd get the pattern out and I learned to do those things for her. She showed me how to put the pattern against the grain of the hide. If you put them the other way they would stretch.

Like Joe, Donald spent his childhood years at Siwash Creek with Doctor William. He married Cecelia, the daughter of Amabile McDougall and Louisa Tomat from Westbank, and moved there after trading his property at Siwash Creek to Westbank's Basil McLeod.[8] The couple raised a large family. Their youngest son, Ben Abel, still lives at Westbank and is a gifted writer. His older sister, Lilly, married Enoch Wilson. They had one son, Lawrence. Lawrence confirmed the story that Donald acted as official constable and produced the following record:

> "Pursuant to the statutory authority invested in me as Commissioner of the Royal Canadian Mounted Police, I have this day appointed Donald Abel of the Okanagan in the province of BC to a special constable in the Royal Canadian Mounted Police subject to the provisions of the said statutes for duty at the Okanagan Indian Reserve in the province of British Columbia given under my hand and the seal at Ottawa this sixth day of November in the year of our Lord nineteen hundred and twenty three."[9]

Before his death in 1994, Ben Louis remembered times when Donald patrolled the Reserve on a high-wheeler bicycle. He said it was strange to see such a thing, but Donald took his work seriously and abided by regulations set out for him by the authorities. Later, it seems Donald had a fascination with wheels. Some tell of how he mixed and matched different kinds of wheels to his buggies and carts. Needless to say he always had transportation. As events would have it, it seems the people respected Donald's position but at times made his work harder. One such person was a Westbank Band member who lived at the ferry dock.

Lawrence Wilson: *He couldn't speak very good English. He saw Donald coming. He had a cookstove at that time and he had it on. He had a fire going. He opened the oven and put his jug of wine in there and he closed it. I guess Donald came in and they were sittin' around there too long and all of a sudden BANG. Right away he hollered at Donald, "That not me that. That not me that." He meant that's not mine. Donald didn't arrest him 'cause he couldn't do anything anyway. The jug exploded.*

In all, Joe and Donald are remembered as kind and generous brothers. Joe's concern for the sick and dying is also part of the nature of his grandson, Louie Fred. His skill at carpentry and working with wood has led him to a sensitive position of casket making. Louie's spouse, Colleen, and their children are also highly involved in preserving cultural aspects such as buckskin preparation, beading and handiwork.

August Andrew, or Ko-mas-ket, meaning "horn" or "antlers in the sky,"[10] the brother of Blind Narcisse Qway-um-qin, died July 5, 1930, about two months after a car accident in Washington State. His wife Madeline Tonasket was born in 1851 and died October 30, 1937.

In 1910, the north end of Swan Lake was the residence of Okanagan people Baptiste Logan, Kimas Kite or Ko-mas-ket, Jimmy Logan and Thomas Lindley.[11] Ko-mas-ket was the brother of Blind Narcisse and had land also at Blacktown. Madeline leased her part of the property to a local woman who pastured cattle there. When it was cut off from the main reserve at Head of the Lake, in 1913, it was sold. At her death the local news wrote:

> "A link with the past was severed on October 30, 1937 by the death at Okanagan Indian Reserve, near Vernon of Madeline Komasket at age 86. She was a well known Indian in the district, her tall commanding figure and well-shaped features demanding respect both from whites and Indians. Her father was the son of Chief Nicola a man 'termed a royal Indian.' The mother of Madeline, a Kamloops Indian, had four children one of these was Joe, being the first Indian to attend the Mission school established in this district. Unfortunately he died at an early age.

> She is survived by Milly Tonasket of Republic Washington. Madeline was born at Blacktown and was interred November 2, 1937 also at Blacktown. Madeline often told of the 'great earthquake' that occurred when she was a young girl, recounting how it was too severe to even permit their sitting on the ground and they had to lie flat as the earth undulated in waves. She was very proud of her membership of the 'Awauk-kane' tribe, from which the word Okanagan is said to be derived and to mean, 'The people who cut their hair at the shoulders,' as distinct from those who allowed it to grow long and wore it in plaits. She was interred with full Indian honors on November 2, at the Indian cemetery at 'Blacktown' which was her birth place and residence until her death."[12]

The Ko-mas-ket property at Blacktown is now known as Ko-mas-ket Park. This fitting legacy includes a large arbour, baseball and soccer field, as well as a new facility named Sn-c-ca-mala-tn, which means "where the children are." The building also serves as a daycare and a pre-school.

ALEXANDER (SMITKEN)

MARGARET

BASIL

MARY ANN

LOUIE

THERESA

WILLIAM

HARRIET

MARY LOUISE

ALEXANDER PLACE

ALEXANDER (SMITKEN)

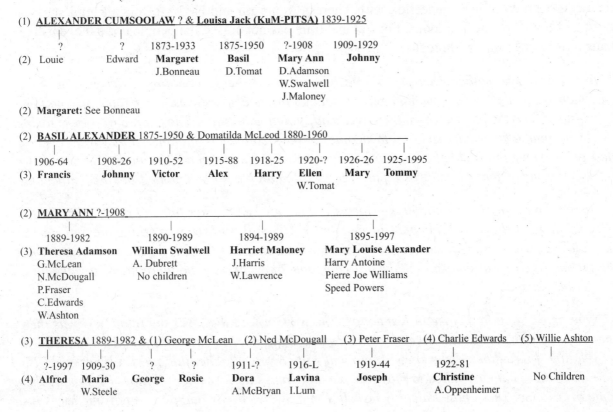

(1) **ALEXANDER CUMSOOLAW ? & Louisa Jack (KuM-PITSA) 1839-1925**

?	?	1873-1933	1875-1950	?-1908	1909-1929
(2) Louie	Edward	**Margaret**	**Basil**	**Mary Ann**	**Johnny**
		J.Bonneau	D.Tomat	D.Adamson	
				W.Swalwell	
				J.Maloney	

(2) **Margaret:** See Bonneau

(2) **BASIL ALEXANDER** 1875-1950 & Domatilda McLeod 1880-1960

1906-64	1908-26	1910-52	1915-88	1918-25	1920-?	1926-26	1925-1995
(3) **Francis**	**Johnny**	**Victor**	**Alex**	**Harry**	**Ellen**	**Mary**	**Tommy**
					W.Tomat		

(2) **MARY ANN ?-1908**

1889-1982	1890-1989	1894-1989	1895-1997
(3) **Theresa Adamson**	**William Swalwell**	**Harriet Maloney**	**Mary Louise Alexander**
G.McLean	A. Dubrett	J.Harris	Harry Antoine
N.McDougall	No children	W.Lawrence	Pierre Joe Williams
P.Fraser			Speed Powers
C.Edwards			
W.Ashton			

(3) **THERESA** 1889-1982 & (1) George McLean   (2) Ned McDougall   (3) Peter Fraser   (4) Charlie Edwards   (5) Willie Ashton

?-1997	1909-30	?	?	1911-?	1916-L	1919-44	1922-81	
(4) **Alfred**	**Maria**	**George**	**Rosie**	**Dora**	**Lavina**	**Joseph**	**Christine**	No Children
	W.Steele			A.McBryan	I.Lum		A.Oppenheimer	

The first written reference to the Alexander (Smitken) family is seen in Father Baudre's census of 1877. Baudre begins with the family head, Alexander "Kamskasoulat" who was then forty years old, and his thirty-six-year-old spouse, Louisa "Keslawitsa." Their eldest son was Louis, who was nineteen, baptized and married to Monique "Cepoulsalay." Louis and Monique had one daughter Lucia. Additional family members were sixteen-year-old Edward and twelve-year-old Mary Ann.[2] It is reasonable to conclude that Alexander must have died shortly after the census was taken for his widow, Louise, received the sacrament of confirmation September of 1882.[3]

Mary Ann met an untimely death in August 1908. In the beginning no inquest into her death was ordered and was called an "unfortunate accident" by the Vernon News. Only after a complaint was made by a family friend did an inquest ensue. In the end, results concluded that she was first killed then her body was laid on the railroad tracks in an act to conceal her murder. Apparently, no suspect was ever charged with the crime.[4]

Lavina Lum is the granddaughter of Mary Ann and the daughter of Theresa Adamson and Ned McDougall. She is the eldest living relative of the Alexander family. Lavina was born in a tent at Okanagan Landing in April 1916. While still an infant she was adopted by her uncle,

Billy Swalwell, and his wife, Annie Dubrett. She spent her childhood mainly at Deep Creek. She never learned of her connection with Theresa Adamson and Ned McDougall until she was registered for school at Kamloops. For Lavina, time has not erased the people nor the events that made a difference in her life today.

Lavina Lum: *My mother Theresa tol' me that ol' Basil, her grandfather, was workin' for a whiteman, a rancher on the commonage, when they started takin' census. The people then had one Indian name and the places where they lived had Indian names too. The people who were taking the census had to know the names of the people. So they tell them in Indian, but they want to know their other name and evidently the man he was workin' for was named Alexander. That's how we got the Alexander name. Basil was a pure-blooded Indian but got his name from the whiteman.*

TaTupa, Kem-pitsa, used to tell me stories. I'd lay my head in her lap and pretty soon I'd fall asleep. I thought she was telling me Coyote Stories; Chaptilk, but she was telling me real stories. She said they'd go away all summer to the Arrow lakes and Kettle Valley. I only remember what she tol' me when I was awake. It's like a dream, you know, first I'd be there then I'd wake up in a different place.

One time I went to a wake in Kamloops. The woman who died was my relation. I was there and this lady came to me and asked if I was lost. I tol' her no. I tol' her that woman who died was my relation. I asked her if she knew Annie and Billy Swalwell. She did, and I tol' her, well, I'm their daughter. That lady yelled to those people there and said I was her relation. Everybody then come over to me. That's how I identify myself. I'm a Swalwell. My dad always tells me I was just little when they took me. And that's who I woke up to. That's who I know. I didn't know Theresa Adamson. I didn't even know my sister Dora until I got really acquainted with her. My brother Joe, I didn't know, I used to see them but I didn't know them. I thought they were just kids who wanted to play with me.

Once in a while, just like I'd been asleep, I'd wake up and we'd be over at Duck Lake. I remember my mom and I went over there. My dad wasn't around. My mom said you got to be real brave 'cause we're going to Duck Lake. I remember we got there and Theresa Adamson was there. We stayed at her log house next to Gramma McDougall's house. She was staying there with Uncle Angus McDougall. Well, I didn't know them from Adam, but she was staying there with Uncle Angus. Seems like I woke up again and Uncle Happy was putting boxes of pears in that root cellar on the side of the hill there and I remember he called that girl Delphine. She was just standing there staring at me. Uncle Happy said, "Why don't you play with your cousin." Well, I don't know what cousin means, because in Indian, you know, your mom is my sister when they are within the same family. And that's what I know. When I grew up, I grew up with the Bessette boys and the Brewer girls. My mom used to always tell me those are your brothers. Or she'd say, here comes your sister from across the creek. That was Jenny Brewer. So you see, that's how I knew. Within the family they were my brothers and sisters. That's how the Indians relate you within the family. I even thought Danny Logan was my little brother.

My mom's mother was Mary Ann. She was killed by a train somewhere near Armstrong. She had four kids, my mom, Theresa, Billy, who adopted me, Aunt Harriet and Aunt Mary Louise. My mother, Theresa, had four different families. She was with George McLean first. He was part of that wild McLean family from Douglas Lake. With him she had Alfred, Maria, George and Rosie. Then she got with my dad, Ned McDougall, and had I and Dora. I found out later that he took off down the States so he wouldn't have to join the army. She then got with Pete Fraser and had Joe. Then she got with Charlie Edwards and had Christine. Her and Willie Ashton, who was an Englishman, didn't have any kids, but they did get married in May 1929 when my sister Dora and I were at the residential school in Kamloops.

When Mom and Willie came up to see us at Kamloops, he was courtin' her already. I didn't know who Willie Ashton was. Then they took us and they went over to town and they got married. Me and my sister Dora were witnesses. Willie Ashton was with Christine Brewer when he purchased that land past O'Keefe Siding from ol' Scotty. He grew potatoes. Back then you could grow a big garden on dry land and it's just like it was watered. Willie built that house and when I first went there I saw it had no insulation, just black paper covered with that thick wall paper that they used in them days. Christine died and before that he was with Coyote Mary; Mary Edwards. He never did have kids from any of those ladies.

Mary Edward's grandson was Johnny Victor. His brothers William and Louie are full brothers, but Johnny is a half-brother, a breed. Two girls died at birth. William Victor used to tease me when I was a kid. He'd say, "when you see an owl, you go 'round and 'round the owl, 'cause the owl has a spring. He won't turn his head. He'll just keepa going 'round and 'round." So when we lived in Deep Creek an ol' lady, I can't remember who she was, came to visit my mom. Mom [Annie] told me, "Go down the spring and get some water and we'll have tea." She gave me a five-pound lard bucket with a lid and said, "You hurry up now!" I said, okay. An' I took that bucket and I run to the spring.

There was a big stump by the trail and there was a big horned owl sittin' there, lookin' at me. I remember what uncle said. So I went 'round and 'round and 'round that stump. That owl kepta watchin' me and I know he didn't turn his head, he just kepta going 'round and 'round and 'round. I had a beaten path around that stump and thought, Yeah uncle, he's right, that owl don't turn his head! I was gone a long time and I ran down to the spring and filled up my little bucket and went back and the sneena was still there. I went 'round and 'round and 'round, once more, then I went home and the ol' lady was gone.

My mom says, "What happened to you?" I said, "I was just goin' down there." My mom said, "I thought maybe you went through the ice an' fell in!" Anyway, I said, "I wasn't gone very long! I just went down there and came right back. Where's that ol' lady?" My mom said, "She left! We were gonna have tea, but you were gone a long time. It's already time to cook for your dad. We better go for some more water before I start dinner."

So we went down there and she seen where somethin' was sittin', and of course, I was followin' along behind her, talkin' and talkin'. The good Lord gave me the mouth to talk and I always use it! When she seen that trail around that stump, she said, "What was here!" I said, "You know Mom, Uncle William tol' me that the sneena, the owl, has a spring neck and he can go 'round and 'round. You can go 'round that sneena and he will never turn his head, an' now I know they do. My mom said, "Oh, that's what you were doin'! That's why you stayed so long!"

I only remember little bits when I was small. I don't remember when we moved from Deep

Creek to Little Rope Ranch. I only remember Mom would cook something for that ol' blind lady, Sqwt-palks, and she'd tell me to take it over there. Sqwt-palks was Frank Pete's ol' lady. Frank was from Penticton and had one arm chopped off. Anyway, Mom tells me, "Holler at Sqwt-palks 'cause she's blind and deaf and put this tea in her cup and don't burn her!" And I'd take the food and go over there and knock on the door and I'd say, "Tupa! Tupa! Here's some dinner!" I'd go in and holler in her ear and take her hand and let her feel it. I was pretty small and Sqwt-palks would be real happy for the food. Then one time Mom went over there with me. She tol' Mom, how happy she was for the food and water and all our help and she gave me her Indian name, Sqwt-palks.

My mom, Theresa, looked after Kum-pitsa, she was partially blind, and Tommy Gregoire's grandmother, Millie's mom, I think, or maybe it was her aunt. They'd go pickin' berries together and come around meal-time, my mom would go get a groundhog for their supper. Then, in the fall they'd go over to Kalamalka Lake. My mom said to them ol' ladies that she wanted to go fishin' there, at Shale Point. Her mom tol' her no 'cause the water will pull you in. I guess Mom didn't listen and was fishin' from the shore when she heard a wooshin' sound and looked out and saw a big swirl of water there close to her on the lake. My mom got scared and said, that's the reason why they tell me not to go fishin' there!

My mother knew her horses. She was good with them and could really ride. One time she was up Douglas Lake with ol' George McLean. She was pregnant then, I think, with Alfred. Anyway, George said, "Theresa I'm goin' go for a ride and I'm takin' your horse." That was her horse, so she said, "What am I gonna ride?" He said, "You can ride that horse in the barn!" Well, that horse wasn't broke and she was real far along with my brother, Alfred. Anyway, them guys were gonna blind-fold the horse and ear him down, but she tol' them to just leave him alone. If you want me to ride that horse, I'll ride him. He wouldn't listen to her and he had just the rope on the horse, around its neck and was raisin' his quirt. Mom said, "I just raced and jumped onto the saddle. I grabbed the reins and reached for the rope and he wouldn't let the rope go. He nubbed it to his saddle." She kepta tellin' him, "You let him go!" He wouldn't. So she said the horse bucked and she said, "Let him go!" Finally, he let it go, and my mom took off with that horse just a buckin'.

George didn't like it that she stayed on. He tol' her, you think you're so smart and raised his quirt against the horse again. My mom said she kepta talkin' to the horse and as soon as that ol' man would raise his quirt the horse would step aside. Then she said they went to the edge of the field where there was a shale bank that went down into a deep ravine. She said, with just the reins, she got the horse to sit down, and went all the way down to the bottom. Then she looked up at ol' George and said, "You come down!" But he wouldn't. He tol' her, "You're crazy to go down there! You could kill yourself." She said, "Come down!" But he wouldn't. He went all the way around.

When she left ol' George, she come from Douglas Lake on a buggy with two horses. One was a tame horse and one was wild. She harnessed them both, and she tied them together, so they don't wreck them. There was no cattle guards in them days. So she had to open every gate. She had my brother George in a board and put him down on the floor in the buckboard. My two sisters, Maria and Rose, were with her, too. She said she just took off. It was pitch black when she come down that canyon. Then she come all the way down to the other side of Falkland and the horses was givin' out. She went to a house and asked those people if she can rest the horses there. She was tired, with two little kids, and hungry, and the horses were just barely goin'. She tol' the man, "If a man comes and asks you if you seen a woman with two little kids goin' by here, don't tell him." So the man hid the buggy and put the horses in the barn. She said they took her upstairs and fixed her bed and she stayed up there for two days. All that time she thought ol' George would come lookin' for her, but he didn't come till quite a while later. Anyway, she left and went on the other side of the lake 'cause that's where ol' Kum-pitsa, her gramma, and her two uncles lived.

Her uncles were big, tall men. She tol' them her story and when George did come they said, "You lay one hand on our niece again, you'll be either nailed to the side of the barn or we'll string you up!" She said he behaved himself for quite a while and then, I guess, he figured he was there long enough and tried to get my mother to go back with him. He got funny with her and my mother's uncles chased him off. He ran away and never did come back.

All those ol' people like my uncles and gramma are buried across the lake. That's where they lived. My mom, Theresa, died in 1982 and is buried at Head of the Lake. Mary Ann's oldest son was Louie. All the Jacks that live over here, those are all my mom's uncles, Mary Ann's brothers.

The reason I left here when I was so young was one time when we lived at Deep Creek my dad took me outside and pointed toward Duck Lake and farther. He said all those people at Duck Lake and as far down as the mountains are your relatives. He said for me to stay away from them when I got older. That's one of the reasons I left here.

Carol Louie: *Our mother Christine was the youngest child of Gramma Theresa. The things I remember about Gramma Theresa was that she was a very beautiful, regal and elegant lady. She always dressed nicely and most of the time she wore a nice dress with stockings and a two inch high-heel. She was always a slim person. She also had a beautiful smile and almost always appeared confident in everything that she did. From as far back as I can remember she wore her hair in braids. She was very traditional and old fashioned. She wove her traditional and Catholic ways into one belief. She spoke the Okanagan language most of the time. She would get exasperated at her grandchildren if they didn't understand when she spoke to them in our language. We all cherish a picture of Gramma in traditional dress that she made herself.*

Other fond memories are of her and auntie Mary Louise Powers tanning hides at Gramma's at O'Keefe Siding. She made buckskin gloves, jackets, moccasins and other Okanagan items that she sold as another means of an income to help feed her grandchildren. She was a hard worker and could ride a horse as good as any man could. She even raised her own horses, cattle, and poultry. She grew vegetables, melons and berries. She dried deer meat and there was always an abundance of dried salmon in her kitchen. She provided well for her family and had great affection for all of us and taught us about our culture and traditional ways. I will always remember her kindness, good works, and her most beautiful laugh. She will always hold a special place in my heart.

QWAY-QWAY TASKET

JOHN ALEXIS

ELIZABETH

ELLA

MARY

ANNIE

CHILDREN OF JOHNNY AND ELLA ALEXIS

ALEXIS / CAMERON

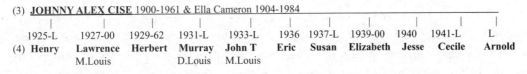

(1) KWITASKET & AMARATKOA
|
(2)   1861-?
        Alexis

(2) ALEXIS (KWITASKET) ? & Mary Ann Qway-um-qin 1873-1937
|
(3)   1900-1961
        Johnny
        E.Cameron

(3) JOHNNY ALEX CISE 1900-1961 & Ella Cameron 1904-1984

1925-L	1927-00	1929-62	1931-L	1933-L	1936	1937-L	1939-00	1940	1941-L	L
(4) **Henry**	**Lawrence**	**Herbert**	**Murray**	**John T**	**Eric**	**Susan**	**Elizabeth**	**Jesse**	**Cecile**	**Arnold**
	M.Louis		D.Louis	M.Louis						

(1) DAVID CAMERON 1876-1953 & **(2) Rosie Louie** & (3) **Elizabeth Edwards** & (4) **Susan Lawrence** & (5) **Mary Anne Gregoire**

1891-1983	1903-1972	1904-1984	1917-83	1919-?	1921-L	1923-?	1925-L	1932-86
(2) **Annie**	**Mary**	**Ella**	**Betty**	**Jackie**	**David**	**Minnie**	**Lucy**	**James**
J.Logan	A.Dubrett	J.Alexis	I. Anderson	A.Swanson		C.Jacobson	G.Brett	V.Cameron

The Alexis and Cameron families are connected through Johnny Alexis and Ella Cameron as well as through David Cameron and Susan Lawrence. As understood, family roots go back to Kwitasket, or High Mountain Cloud,[2] Chief at Head of the Lake in the early 1900s. He was also known as Johnny Kamloops. The most recent finding of the marriage record of Alexis and Marianne reveals Alexis' parents as "Kwitaskret" and "Amaratkoa" and Marianne's parents as "Simon Tlishalsin" and "Anne Hastitwa." They were married July 11, 1886, by Father Lejacq, OMI, at the Indian chapel at Kamloops. The same record indicates that Alexis was from Kamloops and Marianne from Head of the Lake. [3]

Most agree that the Alexis surname was changed from Alex Cise by the Oblates and Indian Affairs. Further research has also disclosed that the Alexis surname is not limited to the Head of the Lake Band, but can also be found in the Similkameen, Kamloops, Nicola and Kootenay Bands.[4]

Tim Alexis: *Kwi-kwi-tasket or Alex Cise was my dad's father. It's possible that he was from the Deadman's Creek area. At one time they were the biggest family in Kamloops. That ol' couple had fourteen kids, but they all died young except for my dad. There are some of them buried at Kamloops, across the lake and below the Arrow Lakes. They travelled a lot and their kids were born all over the area.*

Hank Alexis: *Alex Cise is our real name and I'd like to go back to that name because that is what our dad's name was. Our dad had relatives in Deadman's Creek. He [Edward Enneas] was a chief there, and used to come here every summer and spend two weeks. I remember he was our dad's relative. We have relatives in Kamloops too. Dad was raised by his stepfather, Henry Lawrence, and that is why he was known as Johnny Lawrence. His dad died and our grandmother, Marianne Qway-um-qin, married Henry Lawrence. Dad is a half-brother to Henry, Susan and Joe Lawrence.*

Ned Louis: *I believe Johnny's dad was born at Needles. Back then the people travelled between the Arrow Lakes, the Columbia River and the Okanagan.*

Mabel Alexis: *Ella and Johnny were married May 12, 1925 at St. James Roman Catholic Church in Vernon. She was twenty-three and Johnny was twenty-four. Their kids were all born at home here except for Arnold. Lena Lawrence was midwife for all of Mom's kids except for Banker. Ella was out helping Johnny stook hay and decided to come in and make dinner. By the time Johnny come in, Banker was born.*

Tim Alexis: *Our mom [Ella] was born and raised up here on Cameron Flats. Her mother, Elizabeth, was known as one of the Wilson girls. There were three of them. Old George Wilson was married to the mother, and my grampa, Dave Cameron, married Elizabeth. Tommy B. Struthers married the other one [Sophie] and Frank Gottfriedson had the other sister [Julianne]. I don't know why they went by Wilson, 'cause the Wilson's here originate from ol' Dan Wilson. But ol' Cameron was a real family man, too. My mom said when they were growing up my grampa used to take them to town every year between Christmas and New Year's. They'd get a room and my grampa would give them money and he'd go celebrate with his friends.*

Rose Louis: *Ella Cameron or Alexis was one of the girls from here that went to Kamloops School when the school was known as the Industrial School. Julia Tonasket went there too. They learned how to cook and sew and other things that women do. They also learned how to write in Chinook and English.*

Tim Alexis: *Our dad was a big, strong, hardworking man and a really nice, kind father. He used to play hockey with all of us. He used to buy us all sticks and we'd take the lanterns outside and play for hours. George Wilson and his bunch would come over here and Edward McDougall was on leave from the army and he'd come play. One time he fell on the ice and hurt his head. He had headaches for quite a while and when he went back to the army they x-rayed him and found out he had a fractured skull. That's what happens when you try to learn when you're too old.*

You know our mom always kept up with the times and really loved her grandchildren. With every generation that came along she moved right in with them. She'd dress up with the kids at Halloween and together they'd put on their makeup and have lots of fun. Her and our kids were always laughing. She always talked about Macca, Martha Struthers, her cousin. I guess Macca had an accident when she was little and broke her back. Mom looked after her. That's the way it was long time ago. When someone lost their mom or dad, a relative would always take them in. It's just like Albert Saddleman Sr., he lost his mom when he was young and he used to always come here. When he was killed in the war, the police told my dad and he took it really hard. Albert's brother, Walter, of course, was raised by Pierre and Katherine Louis.

Dad really worked hard. At this place here, my dad logged with ol' Jones and they'd bring the logs here and drag them on the lake to Simpson's mill in Kelowna. He had a timber limit up here at Siwash Creek and sold it to Simpson. When he was just twelve years old he cut wood with ol' Joe Parker. They'd bring the logs down to the place on the shore at Tommy Armstrong's and cut it into firewood. Then they'd load it on one boat and pull it along with the other boat over to

Okanagan Landing to the Chinese. Them Chinese used to make them wait, too, until they were darned good and ready to come pick it up. Those were real tough times for them guys, then. Well, it pretty well had to be if they had to take the wood across the lake just to get money to buy salt, sugar and coffee.

Dad learned to drive truck and then bought his own truck while them other guys still used horses. He built that road up Six-Mile with just a scoop. Ben and Ned Louis and all them other guys worked with him. He surveyed and built that irrigation ditch, too, from Siwash Creek to here. We had that survey thing around here for quite a while until it got broke. It was two sticks made into a Y.

Dad hauled the logs from here to Vernon at first and then to Bell Pole in Lumby. It was a long haul and them old roads up here were pretty steep and narrow in places. Hank and Graden used to drive the truck too and I used to ride along with Dad and he'd tell me when we got to a steep hill to pull the emergency brake. Boy, that was something, I was just small and I'd have to pull with both hands to slow that truck down. One time I got bored and Dad said I could run along side the truck. He had a load of poles on and I was running behind the truck holding on to one of the poles. We hit a dip and that log hit me on top the head. You don't think about those things when you're young but I never did that again.

We all grew up with music. Dad used to say if you can play an instrument and sing a little you will never go hungry, someone will always invite you to their table. I remember when we were growing up, Dad would sit us all down and tell us to play him a tune. This ol' guy Burton used to come here and sing. He couldn't sing at all, but he'd try, and while he was singing, he'd screw up his face. We'd get hit if we laughed at him, but even until just before Murray got sick, he could mock ol' Burton. I'd remind him of Burton and Murray would mock him to the tee.

Long time ago everyone could play an instrument, and if they didn't know the tune of a song, they'd get their wives up there to hum along while they played. My dad used to get my mom up there. He used to say that this McDougall guy used to say, "Babe Ruth can knock 'em a fly and I can knock 'em a tune." In fact, Murray, Banker, Hank, Roy Robins and Lawrence Pierre from Penticton used to sing on the Kelowna radio station. That Lawrence Pierre could really sing. Roy Robins, of course, travelled all over the States singing and playing. He never went hungry. You know that's why our boys could play and can sing a little. Music was just always a part of our lives.

Our dad was killed when his car went over the bank on Six-Mile Creek road. Everyone was out looking for him for a whole week before Lyle Berg from up Six-Mile came and told us. They were driving their kids to school and one of them saw a car over the bank. They went back after taking their kids to school and saw that it was our dad.

Mabel Alexis: *Johnny though lived to see some of his grandchildren. Sheila was born just before he died and him and Ella used to argue over her. Johnny would go look at her and tell Ella that Sheila smiled at him, but Ella would say it was just gas. Johnny would stick up for himself and really believed she did smile at him. Maybe she did, 'cause not too long after he died.*

Rather than leave the Alexis family history open ended, it is fitting to mention in part some of the accomplishments of this family. The eldest son, Henry, more commonly known as Hank, is known for his music ability with the guitar. Along with his brothers, Lawrence, better known as Graden, and Herbert, better remembered as Banker, their brother Murray and their uncle Joe Lawrence earned a reputation as a highly talented group of Okanagan musicians. At one point their reputation led to performances on the local radio stations in both Vernon and Kelowna. Their talents do not end with music but continue in the administrative work on a band level. Murray served the band as chief for many successive years and his brothers John, better known as Timmy, and Graden served as many years as councillors. Their social contribution in the entertainment field as well as their political contributions have benefitted the Okanagan Indian Band in many ways.

David Cameron was born in Eastern Canada. At age sixteen he came west to Vernon to work for his uncle William Cameron. It appears that things did not work out between David and his uncle so David decided to try the cowboy life. Eventually he settled above Siwash Creek. His neighbours there were George Smith, Thomas B. Struthers and for a while Frank Gottfriedson. David, Thomas and Frank eventually married sisters.

David had one daughter, Mary, with Rosie Louie[5] before he married Elizabeth Edwards at the Vernon Army Parsonage on January 27, 1903.[6] He then married Susan Lawrence, March 3, 1926 and had five children. Later he had one son, James, with Mary Anne Nicholas, nee Gregoire. If the calculations are correct, then Elizabeth was just a young girl of fourteen at the time of her marriage. Dave and Elizabeth's daughter, Ella, married Johnny Alexis.

On March 26, 1913, ten years after Elizabeth's death, David married Susan Lawrence.[7] Susan was the half-sister to Henry and Joseph Lawrence, and possibly a half-sister to Johnny James and Manuel Bercie from Enderby. After several years with David, and five children later, the couple separated. Their children all married and had families of their own. Bobby Cameron and his sister Lucy Brett are the lone survivors of David's fourth relationship.

John Marchand: *David and Susan's kids all went to school at Six-Mile. They used to ride down the hill on their ponies. When you see pictures of kids and their ponies you know they are the Cameron kids because they are the only ones who had ponies in them days.*

Lucy Brett: *We used to come down off the hill to go to school at Six Mile. I was too young to remember much. I only remember coming off the hill and making snow angels in the snow. By the time we got to school we were slopping wet and they would tell us to take off our coats and hang them up. All I remember is they gave us this vegetable soup and bread at lunchtime and made us take castor oil.*

As I said, I was too young to remember much but they came and took us away and were going to put us in a home or school or something. Then George Anderson said he would take us. We went to the Anderson Ranch. My brother Bobby worked there. Jackie and Betty went to the Catholic Convent in Kamloops. They sent Jackie home after a while because she got sick. Minnie went somewhere else. Then my mother came and took us to Vancouver. I was nine or ten.

We stayed here until I came back here and stayed with my older sister, Betty, on the Anderson ranch. I worked at there, and at the Vernon Jubilee Hospital, cleaning the kitchen and the nurses quarters. One time I was cleaning the bed pans. I turned on the water and forgot about it. It ran down the winding stairways. I worked there when I was about sixteen or seventeen.

My dad died in 1953. He was the salesman for Watkin Motors for quite awhile. I don't remember too much about him because I wasn't really with him all the time, not until George and I got married, and we went up to the old house. Then there was a the time when Minnie and I we were up there with Mary Anne when Jimmy was born. I don't remember how we got out of there or the date.

I remember George Smith. He had his house past ours. He would bring us penny candies and help decorate the house and tree at Christmas time. He would take us to the pole wharf for swimming. He taught my brother, Bobby, and my sisters how to swim. Of course, I was too small and played on the beach during those times.

I remember more about my mother after she took us to Vancouver to live with her. She couldn't read or write, but could cook without a recipe and knit and crochet without a pattern. She couldn't read, but she could look at anything and make it. She was always truthful and I never heard her swear. I don't know anything about my mother's mother. But I do know that my mother had two half-sisters in the States, but I don't know what name they went by. Ella knew all that stuff, but she's gone now. My mother did talk about her dad, Henry Lawrence, though.

I'm not quite sure, but I was told that my mother was born in 1899 and died about 1963. She died of sugar diabetes. She was here staying with Johnny and Ella when they amputated her toes on one foot. They couldn't find her diabetes. They didn't know about it in those days I guess. She died later in Vancouver. I remember her brother, Joe Lawrence, came to the funeral.

All of David Cameron and Susan Lawrence's children married with the exception of Bobby. He however, raised three stepchildren and served in WW II. Lucy married George Brett and has five children.

SAM & ROSIE BARNES

ROSIE BARNES & FAMILY

DENNIS BARNES

ELIZABETH, EMILY, DENNIS & GEORGE

ANTOINE / BARNES / POWERS

(1) **ANTOINE** & **MARY ANNE**
         | |
    1879-1934   ? -1926
(2) **Rosalie**   **Lucy**

(2) **ROSIE ANTOINE** 1879-1934 & Marcellin (Sam) Barnes ?-1926
              | |
       1901-1938   1914-1963
(3)   **Julie**   **Dennis**
                        C.Tom
                        E.Michele

(3) **DENNIS BARNES** 1914 -1963 & (1) Christine Tom   & (2) Emilie Michele 1919-1969
         | | | |
    1948-L   1952-L   1957-L   1961-L
(4) **David**   **Wilfred**   **Rose**   **Ernie**

Rosie Antoine married widower Marcellin Barnes March 12, 1906 at the Head of the Lake.[2] Their marriage record discloses that she was the daughter of Antoine and Mary Anne who lived at Blacktown. Marcellin too, was living at Blacktown then, but was born in Lillooet and was the son of Julienne. Sam Barnes was a policeman at Lillooet and is seen with revolver and handcuffs in a photo included in the September 1995 issue of the Nicola Valley Museum and Archives Association.[3] His father's identity however is excluded from the record. Marcellin who was also known as Sam, drowned January 6, 1916, while driving his buggy east across the ice of Okanagan Lake to check on reports of hay being stolen.[4] According to oral history, after Marcellin's death, Rosie married a second time to a man named Roberts and had two more sons, Milo and Charlie.[5] More recent research discovered that Rosie also had a daughter Louisa with John Isadore from Washington. Louisa died at thirteen years old, February 3, 1931.[6]

Although Antoine or Mary Anne could not be placed on any particular family tree, the record of Lucy Antoine Powers gives a clue to the relationship of Rosie, Lucy, and a woman known as Julie. A combination of records states that when Julie Spapowcheen, the widow of Michele, died in 1926 she left all she possessed to her sister Lucy Antoine Powers and another concludes that Lucy was also Rosie's sister.[7] Therefore it is in the comparison of these records that we can assume that Rosie, Lucy and Julie were sisters and probable daughters of Antoine and Mary Anne. No records indicate that Lucy or Julie had children.

Lucy Antoine married Speed Powers. A family member was told that Speed's father originated in Kentucky and that he was born on Blue Nose Mountain near Lumby, around 1884.[8] Further information taken from the 1891 Canada Census discloses that Speed's father was Martin Powers. Martin was then a miner and his origin listed as the US. Speed's origin is documented as Red, meaning his mother was of Aboriginal descent. Oral history maintains that Speed was a maternal half-brother to Tommy Armstrong. After Lucy died Speed married widow Mary Louise Alexander after her spouse Pierre Joe Williams died in 1931. Speed died in 1974. He left no children from either marriage.

Conflicting memories cannot confirm that Julianne and Dennis Barnes were siblings. Some say Julianne was Dennis' mother while other say his mother was Rosie.

Millie Steele: *Julienne Barnes, or who we called Wscumnelqs, used to come to my mom's place to trade beads. I used to think that Dennis was Speed Powers' kid 'cause he was always around Speed. But Gramma Marchand said Dennis was Rosie's son. Rosie was Lucy's sister.*

For now we will assume that Julianne was Rosie's daughter and continue with further research results. The October 20th issue of the Vernon News printed:

> "Julia Barnes, middle-aged Indian woman and member of Okanagan Reserve No.1, was accidentally killed, when she was apparently struck by a BC Coach Lines Bus at Barnhart Vale, near Kamloops.... The body was shipped to this city from Kamloops and funeral services were held Wednesday afternoon. Though born in the local reserve and member of the band, she had been living near Kamloops for some years."[9]

Marriage records and oral history maintain that Dennis Barnes married twice. From the record we find that Dennis was first married to Christine Tom. Christine was the daughter of a Douglas Lake man known as Michele Tom and his spouse Emma Lamprow. Emma, it seems, was the granddaughter of Andrew Lamprow.[10] At this time there is no evidence that they had children. However Dennis married a second time to Emilie Michele of Westbank and had four children.

Dennis Barnes Family: *Our father, Dennis Barnes, was a logger, rancher, cowboy, orchard worker and loving dad. He passed over to the spirit world early in our lives. One of the things he is remembered for is his team of Clydesdale horses that he trained and used in the logging industry. Their names were Barney and Dick. Even though our dad was very strict and had a firm hand with discipline, he was a jokester. His nick-name was Senklip, one who plays tricks and jokes on others. Looking back on it now, we believe that he was preparing us to be on our own at a young age. His family was very important to him and he would protect us without question. Dennis was a very spiritual man and sang his own traditional songs. His teachings were very strong and are now being befitted by us and passed down another three generations.*

Emily Michelle had two children prior to her relationship with Dennis. She first had George Michelle with Archie Eli and Elizabeth Lindley-Charters [nee Michelle] with Edward McDougall. George, Archie and Edward are all deceased.

Julianne Barnes' Indian name was Qwen-l-pitsa, meaning "tattered [poor] blanket." Emily Michelle's Indian names was Kl-kem-pitsa meaning "evening shadows." I, Rose Caldwell, am also known as Kl-kem-pitsa. It is a name passed down from mother to daughter.

One last point is that some of these pictures and family information is all new to us. Prior to this book we never knew this information. It is overwhelming and gratifying to finally, after all these years, get in touch with our roots from our dad's side of the family. It sounds kind of corny, but it is so true. Research where you come from. Regardless if it is good or bad. The information will fill a void in your life that nothing else will. I [Rose] shed a lot of tears of happiness when I learned a little more about my dad's family.

BESSETTE

MAGGIE, ROSIE & BESSETTE CHILDREN

MARY HELENE

GEORGE

STEVE

TARZAN

GEORGE

WILLIE

MARGUERITE

MARY

MICKEY

CHRISTINE

HARRY

JOHNNY

CHARLIE, ADELINE & FLORENCE

BESSETTE

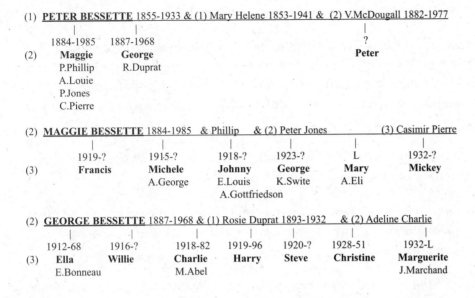

(1) **PETER BESSETTE** 1855-1933 & (1) Mary Helene 1853-1941 & (2) V.McDougall 1882-1977

	1884-1985	1887-1968	?
(2)	**Maggie**	**George**	**Peter**
	P.Phillip	R.Duprat	
	A.Louie		
	P.Jones		
	C.Pierre		

(2) **MAGGIE BESSETTE** 1884-1985 & Phillip & (2) Peter Jones (3) Casimir Pierre

	1919-?	1915-?	1918-?	1923-?	L	1932-?
(3)	**Francis**	**Michele**	**Johnny**	**George**	**Mary**	**Mickey**
		A.George	E.Louis	K.Swite	A.Eli	
			A.Gottfriedson			

(2) **GEORGE BESSETTE** 1887-1968 & (1) Rosie Duprat 1893-1932 & (2) Adeline Charlie

	1912-68	1916-?	1918-82	1919-96	1920-?	1928-51	1932-L
(3)	**Ella**	**Willie**	**Charlie**	**Harry**	**Steve**	**Christine**	**Marguerite**
	E.Bonneau		M.Abel				J.Marchand

Looking back over the family names in the 1891 Canada Census records and reading various historical articles, it becomes apparent that the Bessette family was one of the early pioneer families that settled in the White Valley, now Lumby, before the turn of the century.

White Valley, in its infancy, was populated with primarily French Canadian families who came to the area in search of gold, and later to farm. Being of Roman Catholic denomination, the pioneer Bessette family initiated the first Catholic Church built there and later a son, Herbert, was ordained a priest[2] while two Bessette girls took their vows as Sisters of Saint Ann. The first Bessette to arrive in the area was Pierre Bessette who staked and worked a claim at Cherry Creek, now known as Cherryville. In 1877 Pierre pre-empted 320 acres in the "Upper Coldstream Valley" and in 1888 built a sawmill that produced "the best lumber in the Okanagan."[3] He sold the sawmill to his brother Napoleon in 1890 and continued to farm. Peter Bessette, the father of George and Maggie Bessette, who made his home at Irish Creek, was likely a descendant of this large pioneer family. On the other hand, there is no positive link to connect him with one particular family. Even thorough research of sacramental records discloses nothing of any real connection. By 1920, Peter Bessette was registered as a band member and was married to Okanagan woman Mary Helene.[4] They had two children.

Peter Bessette's second marriage was to Virginia McDougall, the daughter of David and Terese McDougall of Duck Lake. They had one son Peter, who died in infancy of bowel obstruction. A story is told that Virginia could not conceive, so the couple went to Six-Mile Creek to consult a Medicine Man. Virginia did give birth to a son, but after the infant died, Peter and Virginia divorced. Seemingly, as one Elder put it, under the terms of the divorce laws, the wife had to be financially compensated in some way. So Peter gave Virginia one dollar and the marriage was dissolved.

Peter and Mary Helene's son, nineteen-year-old George, married fourteen-year-old Rosie Duprat (Dubrett), May 30, 1910. Officiating priest was Father P. Conan, OMI.[5]

Lavina Lum: *Ol' Peter Bessette had blue eyes. Maggie, his daughter, looks like her dad, Peter. Ol' Peter had crippling arthritis. He was all twisted from that disease. Charlie, his grandson, was his pet. Every time they'd tell Charlie to go pack wood, he'd say Hapa, Hapa, Hapa, [probably a baby word for grampa] and go run under his arm. Peter would say, A gee sqwee, which means "leave him alone."*

Marguerite Marchand: *Charlie had an accident with a horse when he was little. I think he fell off. So he had a bad leg for a long time.*

Rose Louis: *Peter and Virginia were good friends to my mother. They used to visit a lot at Dirty Lake. There was picture of them hanging in my mother's house but I don't know what happened to it. It disappeared after my mother died.*

Lavina Lum: *One time Mom [Annie] and I went over to visit Aunt Rosie. Aunt Rosie was in bed and she had a little baby beside her. I asked Aunt Rosie where she got the baby. She said, "Well, I woke up real early in the morning and there was a big bird sitting on the fence and he gave me this baby girl." After that I was thinkin' about how nice it would be to have a little sister, so I tol' my mom, "Why don't you get up real early in the mornin' and go down there. Maybe that bird will bring you a baby, then I will have a sister." Mom and Aunt Rosie just laughed and went on visiting in the Shuswap language. I couldn't understand what they were saying, but I really wanted a little sister. So we used to steal Silly Millie, Aunt Julia's daughter.*

Jenny Marchand: *I remember when Peter used to take a bucket of nails and staples and a hammer and his grandson Charlie, and early in the morning they would go fencing their property all around their home place. Charlie was little and used to hold the bucket for his grampa. Then in the afternoon they'd go over to their other place, where Rosie Marchand lives now, and fence that place. It didn't take them very long. They did that every fall and spring. That way they kept up their fences and nothing got in or out. Them guys worked real hard to keep up their places.*

Mary Ann Eli: *When I was a kid Mom would take us and go back and forth to Summerland. She was with Casimir Pierre then. We'd come back to Grampa's place here at Irish Creek. She had to look after Grampa Peter because he was full of arthritis. That was her job, to look after him. I remember going to Kamloops School in August of that year and Grampa was real sick. I remember Mom told us then to say goodbye to Grampa because we'd probably never see him again. I guess he died around the first part of September.*

Mom was the first woman to wear men's pants. She was the type that nobody bossed around. She could work like any man and rode a horse really well. Anyway, when we were little, Mom and Julia Tonasket and some others used to go to work in the gardens; sometimes at Lumby, other times at Coldstream and other times in and around Vernon. Sometimes, they'd be gone for a long time, and mostly we were on our own. An old man named Qwi-thum-lukn, who lived with Grampa and Auntie Rosie, used to kind of watch over us but Aunt Rosie was too busy with her own kids. Millie, Julia Tonasket's daughter, used to stay behind with us. I used to think though that she was better off than us because at least she had her gramma, Mary Logan, to watch over her. I remember seeing Mary Logan cutting off long socks and sewing them for Millie. Gee, I used to think, I wish someone would sew me some socks. I remember too, Julia would take Millie and say she was going to Blacktown. I never seen Blacktown and remember thinking I wish I could go to Blacktown with Millie and them.

When we lived at Irish Creek, we used to get visitors for the summer. I remember Joe Pierre, or maybe his name was Pierre Joe, and his wife, Onn, used to come. His Indian name was Ch-choo-kin, and Onn, I think, was related to Alex's mom, Mary [Onn was the daughter of Qway-um-qin and a sister to Mary Ann and Blind Narcisse]. But then they could have been related to Grampa too. Anyway, they used to come every summer from Penticton and pitch a tent in Grampa's orchard and stay all summer.

I remember one incident most 'cause one time we were up at the house at my grampa's. Those people always had a buggy. They came across the bridge, up to the gate and then couldn't open it. Ol' Onn must have been howling, or something, because Mom and them ran down to the open the gate. I guess something happened to Ch-choo-kin 'cause he was foaming at the mouth and Onn thought he was dying. They brought the buggy through the gate. I guess he drank something bad, or something, I don't really know. I just remember them always being camped there in the summer.

Marguerite Marchand: *The old folks didn't believe in the school system I guess. The only one who went to school was Steve, but that is because he wanted to. George sure was mad at him for a while. He went to Kamloops for about a year and a half maybe.*

The other Bessette sons were skilled baseball players. Some say that if they played today they would probably be accepted by the major leagues. Willie was the original old-timer catcher for the Head of the Lake Bluebird team. He was replaced by Ernest Oppenheimer. Willie also played first and third base. Charlie also pitched and often played first and third base. Steve too, played catcher, pitcher and outfield.

When Rosie died in 1932, Marguerite was adopted by her aunt Annie Dubrett and Uncle Billy Swalwell. Rosie's father, George, then married Adeline Charlie from Enderby. The photograph, at the beginning of this family history, was taken at the Bessette home at Irish Creek and includes Charlie Bessette, Adeline and her daughter, Florence.

BONNEAU

JIMMY

ELLA, EDWARD & CAROLINE

BONNEAU FAMILY

JIMMY

JIMMY & SARAH

BONNEAU HOUSE - SIX-MILE CREEK

BONNEAU (BONO)

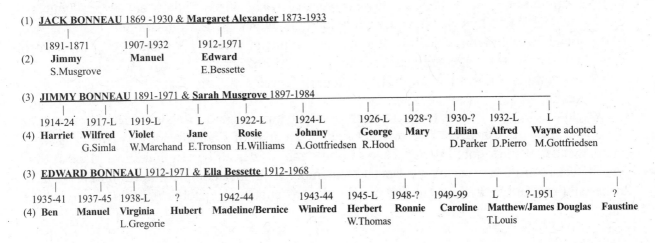

(1) **JACK BONNEAU** 1869 -1930 & **Margaret Alexander** 1873-1933

1891-1871	1907-1932	1912-1971
(2) **Jimmy**	**Manuel**	**Edward**
S.Musgrove		E.Bessette

(3) **JIMMY BONNEAU** 1891-1971 & **Sarah Musgrove** 1897-1984

1914-24	1917-L	1919-L	L	1922-L	1924-L	1926-L	1928-?	1930-?	1932-L	L
(4) **Harriet**	**Wilfred**	**Violet**	**Jane**	**Rosie**	**Johnny**	**George**	**Mary**	**Lillian**	**Alfred**	**Wayne** adopted
	G.Simla	W.Marchand	E.Tronson	H.Williams	A.Gottfriedsen	R.Hood		D.Parker	D.Pierro	M.Gottfriedsen

(3) **EDWARD BONNEAU** 1912-1971 & **Ella Bessette** 1912-1968

1935-41	1937-45	1938-L	?	1942-44	1943-44	1945-L	1948-?	1949-99	L	?-1951	?
(4) **Ben**	**Manuel**	**Virginia**	**Hubert**	**Madeline/Bernice**	**Winifred**	**Herbert**	**Ronnie**	**Caroline**	**Matthew/James Douglas**		**Faustine**
		L.Gregorie				W.Thomas			T.Louis		

The above Bonneau family is maternally connected to the Alexander family as Margaret is the daughter of Alexander Cumsoolaw and Kum-pitsa. Margaret's first son, James, was born prior to her marriage to Jack Bonneau. Jimmy's father, Edward Haynes, originated from the Colville Confederated Tribes near Spokane.[2] James was known as Jimmy Bonneau and passed the surname down to his children.

Indian Affairs Census states that Jack Bono entered the band from Douglas Lake in 1886.[3] Just how the surname Bono changed to the French spelling of Bonneau is unknown. Subsequently, Margaret and Jack had two more sons. Manuel, born in 1907, remained single and died of tuberculosis in 1932. Their second son, Edward, was born in 1912 and married Ella Bessette on April 29, 1935.[4] They continued their life at Six-Mile Creek in a log house built by Edward before relocating later to the Bessette estate at Irish Creek.

John Spotted Eagle: *Our grampa was the first entrepreneur to form a business here on the Reserve at Six-Mile Creek. He operated the store here and was also a successful rancher. He was one of few, I guess, that spoke high Okanagan and hosted winter dances throughout his years. It was him that taught us to be independent and self-reliant. I was told that when they built their house at Siwash Creek, they built it out of recycled material and Mom remembered Gramma Sarah straightening nails for the house. Personally, I remember Grampa taking me to the sweat house and teaching me to make a drum. Also I remember anytime he came to visit us, he always brought us candy bars. When they celebrated their wedding anniversary on November 22, 1963 they invited the whole community. That's the way he was. He cared about the other families on the Reserve. When they were in need he would pack up some potatoes and carrots from his root cellar and give it to the people. So he had a generous nature. He served the community in other ways. He was a Councillor and Chief from 1959 to 1960.*

Edward and Ella had two sets of twins. Madeline and Bernice were born in 1942 and died close together in the same year as their sister Winifred, in 1944. Twins, Matthew and James Douglas, were born in 1951. While Matthew survived, his twin James died at four months old. The two eldest sons Ben and Manuel died of complications of pneumonia in 1941 and 1945. Hubert also passed away at a young age and Faustine died while still in hospital shortly after her birth. The remaining children survived to later marry and have families of their own.

Virginia lives at Head of the Lake with her husband Leonard Gregoire. Herb remained at the home place at Irish Creek. He married Juanita Thomas of Enderby and has two daughters. Matthew, the youngest son, married Theresa Louis and resides at the original home place at Six-Mile Creek. Caroline never married but is remembered for her complete devotion and loyalty to her siblings and their children. She died of a heart attack on October 9, 1999 as a result of diabetes.

Virginia Gregoire: *I really appreciate my family for the care that they gave my sister Caroline, especially in the last five years of her life. My granddaughter Alexis was only twelve when Caroline lived with us. She would help my sister to change her dialysis when we weren't here. And I especially appreciate my husband Leonard for offering to care for Caroline when I had other things to do.*

In their life together Jack and Margaret not only lived on the east side of the lake, but also at Okanagan Landing and later at Six-Mile Creek. This was a time when Indian Affairs, backed up by the church, were pushing the Okanagan toward farming. During this time Indian Agents reported to Indian Affairs on the attitudes of the heads of families toward adoption of Indian Affairs policies. If seen as in favour the agents referred to them as "good Indians" if not, they were referred to as "radicals" or "agitators." Apparently, Jack was a "good Indian" as stated in the following article:

"LATE JACK BONNEAU IS RATED AS A GOOD INDIAN.
One of the few remaining full-blooded Indians passed away on the reserve at head of Okanagan Lake last Friday. Old timers remember Jack Bonneau as one of the best of the Siwashes and will regret to hear of his passing at the age of 64.... Like most of the full-blooded Indians, he was eager for education for the children on the reserve, and did his best to see that they got it. For years he had good cattle and until recently when his health gave out he was an industrious Indian known far and wide for his integrity.... Some years ago he made a trip to the Coast and, as is not infrequent among full-blooded Indians in the strange surroundings, he picked up some germs which worked on his system ever since. His early demise is believed to have been directly due to having made the trip in itself an entirely innocent event and a great adventure. The funeral was held at the Head of the Lake on Monday and the mourners are his wife and three sons. The cynical saying that the only good Indian is a dead one, is shown in its falsity in the life of the late Jack Bonneau."[5]

Both Jimmy and Edward continued in the cattle business after their father died. Edward not only produced fine stock but also leased out his property at Six-Mile Creek to the Chinese gardeners. Some say the produce taken from this property was some of the best produce in the valley. Large crops of tomatoes and subsistence produce were sold to the canneries and packing-houses. Later Edward moved his stock to Irish Creek and both he and his wife Ella and their children continued to live the traditional way of life of the Okanagan. In fact, both Edward and Ella were a key couple who received recognition for their involvement in the resurgence of the Okanagan culture in the decades before their death.

Jimmy married Sarah, the daughter of Lena Lawrence and Jack Musgrove. He also kept a good cattle herd, but unlike his brother Edward, did not lease property to outsiders. In fact, with the help of his large family he grew and harvested hay for his stock and provided food for his family by subsistence farming and cattle sales. His sons and grandsons carry on this tradition today.

Rosie Williams (paraphrased): *Our grandmother, Margaret, used to come and visit when we lived down there beside old Alexis. We didn't know her like we knew Tuma, because Tuma lived with us. One time, after we moved to Siwash Creek, we were going to school and we had to go to Gramma's. She lived here, over by Pierre Jack's. Uncle Edward lived there with her and when we got over there we saw her laying on her bed. She still wore that handkerchief on her head, just like in that picture and Uncle Edward was sobbing. He told us she was dead.*

Millie Steele: *Margaret Bonneau was Gramma Marchand's partner. They both had white horses, like you see in that picture. I remember Gramma Marchand telling Margaret that they would take her team up past the Cameron place on Six-Mile flat. They were going to get moss or something like that, and I used to like to go with them. When we got there, I'd head straight for the strawberries. They grew wild up there. Both of those women had white horses.*

JENNIE

CHRISTINE

BILLY & MILLIE

ERNEST & FAMILY

EMMA

MAURICE LEZARD

CHARLIE LEZARD

BREWER / LEZARD

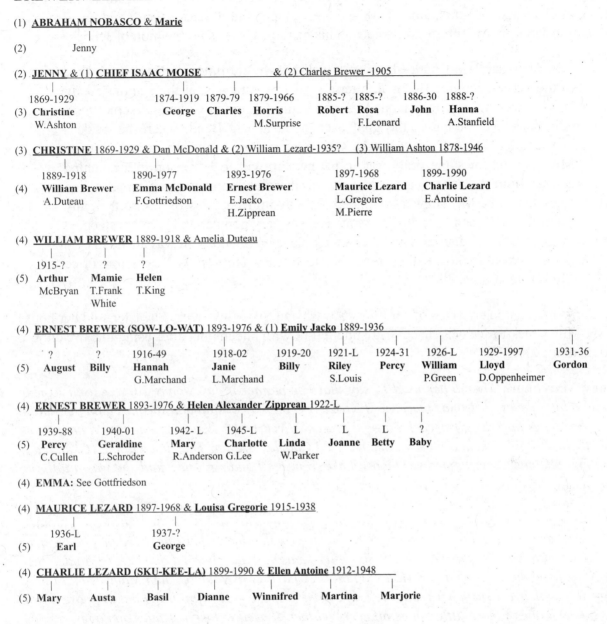

(1) **ABRAHAM NOBASCO & Marie**

(2)   Jenny

(2) **JENNY & (1) CHIEF ISAAC MOISE**   & (2) Charles Brewer -1905

1869-1929		1874-1919	1879-79	1879-1966		1885-?	1885-?		1886-30	1888-?
(3) **Christine**		**George**	**Charles**	**Horris**		**Robert**	**Rosa**		**John**	**Hanna**
W.Ashton				M.Surprise			F.Leonard			A.Stanfield

(3) **CHRISTINE** 1869-1929 & Dan McDonald & (2) William Lezard-1935?   (3) William Ashton 1878-1946

1889-1918	1890-1977	1893-1976	1897-1968	1899-1990
(4) **William Brewer**	**Emma McDonald**	**Ernest Brewer**	**Maurice Lezard**	**Charlie Lezard**
A.Duteau	F.Gottriedson	E.Jacko	L.Gregoire	E.Antoine
		H.Zipprean	M.Pierre	

(4) **WILLIAM BREWER** 1889-1918 & Amelia Duteau

1915-?	?	?
(5) **Arthur**	**Mamie**	**Helen**
McBryan	T.Frank	T.King
	White	

(4) **ERNEST BREWER (SOW-LO-WAT)** 1893-1976 & (1) **Emily Jacko** 1889-1936

?	?	1916-49	1918-02	1919-20	1921-L	1924-31	1926-L	1929-1997	1931-36
(5) **August**	**Billy**	**Hannah**	**Janie**	**Billy**	**Riley**	**Percy**	**William**	**Lloyd**	**Gordon**
		G.Marchand	L.Marchand		S.Louis		P.Green	D.Oppenheimer	

(4) **ERNEST BREWER** 1893-1976 & **Helen Alexander Zipprean** 1922-L

1939-88	1940-01	1942- L	1945-L	L	L	L	?
(5) **Percy**	**Geraldine**	**Mary**	**Charlotte**	**Linda**	**Joanne**	**Betty**	**Baby**
C.Cullen	L.Schroder	R.Anderson	G.Lee	W.Parker			

(4) **EMMA:** See Gottfriedson

(4) **MAURICE LEZARD** 1897-1968 & **Louisa Gregorie** 1915-1938

1936-L	1937-?
(5) **Earl**	**George**

(4) **CHARLIE LEZARD (SKU-KEE-LA)** 1899-1990 & **Ellen Antoine** 1912-1948

(5) **Mary**	**Austa**	**Basil**	**Dianne**	**Winnifred**	**Martina**	**Marjorie**

The Brewer name entered the band membership through Christine, the daughter of Okanagan woman Jenny and Chief Moise. Christine became known as Brewer after Jenny married Welshman Charles Brewer. Oral history claims that Christine was also a half-sister to Johnny Isaac and Christine O'Keefe. Christine Brewer's children thereafter were known by the Brewer name. William married Amelia Duteau and had three children. Ernest married twice and had in total twenty-two children. Emma married Frank Gottfriedson and had seventeen children while Maurice and Charlie both married and took their father's name, Lezard.

Charles Brewer married Jenny, the daughter of Okanagan parents Abraham Nobasco and Marie, at Okanagan Mission, June 8, 1873.[2] The couple had at least seven children. Brewer's obituary in January 1905 pretty well sums up his history. There is no mention of Jenny.

> "On Thursday last, Charles Brewer, a well-known old-timer in this district, died in the Vernon Jublilee Hospital, after a stroke of paralysis, at the age of 75. Mr. Brewer was born in Rockland, ME, and came to British Columbia some thirty odd years ago, taking in the gold excitement at Big Bend, where he made a considerable stake. Coming to the Okanagan valley, he bought a ranch at the Mission, and for some years was in partnership with E.J.Tronson in a ranching and saw-mill business. This partnership was dissolved some twelve years ago, and since that time Mr. Brewer continued the saw-mill business by himself, finally selling out to Wood, Cargill Company. He was very popular and greatly esteemed in all parts of the district. The funeral took place on Sunday and was attended by a number of old friends. Pall bearers were T.Ellis, E.J.Tronson, W.F.Cameron, Price Ellison, J.C.Campbell."[3]

Christine spent many years of her life at Siwash and Six-Mile Creek. She later sold her house at Six-Mile Creek to Joe Marchand. Christine fell ill with pneumonia after using the sweathouse and died in 1929.[4]

Jenny Marchand: *My mother used to say that her mother-in-law Jenny Brewer used to ride horses a lot. Like at Christmas time, she'd have a real big bag of stuff and she puts it on the saddle then she comes and she gives each house a present. Everybody! Wherever she sees a house, she goes there and gives them a present. She married Charles Brewer. They lived at the [Okanagan] Landing. She must have come over Goose Lake from the Landing. They said she was a tall, big woman. I think that's why my dad was so tall and big on the shoulders.*

My grandmother Christine, Jenny's daughter, was not as tall as her mother but she was stouter. Christine has the same father as Johnny Isaac. Our grandmother, Christine, lived in a house over where Joe Marchand's house is now, at Six-Mile. That old house burned down. My grandmother Christine lived there with her son Maurice Lezard. Charlie was younger than Maurice and I used to go stay with her. I knew her really well. She used to make real soft pillows out of goose down. She bit each one of those little things off every feather. It used to take her ages and ages to make one pillow. Then she made two feather mattresses. The one I used to sleep on, you just sink right down into it. She used to knit and crochet all the blankets and bed spreads and scarves, and you should see the sweaters she made. She made the sweaters out of raw sheep's wool that she fixed herself. She'd get raw wool and twist it all into balls. She'd have rolls and rolls of wool all over her house. She'd make gloves too for all those guys like Martin and Casimir Tonasket. She made toques for men and tams for women.

Rose Louis: *My grandmother's son Maurice built that house at Six-Mile Creek. They lived at the Jack place by the Six-Mile church before that and also at Siwash Creek where Sophie and Henry Wilson had their old house. At Siwash Creek they had a little house and then they moved over to Six-Mile Creek where Maurice built a small house out of planks that they took from sluice boxes.*

I used to stay with my grandmother at that house, and I remember she used to pan for gold in Siwash Creek. She'd go up there and pan for enough gold to buy groceries. In one day she'd get about fourteen dollars worth of gold. In them days that was lots of money. She'd then walk to town and walk all the way back with her groceries. She never would take a ride from anyone. Mary Louise Alexander did that too. She'd never take a ride down here to see her sister, Harriet. She'd step off the road when a car went by. I guess they liked to walk.

Jenny Marchand: *My mother, Emily, my brother Gordon, and my sister Hannah's son, Dammy, all died in the same week. The two boys were kind of sickly all the time, but they were both taking medicine. My mother took Gordon and Dammy with her everywhere she went. Hannah stayed at my dad's most of the time and that's why my mother called them both her babies. They were both four years old. Hannah's two other kids, Clifford and Christine, stayed with ol' lady Marchand then. She wanted them, and so Hannah let them go. Hannah couldn't work 'cause she had eczema on her hands up to her elbows. Christine had rheumatic fever, and of course, she done whatever she wanted to do 'cause her gramma was watching her. Christine died when she was about ten years old. So Dammy and Gordon were more like brothers than anything 'cause they were both four years old. On the night we buried our mom, our brother Gordon died. They claim they all died of meningitis and couldn't do anything about it.*

The same night we buried our mother, Gordon was playing on the bed and he wouldn't take his things off. My dad said, "Let me take your coat off." He said, "No I'm not takin' it off." It must have been about ten or eleven o'clock. My dad said, "Come on, let me take your coat off." He said, "No! I'm, not takin' it off, and I'm not going to sleep!" So my dad coaxed him and took off his shoes and in a little while he was jumpin' around and said to my dad, "Dad, look at my mom, standin' over there by those cherry trees and she's whistlin' at me. She wants me to go there. Look she's standin' there!" My dad looked over there and he can't see her. My dad said, "I can't see anything." He said, "She's there, she's whistlin' at me and wants me to go over there." And my dad packed him and he went over to the window and said, "She's not there! I can't see anything!" Not very long after he went to sleep. So we went to bed.

There was a big bed upstairs. I got on the bed and was goin' to sleep and Louie and Gus came up. So Louie laid in the middle and Gus laid on the other side of Louie. And you know, I couldn't sleep. I was wide awake and tried to talk to Louie, but he was sound asleep, so I left him alone. Then, all of a sudden, I heard Mary Louise hollerin' and hollerin' and she said to my dad, "Hurry up, he's doin' the same thing as Dammy." An', you know, I jumped out of bed an' I got my things on and I went down stairs. By the time I got down there he was gone. That's how fast he went. That's when I heard my dad cry. I felt so sorry for him. It was just too many at one time.

He was outside walkin' around cryin' and cryin' and cryin'. He'd come in an' seen their things and he'd cry and cry. So Mary Louise and Annie Logan and my sister Hannah, they got in there and got all their stuff together and did what my dad tol' them to do and they burned it. You know the thing was, my mother had so much done when she got sick. She had so much food canned; all kinds of stuff canned and put away in the basement. Seems to me when she was finished, she started goin' down. She was always real kind to all us kids and weighed only about a hundred pounds.

In them days everyone played the fiddle. Then later they started playing the guitar. Alex Louie played the accordion and it doesn't matter where you go to dances and parties even the young guys would pick up the fiddle and have their turn. Out of all my dad's people, he was the only one who couldn't play the fiddle. The reason why is, in his teenage years, he went to Douglas Lake and worked for Chief Chilheetza till he was about eighteen, then he came home. He said that is the reason he never learned. Horace Brewer and all his boys could fiddle, same as Charlie Lezard, he could do a lot of things, but not my dad. He always wished he learned.

Riley Brewer: *My dad had a combine. He hayed and farmed and worked the land with horses. He had cows, too. I had to work with him. I was driving wild horses since I was ten years old. We had wild horses that we used to harrow the hay fields. Because one of the team was a wild horse, my dad tol' me don't tie the lines together behind your back. I got tired and tied them together and put them behind my back. We were goin' along and the harrows hooked on a root and jumped ahead and the wild horses run away with me. I was down and draggin' behind the harrows when Dad hollered at that ol' horse to stop. The horse stopped and now I know why my dad tol' me not to put the lines behind my back.*

It was in the thirties but we never went hungry. We had milk cows, turkeys, geese and chickens and beef and cherry trees, apples, currants and berries. All planted by my dad. We had everything on the ranch to live on so we never went hungry. We only bought flour and sugar and stuff like that.

Jenny Marchand: *I remember back in those days you could hear the sleighs coming up the road. It was so cold the sleighs made a crackling sound. The people had wood and was takin' it to town. You could hear them from way back there and you should hear the bells. Frank Marchand, Narcisse Jack and Pierre Louis, they all had bells on their horses when they have sleighs. Do they ever sound good! That Frank Marchand, I don't know where he ever got his, but boy were they ever nice. My dad had some bells too and so did ol' Scotty from Round Lake. Chista Logan's wife, Annie, had a cutter and a little thing on her horse with bells on it. They all had different sounds. In fact, you know who's coming up the road.*

When Vera was a baby a big fire started up here at Irish Creek. Dad tol' me to take Gramma Mary Logan and the other kids in the car and drive the other way, away from the fire. That fire was just rollin' down the hill. We ran across the creek and I saw my dad and Louie just a runnin' down the hill. Before my dad's horse stopped he jumped off and ran to the garage and got the car out. I drove away with Gramma, Ella Bessette and the kids. Dad and them guys stayed behind to put out the fire. Then finally the wind stopped and that fire started going down toward Six-Mile on the upper part of the range. It burned all that hill from up here at Irish Creek down to Six-Mile. A big truck came from town and sprayed all over right next to my dad's barn and all the trees. We never had a fire like that since. That's the same time William Louie wouldn't leave his house. He just wouldn't. That fire was so close to his house that it burned his hair. But he wouldn't quit.

Although Christine's younger sons, Maurice and Charlie, were also known as Brewer, when they got older they took Lezard as their surname. In all instances the death journals kept by Mary Abel have confirmed most death dates kept by other sources. Included in Mary's journal is an entry from 1935 disclosing the death of one "W.M. Lesarzard." Although the spelling of the surname differs, it is possible that this entry is the father of Maurice and Charlie. Clara Dubrett, stepdaughter to Charlie Lezard, remembers Charlie mentioning that his father was from Seattle, Washington. Other statistics are not known about this man. Penticton-born Atman, previously mentioned by Rose Louis, is said to descend from the same Lezard line.

Maurice married Louisa, the daughter of Herman and Angelique Gregoire. They had three sons. Billy died in 1934 and is buried at Head of the Lake cemetery. Earl and George remained in the area and worked at haying for others on the Reserve.

By his own account Charlie was named after Louie Jim's father Sku-kee-la, which means, "dead tree still standing."[5] Perhaps unknowingly, others nicknamed him Nuyr-qilps, which means, "twisted neck."[6] Charlie married Ellen Antoine the daughter of Jimmy and Mary Louise Antoine on April 29, 1935. Together they had several children and lived at Blacktown. Clara remembers too, when her mother died and how life changed for her and her siblings.

Charles and Jenny's children can be seen in the family tree, and the only one of the second generation to marry back into the Okanagan bloodline was Horris Brewer. He married Matilda Surprise (Supernant). Matilda's mother, Sophie Stinwisket, was first married to Chief Edward, the son of Penticton's Chief Francois. Edward and Sophie had two daughters, Mary Anne and Margaret Edwards. Mary Anne married William Cohen II, the son of William Cohen Senior and Stalo woman, Lkometamat. William Cohen III married Alex and Helene Marchand's daughter, Laura. Sophie Stinwisket married a second time to Francois Supernant. (The surname Supernant evolved into Surprise as the Indians could not pronounce Supernant.) Matilda's sister Julia married Charles Richter, the son of Okanagan woman, Lucy Simla, and cattle baron, Frank Xavier Richter, while another sister, Lena, married William Shuttleworth, the son of Henry Shuttleworth and Josephine. They settled at Okanagan Falls.

TERESE QUALTIER

ALPHONSE LOUIE

JOHNNY PANTS / ANDREW

KATHERINE LOUIS

EDWARD FRED

ELIZABETH FRED

LENA FRED

MAGGIE EDWARD & JOHNNY VICTOR

LOUIE VICTOR

WILLIAM VICTOR

FRED / MICHELE / QUALTIER / ANDREW / VICTOR

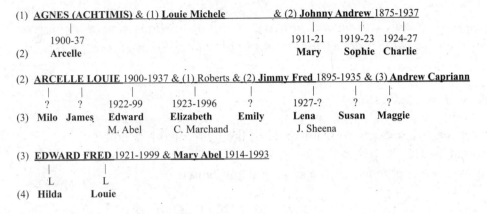

The Fred, Michele, Qualtier, Andrew and Victor surnames are all part of the above family history. At present only the Fred name survives at Head of the Lake, embodied in the son and grandchildren of Edward Fred and Mary Abel. The other names were present in the early years, but no longer exist here because of death and name changes.

The marriage record says that Jimmie Fred was the son of Fred Ishahan and Lizzie. He was twenty-six when he married twenty-year-old "Angela." Angela was the daughter of Louie "Coulter" (Qualtier) and Agnes Michele of Westbank. They were married May 30, 1921 at Head of the Lake Church by Father Le Jeune, OMI.[2] A further record of 1905 explains that Louie Qualtier married Marie Alexis at Penticton. Louie was forty, and the son of Cyprien Qualtier and Angelique (Kalamalka?). Marie was twenty-eight and the daughter of Abraham Alexis and Marianne. The record goes on to point out that Marie was born at Duck Lake.[3] and confirms testimony of Mary Jane Lawrence when she said that her mother Katherine was the niece to Louie Qualtier of Penticton.

Michele

Edward Fred was the first person contacted in regard to the Fred family name. He told me his story which included Louie Michele, or Spe-pa-cheen. He said Louie Michele (Qualtier) was his granduncle on his mother's side and he was related to Ned and Ben Louis through the Qualtier side. Henry and Millie Jack of Westbank added that Spe-pa-cheen means "echo" or "his voice echoes and can be heard across the land."[4]

In spite of his family relationship Edward could not form an accurate ancestral line. With the help of the records and oral history, a sketch of the families involved was formed. Ned Louis begins here with his memories of Louie Michele, or Spe-pa-cheen. Edward follows with his current family history and then we move back in history through the memories of further family.

Ned Louis: *Ol' Louie died comin' down O'Keefe Hill. His horses gotta comin' down that hill too fast, and ol' Spe-pa-cheen and his wagon took a wreck and Spe-pa-cheen died there. When that ol' fella died, Alex helped that ol' lady with the hay. It was just a little meadow then, all the rest of that property was bush. After Alex and Helene Marchand's house burned they stayed for a while at Julia's.*

Records found later confirm Ned's story.

> "Michel Spapowcheen (Chuckatchen) from Head of the Lake died November 19, 1920 at O'Keefe ranch. The 70 year old deceased was killed when the young man who was driving became frightened on the steep hill and bolted."[5]

Julia Spapowcheen died in Vernon hospital October 20, 1926 at sixty-two years of age.[6] No parents are mentioned for either person.

Fred

Edward Fred: *When I was young I didn't care to know who was related to me. Now I wish I studied it long time ago, then I'd know when people tell me they are my relations. It makes me scratch my head. It's like the Pierre's and Alex's at Penticton, they are all my close relations on my mother's side, but I don't know exactly how.*

From my mother's side, I am from the Qualtier family and am related to Pierre and Katherine Louis' family. Katherine is a Qualtier through her mother Terese. I think they originated from Penticton.

My mom Arcelle had two sons by a first marriage. They were Milo and James, and they died before I was born. Then my mom met my dad down here, and went back to Chapperon Lake, where I was born. I'm the oldest of Jimmy Fred's kids. After my dad died in 1933, my mom took up with Andrew Caprian and had Susan and Maggie. They both died too, and I am the only one left.

I don't know who my dad's father was but he had a brother named Stroney Fred. Lottie Lindley [Boston] from Quilchena is from that family. Her mother's name is Christine. The Yumlst's from Spences Bridge are my first cousins. I only met one of them at Round Lake Treatment Centre when I was speaking. I see him now and again and he stayed sober all this time. Lottie's husband Isaac is also my cousin. His mother is Louise Roper. I am also related to the Tom, McLeod, McLean and Stewart families from Douglas Lake.

My son and his boys are the only ones to carry on the Fred name. On my father's side, the Fred's originated from Spences Bridge. My dad was a small man and so was Mary Abel's dad Joe Abel, my son's grandfather on his mother's side. My son Louie takes after his grandfather Joe Abel. My Hilda though took after me. She's taller. All my family is small. I'm the only one who is big. They say I took after my Uncle Alphonse, my mother's brother. [The son of Louie Michele and Susan Felix][7] I even walk like him, but my mother she was shorter and a little stouter.

My dad had a farm at Chaperon Lake. He had a house, a little barn, and a corral and about twenty to thirty head of cows and horses and a wagon, mowing machine and rake. That place had a lot of muskrats, beaver and lynx. In the fall, he had a mountain trap line at Beaulea Lake. He rides up and spends two days up there then comes home. He brings home pelts, mink, and lynx. Sometimes down along the lake and creek he has traps there, he traps otter too. He sells the pelts to a fur buyer from Kamloops, whose name is Tom Bulman. That was in the late twenties and he was getting old then. I remember when he set his traps, sometimes he'd catch his fingers in there. That was in the 1920's and he was gettin' blind.

Sometimes I think if my dad didn't have to go out and do the things he did, he might been better and lived longer. I don't know exactly how old he was, but he died in 1933. I remember in them days it was cold and it was only by sleigh and horses that you could get there. We were already down here, and my grandparents couldn't take us up there to his funeral. After he died and my mother went with Capriene, the farm went to pot. They wanted to send us to Kamloops school but my grandparents said no way and brought us here. It was June 10, 1937 when my mother died and Father Scott came and drove us up there to her funeral at Douglas Lake.

Andrew

Johnny Andrew got with my grandmother Agnes [Achitmis] Michele after my grandfather Louie Michele [Qualtier] died. Johnny was Mexican and running from the law. In the early days when Douglas Lake first began, Johnny Andrew came over there and asked for a job and changed his name to Johnny Pants. The Mounties came around there lookin' for him. They went down the line asking the names of the people and they come to Johnny and asked the people what his name was. Well, they said his name is Johnny Pants. All the people just knew him as Johnny Pants. Only here, did they know him as Johnny Andrew.

When Johnny married my grandmother and their first child was born, he got rid of his outlaw outfit. I know 'cause he told me himself. His sword, his big knife, his revolver and his belt and cartridges were all there, like John Wayne, you know. He took all his weapons down to the mouth of Six-Mile Creek, where there was deep blue water, and threw them in there. He came back from the lake no more an outlaw. From that time on he kneeled down and stayed with the church till the day he died. Him and my grandmother had three kids but they all died when they were babies. The last one was named Casimir. I still remember him even though I was real young.

Johnny was pretty good to us, but the only thing wrong with him is too much church. Well, people around here didn't like him, he gets in the church and he prays too damn long. The people get tired of him. My grandmother was real strict with us. When I was young, I went along with the punishment but when I got older I said enough of that. We do everything for you and help you, now you don't have to treat us like that. Teach us something better, not that kind of stuff!

My mother died when I was sixteen, but I never missed her because I was being raised by my grandparents. My sister Elizabeth later married Charlie Marchand, the son of Frank and Christine Marchand. And my sister Lena went to Quilchena and married one of our distant relatives, Johnny Sheena. They had kids and a lot of her family is still there. When she left Johnny she came here and stayed with me for about one year at Dry Creek. Then she went to live with someone at Salmon Arm for a couple of years, then came back here for just a little while, then she just disappeared. I heard she was down across the line and died down there somewhere. I never heard from her, no card, no letter, nothing. I don't even know where she is buried.

Ben Louis: *Johnny was standing too close to the road, around Alfred Bonneau's place, when a car went by and the door handle caught his pocket and pulled off his pants. We just called him Johnny Pants after that![1]*

Millie Steele: *That Johnny Pants used to pray for hours and hours. I used to tell Gramma Marchand, you pray. Johnny Pants prays too long. She'd just tell me, "Well, he prays like that so you will learn. If he wants to pray then just let him."*

Eva Lawrence: *Sqwnim-te-nalqs was Kalamalka's daughter and she was the mother to Mary, Nancy and Julianne Qualtier. But I don't know how they got the name Qualtier. I just know that she was related to Katherine Louis. According to Tommy Gregoire, Sqwnim-te-nalqs got her name from the area what is now the north end of Kalamalka Lake. The area there was her playground and when she stands against the hillside, against the rising sun, her skirt changes colours and that is what her name means, a skirt of changing colours. She told me that her English name was Angelique, but because the Indians couldn't say that, they called her Arcelique [Aschelle].*

Ned Louis: *Mary, Sqwnim-te-nalqs' daughter, was a Qualtier. That's the reason why my mother [Katherine Louis] is her closest relative. When Mary died she left that place to my mother. Before that, the Indian Department built that little house for her and you know, once the Indian Affairs builds you a house you can't will it to anybody. So that's why I got that place. Mom said, "What would I do with that place now, at my age!" She was old then, and when it came around she was the last and oldest relative. So she said just pay them for the house and take the place over, and that's what I did, and then turned it over to Fred. Mom was the closest in that part. [meaning Mary's father] But when you're thinkin' of the other part, Mary and Nancy's mother, she married Big Louie from Enderby. They didn't have any kids though.*

The mother of Nancy and Mary Qualtier was married to Big Louie in Enderby. That little grave yard, this side of Enderby, is her place. Mary, her daughter, married Alexander Victor and when he died, Mary lived with Allen Edwards. The ol' lady, their mother, went back and forth between here and Enderby. Every time I went by her place, she'd call me, tell me to come in, she was makin' pancakes. "Sn-qws-u-lawh," she'd say, "I'm makin' pancakes." I used to leave my team at her place and go back and forth across the lake on my saddle horse.

Eva Lawrence: *Sqwnim-te-nalqs was not my grandmother, but I called her Tupa. I was a year old when my mother Edith Nicholas died. After that I lived with my grandmother Mary Nicholas. Then when I got a little older I was taken in by Nancy. She was a first cousin or something like that to my mother's mother, Mary Nicholas. Nancy told me to tell the Indian Agent that I wanted to live with her instead of my mother's mom. I remember, I was really glad 'cause that meant that I could live with Tupa too. I really liked her. She was really kind and had a good sense of humour. She always taught me never to gossip or tell lies. She believed in the church and was a real good woman.*

From the time I come to remember, Sqwnim-te-nalqs lived in that log house a little ways from Neehoot with Mary Edwards and we lived in a house out in the field the other way from where my son Dave lives now. She'd walk with her two daughters from there. So I grew up knowing her. She was so kind and had a good sense of humour. Sqwnim-te-nalqs was fun, we played with her. One night we went to church at St. Theresa's in Six-Mile or Snklahootan, and Millie Steele and I went behind her and we'd sneak ahead of her. We'd hide in the bushes. There's lot of rose bushes along there and then we'd pretend we were ghosts. Tupa had a little cane and when she goes, she kind of trots. It's dark and it's evening mass; benediction. She'd come up and she'd say, "I'm gonna use my cane on you when I catch up." And we kept doing that till we got to the church. Coming back we didn't do that. But she came home and went to bed and slept, I guess three days, and she died.

When she died they got the doctor and she wouldn't wake up. Then they got the priest, and she still wouldn't wake up. Then they took her and had an autopsy and they said she was so old that she just faded away. There was no illness. She had no teeth decay, she can thread a needle, no arthritis, no heart problems. Nothing! I used to get whippings from my grandmother [Nancy]. And when she tells me you get in there and you do the dishes and I say I'm going, and at the same time I'm lazy, Tupa would jump up. Well, she is the size of me, and she'd go and she'd do the dishes. Or sometimes my granny would get a stick and she'd get ready to whip me and Tupa would tell her daughter, "You gotta hit me first!" When she died, I cried for that. We used to have an old barn there and I cried my eyes out and I thought, who's gonna take my part. Who's gonna do dishes. That is so selfish, now that I think of it.

Neither Granny or Tupa could speak English. I remember when Granny Nancy would try to sell gloves. When we lived over there, at Neehoot, she'd stay up all night sewing gloves and we'd go in a buggy and go to town the next day. She'd go on the street and check the Bay and all those stores and my Tupa – she was getting short – she'd tell her daughter give the gloves to me! She'd go and walk on the street and, of course, I'd be with her, 'cause I loved being with her. There was nice dressed guys walkin' with their heads in the air along the street. Well, she's short and she'd grab them and put the gloves up to them and they'd laugh and they'd buy it from her. She'd get fifty cents a pair.

Sqwnim-te-nalqs' daughter, Mary, married Alexander Victor from Enderby. They had three sons Johnny, Louie and William. Alexander died and Mary got with Allen Edwards. He was from around Kamloops. Mary stayed at Deep Creek until she died in 1963.

I remember Mary Edwards when she died. She was going with Mary Louise and her daughter, Susan Joe, up to what they called "Huckleberry Mountain." That is Silver Star. They said they camped at the bottom and made supper and Mary rolled up her sweater and used it as a pillow. Later they called her for supper and she didn't wake up. So they took her to the hospital in Vernon but she was already dead.

Granny Nancy married Francois Gregoire. They had two kids but they died when they were young. I never knew them. After the kids died Nancy and Francois parted and she went back to Deep Creek to live with Sqwnim-te-nalqs.

When Granny Nancy got sick she wanted to die like her sister Mary and her mother Sqwnim-te-nalqs. She used to pray for a death like that. She knew too, when she was going to die. She called all the people together here. There was lots of people here and they were sitting around her bedside. She said goodbye to me and the other people but when it came time to say goodbye to Willie she sure broke down. She really liked Willie. He used to do a lot of things for her. She told him he would have to take full responsibility for me and the kids.

Rose Louis: *That old lady Sqwnim-te-nalqs liked to call herself Tootsie Allen. She was no relation to Allen Edwards. He was just the husband of her daughter Mary. After Mary's son, Louie Victor, got with Martha [Tootsie] Simla, the old lady thought that name was so pretty that she called herself Tootsie Allen.*

The last time I saw Louie Qualtier and his wife was when they came up here for me and Ben's wedding. They were old then and he was all crippled up with arthritis. They camped at Pierre and Katherine's place. They were from Penticton and were here because they were fencing that place at Duck Lake. That was their place then.

Victor

Johnny, William and Louie Victor were Mary's sons. Johnny Victor also known as, Barcette or Barney Alexander, married Penticton's Maggie Edward, the widow of Alex Paul and daughter of Edward Michel and Sophie. William Victor, also known as William Alexander, married widow Cecile Baptiste, nee Clemah, on September, 26, 1924.[7] Cecile's first husband was Washington born Narcisse Baptiste. He died April 7, 1923.[8]

Although the next story takes another route it is relevant here as the couple's names are within the band membership. The story is also an example of the standards set out by the early church.

Rose Louis: *That old couple, Baptiste and Cecile, lived across the lake and we used to see them sometimes come by our place at Spider Ranch. They had a single buggy and they would go to town over the hill from where Wilfred Bonneau has his place now. Sometimes at night they came back the other way, further north over Goose Lake road. They didn't need to drive the horse because that old horse would take them home. You could watch that horse stop and eat and go a little further then stop and eat again. They lived across the lake and that old man died and William married his widow Cecile. She was a chief's daughter from Enderby. She was a lot older than he was. Back then if you were ever caught with someone they made you get married. That's why they got together. Louie never married, but lived with Martha Tootsie for a while. None of the Victors had kids.*

Edward Fred died of cancer in 1999. He was a man who followed his own convictions and was very proud of his heritage as an Okanagan man involved with Okanagan rights and customs. He served in the army as a driving mechanic, was involved with Alcoholics Anonymous, and served on the board for some years at Round Lake Drug and Alcohol Treatment Centre. He was a loyal and active member of the Inkamuplux Elder's Society. Edward's knowledge of Okanagan history, place and people names and his ardent support to see this book completed will always be appreciated. Edward leaves behind his daughter, Hilda Belanger, and son, Louie Fred. The Fred name is carried on through Louie's children.

TOP: FRANK, CLARENCE, JOSEPHINE, GEORGE

MIDDLE: GUS, ROSE, TEDDY, ADELINE

BOTTOM: ANGELINE, JOHN, JANE, CLEMENT

RIGHT: SPIDER RANCH

GOTTFRIEDSON (GOTTFRIEDSEN)

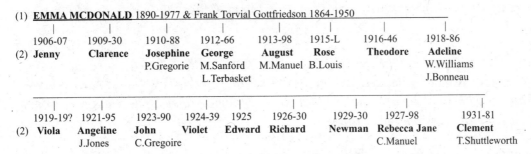

(1) **EMMA MCDONALD** 1890-1977 & Frank Torvial Gottfriedson 1864-1950

1906-07	1909-30	1910-88	1912-66	1913-98	1915-L	1916-46	1918-86
(2) **Jenny**	**Clarence**	**Josephine**	**George**	**August**	**Rose**	**Theodore**	**Adeline**
		P.Gregorie	M.Sanford	M.Manuel	B.Louis		W.Williams
			L.Terbasket				J.Bonneau

1919-19?	1921-95	1923-90	1924-39	1925	1926-30	1929-30	1927-98	1931-81
(2) **Viola**	**Angeline**	**John**	**Violet**	**Edward**	**Richard**	**Newman**	**Rebecca Jane**	**Clement**
	J.Jones	C.Gregoire					C.Manuel	T.Shuttleworth

The surname Gottfriedson is of Danish origin and comes to be a prominent name at Head of the Lake through Frank Torvial Gottfriedson. Frank's parents were Frank Henrich Gottfriedson and Stalo woman, Yetta. He was born April 7, 1864, at Spitlum Flats near Harrison Lake.[2] Frank had two brothers, November and Henry. All seem to have come to the Okanagan about the same time. Gottfriedson Mountain, southwest of Vernon, was apparently named for November.

"Gottfriedson Mountain is named after November Gottfriedson; a Danish half-breed and the first settler on the wild hay meadows at Hatheume Lake....There is story, probably started by himself, that since he was born after his brother August he was named September, but because he was 'always late' he was generally called November.... He died at Kamloops in the late 1940s."[3]

As the story goes, Frank and his brothers went to school somewhere near New Westminster but Frank left home and school at fourteen and became a longshoreman off the mainland. After working on the ships for a few short years he went to Clinton where in 1883 he married a local woman, Susan Jane Grinder.[4] They had one son Francis. For the record, Francis married Rosie Haller at Big Bar in 1915.[5]

Frank Torvial married a second time to Julianne Edwards, aka Wilson, in Vernon, 1902.[6] They lived on the Six-Mile flat and were good friends to David Cameron, as Julianne and Cameron's second wife, Elizabeth, were sisters. However, Frank and Julianne had no children and she died shortly after the marriage.

Three years later, Frank married Emma McDonald, the daughter of Christine Brewer and Dan McDonald, on the September 5, 1905.[7] Emma was born at White Valley May 1, 1890.[8] Subsequently, Frank and Emma had seventeen children; eight daughters and nine sons. They also began their marriage on the Six-Mile flat at Frank's log cabin. Later they moved to the east side of Okanagan Lake. They moved back to Siwash Creek so their children could attend the Six-Mile Day School. After that they moved to what they called Dirty Lake on the corner of Highway 97 and Westside Road.

Rose Louis: *Mom told us that her father, Dan McDonald, came to see her before he left Vernon. He brought her a tin plate with pink roses on it and an enamel cup. She never saw him again after that.*

My mother worked really hard all her life. I guess she pretty well had to, to raise all us kids. When we lived at Spider Ranch, Mom dressed the boys like girls in dresses. It was hard, I guess, to diaper them all, so with only dresses she didn't have to change diapers. They just ran around without pants and wore diapers only at bedtime.

My mother and dad moved from Six-Mile flat over to the east side of the lake. For a while, I guess, they lived in a tent on the bench above Ben's place then moved closer to the lake. They called that place Spider Ranch. There was a log house already built there and that's where we slept. My dad built another place next to it out of lumber and that was where we cooked and ate.

My dad mostly farmed. He worked that land across the lake and my mom had lots of chickens. Some people said that when you look across the lake to Spider Ranch it was just white. That's how many chickens they had, I guess. They had milk cows too, and a separator and churn with a hole covered with glass. I remember that hole had to be covered tight or you could loose the cream. When you wanted to see how well the butter was churning then you looked through the glass. Anyway, Mom had little wooden boxes that we lined with paper and when it was ready you just wrap it up into one pound cubes. Mom would take the eggs and butter and go on her buggy over Goose Lake road and sell it in town. She went to town quite often. I remember she sold the butter for thirty-five cents a pound.

When we were living at Spider Ranch, ol' Atmin would come around there. He was from Penticton, from the Lezard family. We knew about him and heard that he could run really fast. He never wore shoes and always had a rooster sitting on his shoulder, on his back pack. Anyway, he came to our place and Josephine had some chickens that she really liked. And she thought that if she raced with Atmin she could win. So she told Atmin to race her. My dad put stakes in the ground to mark out where they were going to race. Atmin and Josephine lined up at the starting place and my dad said go. Right away Atmin got way ahead of Josephine. In fact, Atmin was coming back already and Josephine was still running the first half. He won Josephine's favourite chickens and walked off with them under his arms. Poor Josephine she was so pitiful. She cried and cried, but Atmin never even looked back.

Atmin always had his dog with him too. The dog's name was Tetwit. It was a male dog and his name means boy. He had another dog that he left in Penticton. Her name was Hehootem which means girl. He'd be around for a while then he'd say, "I'd better go home, Tetwit is lonesome for Hehootem." We were just kids and we used to laugh, but never in front of him 'cause that would be an insult. But when you're just kids, those things are real funny. Then he'd teach us to count and he'd always say, eleven, eight, seven. He always said the same numbers, even if they were out of order. There's lots of stories about ol' Atmin.

He was really scared of snakes, and Ben said he had a house on stilts across the lake. Ben said he built it out of rails and stuff. He put it up in the thorn bushes because I guess he thought the snakes wouldn't go up there. He'd run and jump over the wall to get in there. And he'd sing really loud too. You could hear him from a ways off. He lived like the old timers and took baths in the morning. He'd even cut holes in the ice and run really fast and jump in. You could hear him yelling from a long ways off. ·

Josephine married Pete Gregoire. They never had kids. They used to travel all over the country, even down the States to all the places where Indians gathered. Sometimes my mother would go with them. Nothing stopped them, they'd be here one day and the next I'd hear they were gone.

One time when we were little our grandmother, Christine Brewer, took Josephine and I up past Silver Star. She showed us these flowers that the Indians used to get people together. That place was a long ways up Silver Star Mountain, just below the lookout station. They were supposed to be some kind of love potion flowers with bright pink petals. I barely remember that time, but it was around the time that I guess they wanted me to take that ceremony for girls that were going into their woman stage. I never though. I don't know why. One time Pete and Josephine got charged with hunting off the Reserve out of season. They fought that case though and they won because they proved that place at Silver Star was a traditional hunting and berry picking territory. Josephine learned a lot about tanning hides and making gloves and beading from our mother. She got really good at doing traditional stuff like that.

In 1921 Clarence, Josephine, George and I were sent by train to St. George's Anglican Residential School in Lytton. I was six and a half years old. I stayed there until I was eight and a half then came back and went to Six-Mile School until 1929.

I don't know why but I left home before going to Kamloops School. I guess it was because my uncle got me a job at Minnie Lake, just past Penask Lodge, to stay with this woman. She was going to have a baby. Then they brought in a baby-sitter and took her to the hospital by buggy. She was gone for a month. I was fifteen and milked the cow and fed the chickens. That's all I did. Then when my brother Richard died I came back. Within four months, Richard and my youngest brother, Newman, died. After that, I was sent to Kamloops School.

In 1923 we moved to Siwash Creek so we could go to school. My dad bought some land from my grandmother, Christine Brewer. He later sold it to Johnny Bonneau then he sold it to his sister, Rosie Williams. At Siwash Creek my mom grew lots of beans, peas, raspberries, strawberries and chickens. She made butter and sold beans and the berries in Armstrong and Vernon. We all had to help in the garden, picking the beans and the berries. All of us girls helped her to tan hides and she'd make gloves and sell them in town. In the summer she'd load up all the stuff in her wagon and in winter she'd use a cutter with a single horse. Sometimes she'd leave early in the morning and wouldn't get back till late at night.

The boys mostly cut wood and worked with my dad. My oldest brother, Clarence, worked building train trestles in Elbow, Saskatchewan. Then he came back and was working for Johnny Alexis over by the Landing somewhere. That winter he caught a cold and must of picked up TB and he died in 1930. Two of my other brothers, Richard and Newman died that same year spring too... all within three months of each other.

I was eighteen when I left Kamloops School and got married when I was nineteen. Ben and I were married on June 26, 1933 at St. Theresa's at Six-Mile, in a double ceremony with Ben's brother Ned and Irene McDougall. It was funny we were there and here comes Irene on horseback, just flying up the road. She looked so funny with her wedding veil just a flyin' in the wind. We got married by, I think, Father Cullanen and after that we went to Pierre and Katherine's. Both Ben and Ned went to work in the afternoon and we never saw them for quite a while. I stored my wedding veil upstairs at Pierre and Katherine's. The crown of my veil was made of wax and it had dogwood flowers on it. Anyway one day I went up there and saw the crown all crumbled up and the veil torn to shreds. I sure felt sad when I saw it there all broken and torn.

Ben and I lived up at Six-Mile Creek road, where the Haworth farm is now. Ben was logging up there with his dad and Ned. That's where Mike was born. I named him after my brother Clarence, but everyone called him Mike. Then Evelyn came along and May was the baby when I remember coming back from Peachland in the buggy. Ben was working down there that time. We were coming back on Westside road and Mike got all excited and was yelling and hitting us from the back of the wagon. Ben and I looked back and there was Evelyn running after us. She was crying and screaming her head off. I guess as we went by a tree or maybe a bush, she grabbed the limb and it drug her off the wagon. Ben and I laughed and laughed.

My brother Gus worked at logging and ranching. He helped my dad in the bush while he was still living here. After he married Mildred Manuel, he moved to Kamloops. Him and Mildred had thirteen kids. Gus really liked horses. He was a stock contractor and put on Indian rodeos at his place at Paul Lake, near Kamloops, every year. Most of his boys rode buckin' horses too. Bobby was the Indian champion for while. Mildred got the Mother of the Year award too, but I can't remember what year that was. They had lots of kids of their own but they still took in foster kids. Gus was part of the North American Indian Brotherhood and was the chief at Kamloops for a long time. He had a real good memory and when he got with Ben they'd tell stories all night. Mildred and Bobby died before Gus. He died of heart disease in 1997.

Teddy died of typhoid fever in 1946. He was down the States when he got sick and he told us he thought he might have drank some raw milk. He used to walk from Dirty Lake over to where Ben and I lived across the lake. He didn't look good then.

John Marchand: *Teddy and Emery Louis and Raymond Simla and I worked down the States for a while together. We used to live beside the Gottfriedson's at Siwash Creek in our younger days. Teddy and I were good friends, even though he was a few years older than me. He never had his own horse but we'd borrow one and go riding all over the place together. Finally one time my dad had a horse there and he gave it to Teddy. Then we'd go across the lake and round up horses and ride them in a corral there at Head of the Lake. I remember when we got back from the States Teddy got sick. He'd drive his car over to Head of the Lake and watch them guys ride. He'd tell them how they could ride better then he'd leave. He had to be pretty sick to leave the corrals. I missed him after he died. We were good friends.*

Rose Louis: *Adeline married Willie Williams and had three sons. After Willie came back from the war, they divorced and she married Johnny Bonneau. They had three kids. Angeline married Johnny Jones and they adopted my sister Jane's son Truman and a girl that they called Sandy.*

Angeline died of heart disease in 1995. John married Baby Ann Gregoire and mostly ranched and logged until he died in 1990. They had three boys Newman, Harvey and Deb. Jane married Clarence Manuel and moved to Chase. They had one daughter. My brother, Clement, married Theresa Shuttleworth. He died of a heart attack, too, in 1981 between Orville and Tonasket, Washington.

George Gottfriedsen Family: *George was the fourth child of Frank and Emma Gottfriedsen. Like his siblings, George learned from his parents a strong work ethic from helping out on the family and and other family ventures and the value of family and community. Like his parents, George was proud and independent. He had many skills and attributes besides his good looks. He was easy going and was a little on the quiet side until one got to know him. He had many interests ranging from baseball [he enjoyed playing on the local Bluebirds team with more than one brother], music [he was self-taught and played the violin, banjo and ukulele] like his father, loved to read and study a variety of subjects. As most Okanagans of that time, George was limited to manual labor jobs and from a very young age onwards, worked in orchards, sawmills, logging camps and at other physical labor jobs [e.g. the building of Grand Coulee Dam].*

George's first wife was Margaret Sanford; they never had children. George later married Lucille Terbasket, from the Similkameen, a strong and powerful woman with the same sense of pride and independence as he. They lived in his home community for a few years and after the birth of their third child, sold their land and home at Salmon River to his sister Angeline and transferred to the Similkameen. They had nine children and raised two foster daughters as well. George and Lucille owned and operated a cattle ranch and a school bus business. Both worked out periodically in order to support and raise their family. George, like his parents and subsequently his wife, was ahead of his time. He learned carpentry and all told built three homes with his own resources for his family. He was one of the first to initiate and coach a girl's softball team but this was a short-lived venture due to local politics and his familial responsibilities. George and Lucille both valued formal education in spite of their residential school experiences. George encouraged his children to work hard in school. He also served as President of the then Parent Teacher Association. He was also a member of the Native Indian Brotherhood and participated in Aboriginal politics as much as he could. He was proud of the fact that back then, the members paid their own way by passing a hat around – that strong sense of independence again!

It is a challenge to provide a very short biography on our Dad – we can only hope that this one portrays him as the strong Okanagan family man that he was. Life was not easy for any of our people in his time but through determination and hard work, George and Lucille provided for their family an alcohol-free home, served in their communities and enjoyed their lives, hard work and all. With all considered George was an exceptional person. To speak of George is to also speak of his exceptional parents and the ways that they lived their lives in very challenging times. It is sad but in retrospect, no real surprise that he literally worked himself to death; he died of a heart attack on the ranch in August 1966. He is loved and missed by his family, friends and communities.

MARIETTE, HARRIET & JOHNNY

FRANCOIS

ALICE & UNIDENTIFIED

TOMMY

FELIX

DAVID

MARY ANNE

PETE

LOUISA

HECTOR, BERNICE & LOUIE LEWIS

GREGOIRE / LEWIS

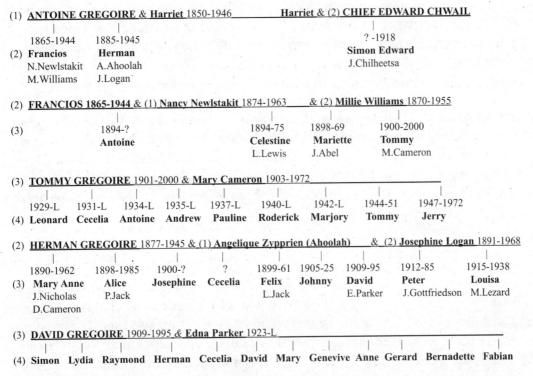

(1) **ANTOINE GREGOIRE** & Harriet 1850-1946   Harriet & (2) **CHIEF EDWARD CHWAIL**

1865-1944	1885-1945	? -1918
(2) **Francios**	**Herman**	**Simon Edward**
N.Newlstakit	A.Ahoolah	J.Chilheetsa
M.Williams	J.Logan	

(2) **FRANCIOS 1865-1944** & (1) Nancy Newlstakit 1874-1963   & (2) Millie Williams 1870-1955

(3)	1894-?	1894-75	1898-69	1900-2000
	Antoine	**Celestine**	**Mariette**	**Tommy**
		L.Lewis	J.Abel	M.Cameron

(3) **TOMMY GREGOIRE** 1901-2000 & Mary Cameron 1903-1972

1929-L	1931-L	1934-L	1935-L	1937-L	1940-L	1942-L	1944-51	1947-1972
(4) **Leonard**	**Cecelia**	**Antoine**	**Andrew**	**Pauline**	**Roderick**	**Marjory**	**Tommy**	**Jerry**

(2) **HERMAN GREGOIRE** 1877-1945 & (1) Angelique Zypprien (Ahoolah)   & (2) **Josephine Logan** 1891-1968

1890-1962	1898-1985	1900-?	?	1899-61	1905-25	1909-95	1912-85	1915-1938
(3) **Mary Anne**	**Alice**	**Josephine**	**Cecelia**	**Felix**	**Johnny**	**David**	**Peter**	**Louisa**
J.Nicholas	P.Jack			L.Jack		E.Parker	J.Gottfriedson	M.Lezard
D.Cameron								

(3) **DAVID GREGOIRE** 1909-1995 & Edna Parker 1923-L

(4) **Simon**   **Lydia**   **Raymond**   **Herman**   **Cecelia**   **David**   **Mary**   **Genevive**   **Anne**   **Gerard**   **Bernadette**   **Fabian**

Oral history and historical articles agree that Antoine Gregoire was a resident from the Shuswap region of Neskonlith and Adams Lake. He died August 1862. Within the Hudson's Bay Company journals some information is written as to the family lineage. This same information is re-told in Volume Two of the Shuswap Chronicles. It reads:

> "Chief Sehowtken was given the name Adam, when he was baptized by Father Nobili in 1849. The H.B.C. journal entries show that he was a powerful chief who supplied the company with many furs and was a hard bargainer who demanded respect. By 1867, Adam had died and the river and lake is named after him. Antoine Gregoire (by legend was Adam's oldest son) was an equally powerful and respected chief, whose son Niskonlith gained extensive reserve land on the South Thompson and along side the lake named after him."[2]

Antoine came to the Okanagan with the Royal Commission to mark out the boundaries of the Douglas Reserve in 1861.[3] He married Harriet, the daughter of Chief Edward Chevely at Neskonlith. Antoine and Harriet had two sons, Francois and Herman. After Chief Edward died, Harriet came to Head of the Lake and married Chief Edward "Chwahil" on September 14, 1884.[4] They in turn had one son, Simon. Simon married Julianne Chilheetsa but left no descendants.

Francois married Nancy Newlstakit,[5] the daughter of Sqwnim-te-nalqs and the sister to Mary and Julianne Qualtier. After losing three children at a very young age, Francois and Nancy parted and Nancy went back to Deep Creek to Sqwnim-te-nalqs'. Francois then lived with Millie Williams and had three more children Celestine, Mariette and Tommy.

Francois Gregoire was a successful farmer, rancher, prospector and guide. His name appears in the Vernon newspaper several times in connection to his business affairs with both Indian and white residents of the time. He owned a large herd of horses, some of which he raced locally and beyond. He did not limit himself to racing but equipped himself with fine teams of work horses. By 1915, he owned a threshing wheat separator that he rented out to local ranchers.[6] His skills at guiding and prospecting also landed him jobs from distant hunting and prospecting parties.

Tommy Gregoire: *My father told me he saw gold on that mountain in the Revelstoke. He go up there with Henry McDougall, your great grandfather's brother. They go together. One time my father tol' me he was walkin' on the ice on that mountain and he heard his dog far away. He go over there where he hear the dog and I guess he fall in that deep hole. My father, Francois, fell down in that hole too and they can't get out. Then something help them, he say he don't know what but it must be God 'cause that's how he come out of that hole.*

Lewis

Celestine married Louie Lewis who was born in 1893 at Douglas Lake to William Lewis and Louise Shinitko.[7] They had five children. Louie worked for the various ranches rounding up cattle, branding and putting up hay. At home he served on council for many years. The couple's son Hector married Bernice Marchand and together they had six children Vince, Roger, Brian, Suzanne, Frank and Todd. While giving birth to their seventh child Bernice died. Hector too, died tragically while working at Lavington Planer Mill in Lavington. It is through the children of Hector and Bernice that the Lewis name continues as it is today.

Tommy married Mary Cameron, the daughter of Rosie Louie and David Cameron. Mary was raised by Jimmy Joseph, better known as Scotty, and his wife Mary Ann Francois. Scotty is remembered as being an excellent fiddle player, good dancer and of Shuswap descent. He died at ninety-nine years of age December 30, 1940.[8] His spouse, Mary Ann, predeceased him just three months earlier on September 13, 1940.[9] She was eighty-three years old.

Mary Jane Lawrence: *Mary Cameron was raised by ol' Scotty and his wife at Round Lake. I don't remember his wife, but I remember dancing with ol' Scotty down here at Six-Mile. I was just a kid when ol' Scotty would come to my dad's. All us kids used to dance with him. Then I remember when ol' Scotty had dances at his place at Round Lake. I don't know how the people would hear about it, but everyone would go and they'd dance all weekend.*

Tommy Gregoire: *Scotty was a real good jockey and he was a Shuswap. Ol' Scotty and Ko-mas-ket used to drive horses down to California. One winter they got stuck down there. They went over the mountain and when it was time to come back there was lots of snow on that mountain. Ol' Ko-mas-ket, my father said, cried 'cause he thought he's gonna die down there. Ol' Scotty says, "No, we not gonna die down here. The snow will be all gone and we can go home." Sure enough next week they come home.*

Tommy Gregoire was the last of his era to pass on. He died March 14, 2000 at nearly one hundred years old. Many people from far and wide came to pay their respects to the icon who never stopped promoting Indian rights and freedoms and to the man who held firm to family and cultural values. Tommy was also highly respected by the people for being one of the last who could speak high Okanagan. In explanation, some have said that high Okanagan is really hard to understand and equally hard to speak, but Tommy could speak it well, and it seemed that sometimes he was lonesome for the language.

Throughout his life Tommy was never idle, nor was he content to live in a cocoon. He spoke often of his trips to California, Montana, Ottawa and even New York City. From the twinkle in his eyes and the humour in his stories it is clear that he thoroughly enjoyed his adventures. This is not to say that Tommy did not enjoy his surroundings in the valley. His historical knowledge of the Shuswap and Okanagan people helped others to understand the importance of preserving Aboriginal culture and tradition. In doing so, he gained the respect and admiration of both the white and Aboriginal neighbours.

Herman married Angelique Zipprien from Spallumcheen in 1895.[10] After the couple had ten children, Angelique became pregnant with twin girls. Louisa was born at home while the other died with her mother in the buggy on way to hospital.[11]

Herman and Angelique built their first home on the flat on O'Keefe Siding. They got their water from the bottom of the hill near to where the highway is now. After the spring dried up they built a second house on the edge of the flat. Water was then obtained from the well and later from the reservoir that supplied water for irrigation needs. This second house was torn down by Herman's son Pete and used in the construction of his own house at Deep Creek. The barn too was sold and taken apart log by log and reassembled at John Gottfriedson's place on the corner of Westside Road and Highway 97. Michael Marchand remembered that, "We hauled them (logs) by sleigh over to John's and put them all back together. That barn burned later."[12] Although Herman was blind most of his life, his handicap did not prevent him from working his land.

Jenny Marchand: *Old Herman was blind, but that didn't stop him doing his work. He used to walk from that big two story house up at O'Keefe Siding all the way down here to that property on the corner of Westside and Head of the Lake road. He never came in a buggy, he walked all the way and he couldn't see a thing. I remember seeing him walking down the road carrying his bucket and hammer. That ol' man was blind, but you know, he kept up that fence till he died.*

Edna Gregoire: *Herman and Dave used to take me along to line up the fence posts and make sure it was straight. He used to wash clothes too. He'd wash his grandson's clothes and his own on a washboard. He couldn't see but he'd scrub them and then hold them up and ask me if they were clean yet. He used to say I had enough to do, so he'd wash the clothes and boy could he ever make bread. I used to think, for a blind man he sure could get those loaves just right. He sure did help me. Dave and them used to take him out to get cordwood and firewood. They'd mark the log every eight feet then Herman would come along behind them and cut those logs with his cross cut saw. I seen that saw laying over there by where the old house was. I remembered that was Herman's saw, so I told my boys to bring it over here and put in on the side of the shed. It's still there. That was his saw.*

Herman's daughter Mary Anne first married Joseph Nicholas. After his death she became the spouse of David Cameron and had one son, James. James married Vera Marchand and had six children.

HARRIS

ISAAC

CHRISTINE

HARRY

JOHNNY

EDITH

CHRISTINE, BABY & LESLIE

FLORENCE

WILBUR

HARRIS

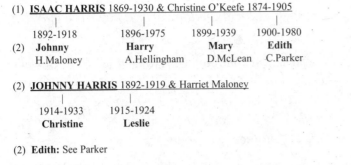

(1) **ISAAC HARRIS** 1869-1930 & Christine O'Keefe 1874-1905

	1892-1918	1896-1975	1899-1939	1900-1980
(2)	**Johnny**	**Harry**	**Mary**	**Edith**
	H.Maloney	A.Hellingham	D.McLean	C.Parker

(2) **JOHNNY HARRIS** 1892-1919 & Harriet Maloney

	1914-1933	1915-1924
	Christine	**Leslie**

(2) **Edith:** See Parker

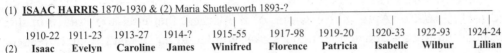

(1) **ISAAC HARRIS** 1870-1930 & (2) Maria Shuttleworth 1893-?

	1910-22	1911-23	1913-27	1914-?	1915-55	1917-98	1919-20	1920-33	1922-93	1924-24
(2)	**Isaac**	**Evelyn**	**Caroline**	**James**	**Winifred**	**Florence**	**Patricia**	**Isabelle**	**Wilbur**	**Lillian**

Isaac Harris was a good-looking individual who had two wives and fathered fourteen children. He was born around 1870 and died at sixty years old, in 1930. Throughout his life he engaged in farming, acted as interpreter, special constable, taxi driver and registrar of the Okanagan Indian Band. He built his home of concrete at Prairie Reserve at Larkin and was singled out by Indian Affairs in 1916, for having "the best kept farm in the Okanagan Agency."[2] On the social front, he was involved in the Roman Catholic Church and donated the infamous Bluebird trophy cup for the best Okanagan baseball team. But it was the mystery around his relationship with Christine, the daughter of Cornelius O'Keefe and Okanagan born, Rosie that kept the Harris name in the forefront throughout the years to come.

Father Carion, OMI, married Isaac Harris, son of Harris "English" and Mary "Indian of Lillooet" to Christine O'Keefe, age seventeen, daughter of O'Keefe and Rosie "Indian" on May 15, 1891.[3] Thereafter, they had four children. Johnny was born in 1892, Harry in 1897, Mary's birthdate is unknown but Edith was born in 1900. Some sources maintain that Isaac had a brother, Tommy, and perhaps, a half-brother who was often known as Harry Joe or Cultus Harry. However, there is doubt that Tommy and Isaac's mother were the same person for Tommy's mother is Rosie Arlchelqua at Lillooet. She was a twenty-six-year-old widow when she married Thomas C. Harris in 1889.[4] Isaac was then nineteen years old. As Harry Joe could not be connected to Isaac Harris, his parentage must be left to further research.

In the past, others have tried to verify the relationship between Rosie and early rancher Cornelius O'Keefe. However, recent findings have clarified what descendants of the Harris family have known all along; Cornelius O'Keefe did take an Okanagan woman, to live with him in an informal relationship and their daughter, Christine, did marry Isaac Harris and leave descendants among the Okanagan Indian Band at Head of the Lake. Further verification of Christine's parentage is given within the marriage records of their daughter, Mary, to Donald McLean, and Edith to Christie Parker. Rosie's parentage, too, is rather vague. However, oral history leaves some clues as to her heritage.

Edna Gregoire: *My grandmother's name was Christine. She was Rosie and Cornelius' daughter. Rosie, my great grandmother, was also the mother to Alex Simla from here, Sitpitsa, who lived at Penticton, and Nancy Simla, who was Johnny Isaac's wife.*

My grandmother, Christine O'Keefe, and my grandfather, Isaac Harris, had four children. They were Johnny, Harry, Mary and my mother Edith. My mother's half-sisters and half-brother Wilbur, were from my grandfather's second marriage to Maria Shuttleworth. They were married after my grandmother died.

My mother believed she was four, maybe five, when her mother Christine died. She said her only memories about her mother was when she went over to her mother's bedside and she was talkin' to her. She didn't know that her mother already passed on, that she was dead. She said she was standin' by her mother's bedside and was talkin' to her and her grandmother [Rosie] went over there and took her away from there and said her mother was gone.

Christine Harris died in 1905. The Vernon News reported that "... the funeral at the Head of the Lake was held on the 16th of April and was one of the largest that ever took place in this vicinity, over three hundred friends and acquaintances... assembled to pay a last tribute of respect and esteem to Mrs. Isaac Harris."[5]

Jenny Marchand: *Isaac Harris was a real smart man. He had that place over there at Larkin. He built that house and he used to have lots of farm stuff around there but only the house is left now. He was the first one that I can remember to have a car on this Reserve. It was a car that had windows all round it. His family used to be always dressed so good and you'd see them in church on Sundays. Isaac Harris was a leader in church. If the Father wasn't there he'd tell the people what is happening and what shouldn't be happening. When the priest is there, he helps him on everything.*

Edna Gregoire: *My mother said her father was strict, too. He knows his family. He made sure they didn't shack up. He wanted them to be married before they lived together. Our mother was nineteen when she got married to our dad, Christie Parker.*

You see, my grandfather wasn't always there at home. He'd go out and work as a jeepie – a taxi driver. He'd drive people to town and home and he'd work on his place. He also had a phone in his house. Like my mother said, when they were little, when they were goin' to school, she said they had clothes to wear at home, everyday clothes, but when they went to church they had a different pair of shoes and clothes to go to church.

The newspaper said that my grandfather committed suicide. My mother said he wouldn't do that. She said he was going to court that day. He got all dressed up to go, but he never even went out of the house when he was killed.

Johnny, the eldest son of Isaac and Christine, married Mary Harriet Maloney, the daughter of Mary Ann Alexander and Irishman Jack Maloney. Johnny enlisted in the army at Ewing's Landing in 1918 with the 30th B.C. Horse Re-Enforcements C.E.F.. Unfortunately, after only a few days in combat with the 47th Battalion of the Canadian Infantry in France, Johnny was wounded and died of head injuries August 15, 1918.[6] Johnny left behind his wife Harriet and two young children. Unfortunately, Leslie died in 1924 and Christine at age nineteen, September 28, 1933. Harriet later married William Lawrence and had several more children.

At nineteen, Mary Harris married fifty-year-old Donald McLean at Penticton.[7] Donald was the son of Roderick McLean, a Hudson's Bay man, and his wife Mary, the daughter of Penticton's Chief Francois.[8] It has been written that Roderick McLean was from the Isle of Mull. He worked for the Boundary Commission surveyors and in 1863 was hired by the Hudson's Bay Company at Similkameen trading post at Keremeos. His duties there included such projects as supervising the ranch of cattle and horses, organizing and preparing pack trains and also as trader and post master.[9] Following the end of his contract, he acquired a ranch at Okanagan Falls. Mary and Donald McLean had three children.

Harry's marriage announcement in the Vernon News to widow Agnes Fellingham at Lumby, caused a stir among at least one member of the O'Keefe family when it was announced that the groom Henry Harris was the "... grandson of the late Mr. O'Keefe."[10] The offended one informed the News "... that there was no basis for the statement that Mr. Harris was related to the late Mr. O'Keefe, and that no relationship whatever exists between the Harris and the O'Keefe family."[11] However, since Harry's origin has now been established, we now turn to some of Harry's achievements. The couple leave no Harris descendants.

Harry was the first Okanagan individual to receive an education at the post secondary level. He graduated from Vernon Secondary School and went on to the University of British Columbia where he excelled in agricultural studies. From there he went to Toronto where he continued his education. Just one month before Isaac's death in 1930, Harry gained notoriety for his agricultural abilities at the Kamloops Fall Fair. The News noted the high quality of his seed grain and went on to say "... if the produce of the Indians in the Agency was cut out from the whole, it would make a big difference to the total production of the Valley."[12]

Isaac Parker: *Uncle Harry used to live up the Six-Mile flat past Cameron's place. He had an old Model T and to get through that deep snow he took bigger tires than he had on his car and cut slits in them and then put the bigger tires over his tires. And that's how he got through that snow.*

Edna Gregoire: *Someone burned down Uncle Harry's cabins up there above Six Mile. I used to always see that picture of our grandmother Christine, hangin' on the wall 'long side the door. My mother said the dress she is wearing in that picture was her wedding dress. She made it herself for her wedding to my grandfather Isaac. Uncle Harry got sick when he was livin' up there. After he got out of the hospital he stayed awhile with Tommy Gregoire.*

Isaac Parker: *My mother was in the fifth grade, fourteen years old, and attending that little school house at Larkin when the Titanic went down in April of 1912. Her teacher was from England and was over there when that ship was gettin' ready to come across the ocean. She got on that ship and when that ship hit that iceberg that ended that part. She was my mom's fifth grade teacher.*

Father Le Jeune married Edith to Louie Christie Parker, June 24, 1919.[13] They had ten children who were raised at Whiteman's Creek. Edith died in 1989 and Christie in 1978. Their two sons, George and Arthur died in the year 2000.

Isaac married a second time to Maria Shuttleworth. She was the daughter of Similkameen's George Shuttleworth and Penticton's Angeline Michele. They had ten children. Winnifred, Florence and Wilbur enlisted for Service during WW II. Evelyn, Caroline, James, Patrica, Isabelle and Lillian all died before reaching adulthood. The eldest son, Isaac, was killed in a traffic accident on his way home from school in 1922.

The News explained the event:

> "A sad fatality occurred on Tuesday night near Larken, whereby W.M. Harris aged 14, the son of Isaac Harris lost his life. It appears that the boy was riding home from school at Armstrong in one of the consolidated school trucks. He got off the truck for some reason and in trying to jump on the running board he slipped and the truck passed over him."[14]

ARCELLE & DICK

ALEX

ROSIE

DICK

MARTHA

GLADYS & DOROTHY

RAYMOND

HAZEL, ROSIE & VIOLET

ISAAC / SIMLA

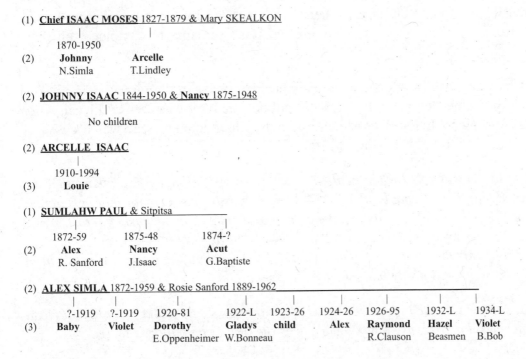

(1) **Chief ISAAC MOSES** 1827-1879 & Mary SKEALKON

                  1870-1950

(2)   **Johnny**   **Arcelle**

        N.Simla   T.Lindley

(2) **JOHNNY ISAAC** 1844-1950 & **Nancy** 1875-1948

        No children

(2) **ARCELLE ISAAC**

        1910-1994

(3)   **Louie**

(1) **SUMLAHW PAUL** & Sitpitsa

     1872-59   1875-48   1874-?

(2)   **Alex**   **Nancy**   **Acut**

     R. Sanford   J.Isaac   G.Baptiste

(2) **ALEX SIMLA** 1872-1959 & Rosie Sanford 1889-1962

?-1919	?-1919	1920-81	1922-L	1923-26	1924-26	1926-95	1932-L	1934-L
Baby	**Violet**	**Dorothy**	**Gladys**	**child**	**Alex**	**Raymond**	**Hazel**	**Violet**
		E.Oppenheimer	W.Bonneau			R.Clauson	Beasmen	B.Bob

(3)

The Isaac and Simla families are connected through the marriage of Johnny Isaac and Nancy Simla. Johnny was the grandson of Chief N'Kwala. He was also the son of Chief Moise and Marie.[2] After Chief Moise died in 1879, his half-brother, William, or Basil, as he was often known, succeeded as Chief. A succession of chiefs followed until Johnny, or Tchlopa, meaning "old man," was appointed in 1924. He would have then been close to fifty years old.[3] His mother Marie died a victim of the Spanish flu.

The news reported that among those who fell victim to the Spanish flu, in October 1918, many were from different agencies. Seventy-one lives were lost in the Lytton agency and nineteen from the Kamloops agency. The same report explained that the Okanagan people were spared until November, when five perished. Among them were Mrs. Louie Jim, Johnny Brewer, Pierre Michel, and the granddaughter of Mrs. Johnny Andrew, and Marie, the mother of Johnny Isaac.[4] The toll was far worse, however, and coupled with tuberculosis and related diseases did not discriminate, but took lives on the whole North American continent. For this reason it was called a pandemic.

Nancy Simla was the sister to Alex Simla and the daughter of Sumlahw Paul and Sitpitsa, of Penticton. She and Johnny had no children of their own but raised Johnny's sister's son, Louie. Louie, or Dick, married Louisa Marchand, leaving the Isaac surname to continue with their sons.

Johnny was Chief for seven years and saw many changes occur in the reserve system. The Indian Act of 1877 was amended and all on-reserve political activity was seen as illegal. After a large amount of jostling by Indian Department officials, Chief Johnny Isaac was accused of intemperance and removed from his position in 1931.[5]

Ned Louis: *Johnny Isaac was blind when he died. He went to visit ol' Sumlahw, his brother-in-law, and left there. At that time all that land north of Neehoot was bush except for that part across the road from Pete Gregoire's. It was in the middle of the hot summer and he musta got lost. Willie Williams happened to be workin' across the lake and saw the birds circlin' above. He came over there to check it out. It was there that he found Johnny's body stuck in the fence. He musta been dead for a while, 'cause he was pretty bad when Willie found him.*

Gladys Bonneau: *Johnny was the first to be buried out of the new St. Benedict's Church, at Head of the Lake. I remember that, because my boy Gary was the first to be baptized there.*

The Simla surname seems to be a corruption of the Okanagan name Sumlahw. Sumlahw Paul was from Penticton and he and Sitpitsa had three children. It is possible, however, that there were two more sons who are not listed here. A family member heard tell that two of the Simla sons went to live in the States and never returned to the Okanagan Band.[6] Alex Simla married widow Rosie McDougall, nee Sanford. Her husband David McDougall Jr. died of a gunshot wound in 1912.

Rosie's parents were William and Janie Walker. All accounts claim that William and Janie Walker were from Lillooet. On the other hand, family attest to their existence at Deadman's Creek in the Ashcroft and Kamloops area. In total, they had ten children. In the early years, the Sanford family moved to O'Keefe Siding on Highway 97, north of Vernon. The property changed hands several times and is now the property of the Tonasket family.

Alex and Rosie were married April 21, 1919, by Father Le Jeune.[7] Their children were all born at the Head of the Lake, but the surname ends with the death of their son Raymond in 1995. Rosie's sister, May, married band member, Andrew Thomas, or Thomar. Andrew was the son of Lena Lawrence. May's sister, Margaret, married George Gottfriedsen. Neither couple had children.

On the maternal side, the Simla line does not end with Alex and Rosie's descendants, but extends to include the first family of Francis Xavier Richter and Lucy Simla.

Francis Xavier Richter was born in November 2, 1837, at Friedland, Austria and later emigrated to the United States. Thereafter, he worked at placer mining near Colville, Washington and in 1864, came to the Similkameen Valley with a herd of forty-three cattle. Since his first choice of pre-emption was planned as the Penticton Indian Reserve, Richter chose 320 acres at present day Cawston. Later, he bought an additional 1500 acres, and still later, bought the Inglewood ranch at Keremeos. He moved to the Inglewood ranch in 1898. But it was at the original ranch, on the Richter Pass, that he and his first spouse Lucy Simla raised their five sons.[8] According to the 1891 Canada Census, Charlie was born in 1870, William in 1872, Joseph in 1874, Edward in 1877 and John in 1880. In retrospect, Joseph Richter remembered his parents' relationship as an affectionate partnership when he said,

> "When I was little, coal oil was brought 70 miles from Hope on the backs of horses. It was used sparingly. My mother made candles in a special mold and after the cotton wick was threaded it was filled with our own tallow. She made soap from waste fat and lye. Some of our clothing was made from buckskin traded with Indians…Buckskin garments are warm soft and comfortable. I suppose that today most people think that our early days were rough. We worked hard, we had everything we needed. We were a closely knit, affectionate family, self-sufficient, yet depending one another, each respecting the other's worth under the guidance of wise parents."[9]

Frank and Lucy's relationship endured until 1894 when Frank Richter married a young woman from the Similkameen area. However, he did not abandon his Okanagan spouse, but made a home for her on the original ranch and provided for her until the day she died. He also provided his five sons with their own ranches. Barman used the following story to demonstrate Lucy and Frank's relationship. She said, "While swimming the Similkameen River in high water Richter nearly drowned. Lucy reached him with a fence rail and pulled him out then succeeded to beat him for risking his life unnecessarily."[10] Lucy died about 1904 and is buried on the original ranch on Richter Pass. Frank died Christmas Day, 1910 at St. Joseph's hospital in Victoria.

JACK / JIM

MADELINE

PIRRECHE   ANGELIQUE

PIERRE   CHRISTINE   NARCISSE   ONN

FRANK   PHILLIP   LIZZIE   ETHEL

ROSIE   ANDY   ANGIE

JACK / JIM

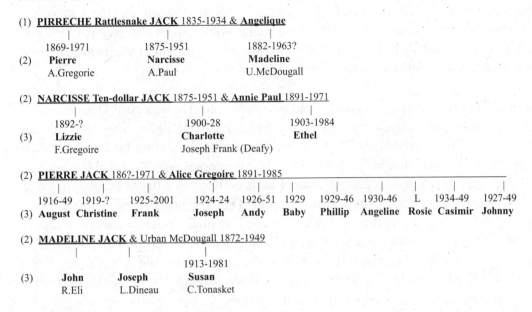

(1) **PIRRECHE Rattlesnake JACK** 1835-1934 & **Angelique**

1869-1971	1875-1951	1882-1963?
(2) **Pierre**	**Narcisse**	**Madeline**
A.Gregorie	A.Paul	U.McDougall

(2) **NARCISSE Ten-dollar JACK** 1875-1951 & **Annie Paul** 1891-1971

1892-?	1900-28	1903-1984
(3) **Lizzie**	**Charlotte**	**Ethel**
F.Gregoire	Joseph Frank (Deafy)	

(2) **PIERRE JACK** 186?-1971 & **Alice Gregoire** 1891-1985

1916-49	1919-?	1925-2001	1924-24	1926-51	1929	1929-46	1930-46	L	1934-49	1927-49
(3) **August**	**Christine**	**Frank**	**Joseph**	**Andy**	**Baby**	**Phillip**	**Angeline**	**Rosie**	**Casimir**	**Johnny**

(2) **MADELINE JACK** & Urban McDougall 1872-1949

		1913-1981
(3) **John**	**Joseph**	**Susan**
R.Eli	L.Dineau	C.Tonasket

The Jack family have a long and varied history on Okanagan soil. Oral history claims that kinship ties stem back to the Okanagan Bands at Penticton, Westbank and the Nicola Valley region. "They are all part of the same family. I'm not really sure, but I think Margaret Bonneau is part of that family."[2] No record has been found of the bloodline of Angelique, but some claim she is an original band member and probably a daughter to Louie Jim.

Rosie Jack: *I knew we were related to the Bonneaus but I didn't know how. All they told me is we are related. Maggie Bonneau is buried here in our graveyard, so that must be how we are related, through her.*

Pirreche and Angelique seem to have inherited property at Six-Mile Creek from Louie Jim. Evidence put forward during the investigation of the Royal Commission in 1913 notes that Ten-dollar Jack and his son Pierre worked land at Priest Valley and at Head of the Lake.[3]

Narcisse Jack had one daughter, Lizzie, with Washington-born Annie Paul. Annie was known as Ettel Onn because she was the mother to Ethel. Onn was the first wife of Narcisse's half-brother Edward, who apparently originated in Washington. Ethel and Charlotte are Annie and Edward's daughters and are nieces to Narcisse. Ethel never married or had children. Charlotte married Joseph Frank of Douglas Lake in 1920 and at aged twenty-eight was killed by a CPR train in Kamloops.[4] Lizzie married Felix Gregoire, but had no children. She was a favourite aunt to her niece Rosie.

Both Narcisse and Pierre left a lasting impression of men with ranching abilities and good horse sense. Narcisse raised well bred colts for use on the range and racetrack. He was also a gambling man and used his expertise and skill at horse races, stick games and five card monty. He and Pierre passed the same skills to Terry Jack. Terry continues to raise many horses and cattle and can be seen putting up hay in the summer and feeding his stock in winter.

At his death in 1971, Pierre was one hundred and two years old. He was born December 16, 1869 and before the turn of the century married Penticton born Louise Felix. The two children of this union predeceased Pierre. In August 28, 1916 he was married by Father Le Jeune to Alice Gregoire, the daughter of Francois and Millie Gregoire. Their witnesses were (Castor) Gaston and Helene Louie.[5] Pierre was employed by early ranchers such as Thomas Ellis at Penticton, Price Ellison, Cornelias O'Keefe, and later O'Keefe's son, Tierney. On the whole, his knowledge of the terrain and trails, horses, cattle and ranching techniques made him an asset when it came to duties such as haying, breaking horses, branding, roundups and cattle drives. In addition, his familiarity with the early Indian trails put him in a position to assist with freight and cattle drives through the mountains to Hope and the Kootenays.[6] Terry remembers Pierre saying that he could remember back to the day when there were only two white men in Vernon.

Pierre and Alice established a family of ten children. A quick glance at the family tree, however discloses the death of many of the children at a young age due to tuberculosis and pneumonia. Sadly they lost five children within the three year period from 1946 to 1949. Tuberculosis took many lives, but as one person said, "if they could remain healthy until they were around two or three years old then generally they would survive."[7] In this case, the dreaded disease took several sons and daughters while still in their early adult years.

Pierre and Alice are remembered as kind and generous people, sharing their home with visitors and relatives alike. Their friendly and cordial hospitality provided many with the opportunity to re-experience traditional values and customs in stories, songs and dance. Up until the time of Pierre's death in 1971, the voices, with rhythm to the drum, resounded throughout the area filtered by the trees and waters of Six-Mile Creek. After a long lapse of time the same sound could be heard when daughter Rosie, and grandson Terry hosted traditional stick games in memory of Christine Jack and her son Jack Struthers. The sound re-created by new voices is a reminder of the voices within an era long since gone. Pierre and Alice shared in the raising of many of their grandchildren and relatives. Tradition and customs were important to them. Many speak of the influence Pierre and Alice had upon their lives. Accordingly, they appear to be the kind of peers spoken of by Mourning Dove in her book, *MOURNING DOVE: A Salishan Autobiography.*[8] Without them in our past the present would surely be incomplete.

Rosie Jack: *My uncle Narcisse, my dad's brother, raced horses. There was always horses here. We have pictures of Uncle Narcisse at the race track in Vernon. We were like anybody else. We had a hard time and had to scrounge like everybody else. My papa worked for Cornelius O'Keefe. So did my brothers. My mom made gloves and sold them for a dollar twenty-five a pair. That really helped my papa and brothers pay the bills. She sold gloves anywhere. In grocery stores she* *traded them for groceries; she'd have piles of them. Every two weeks she'd take them to town and sell them. The only time she beaded them was when she had an order for them fancy gloves, but she made mostly plain work gloves. She made gauntlets too, but only when she got an order for them. Yeah, we had a hard time, but we were happy.*

My brothers went to Kamloops School, too. They never did tell me if they liked it or not. August, Phillip and Frank were all called to service in the army but didn't go because of their health. There was TB and stuff like that in those days.

Pete Marchand: *Pierre Jack and them were over at Alice's dad's. That's where they started out. Then, the Band gave out those permits to build house. The houses were built pretty high with just straight stove pipes. I guess they built a fire too hot and it caught fire. I guess it caught on the wall paper and that's how it burned down. The house they have now was built after.*

Because Louie Jim, or Kemitiken, is likely the head of the Jack family, he is included here. Louie Jim and his spouse Mary were large land-owners when the first settlers came to the area. Sources refer to him as an individual involved in the political, economic and social climate of reserve life at Head of the Lake and in particular at Six-Mile Creek. Politically he held the Chief's seat for three years from 1898 to 1901. He supplemented his income by growing large fields of grain, both on the east side of Okanagan Lake and at Six-Mile Creek. Milling of the grain was done at a flour mill that he set up next to Six-Mile Creek. Oral tradition has it that he purchased the mill from the Hudson's Bay Company at Kamloops. In later years, the sifter was sold to Hoover's Flour Mill in the Spallumcheen and the grinder sold and set up as part of the historic grist mill in the Similkameen.[9] Louie built St. Theresa's Church also at Six-Mile Creek and some say he built it for his people and not for the priest.

The life of Louie Jim is far beyond the memory of present elders. Therefore we have to depend largely on written sources. Rather than rewrite history as presented by Thomson and Carstens we will allow the excerpts from the Vernon News to present an outside glimpse into the life and times of Louie Jim. Even then it seems the Okanagan were seen as a distinct society. The local newspaper at three different times discussed the approval of Louis Jim as Chief of the "Siwashes" at Head of the Lake.

The following excerpts also disclose the attitude of the time:

"Since old Chief William died two years ago, no successor has been appointed, and the camp has been divided into factions, each favouring some favourite candidate for office. Due notice having been given, an election was conducted on Monday under the supervision of Mr. Wood. The contest had by this time narrowed down to two aspirants, Louis Jim, and Isaac and after a count of the votes the former was declared elected, subject to the approval of the department. It is doubtful, however, if the approval will be given, as the successful candidate is a thorough old pagan and refuses to recognize 'white laws' still clinging to the customs of his tribe. He possesses the merit of being a thoroughly sober and industrious Indian and has considerable influence among the Siwashes. Isaac, his opponent, is much more civilized in his ideas and is a member of the Roman Catholic church, but does not hold the sway over his associates that his rival possesses."[10]

"Father Marechal, the Roman Catholic missionary who labours among these Siwashes, has informed us that Louie Jim is not chief, he having failed to be accepted by the government, although elected by the Indians. Father Marechal states that his turbulent nature can brook no inference with his authority, and his character is such that the Indian department were perfectly right in refusing to accept him."[11]

"Louis Jim, the present incumbent, was provisionally elected last fall, but has not given satisfaction to the authorities, and now that the voting strength of the Indians has been materially increased owing to the return of the number of Siwashes who were absent at the time the vote was taken. It is thought probable that Louis Jim's election will not be sustained, but that some more tractable Indian will be installed into the office."[12]

Louie Jim was replaced in 1901 by Chief Chwail. Chwail it seems was a descendant of N'Kwala from one of his south Okanagan wives.[13] No death record could be found for Louie Jim unless he was buried under a name other than Louie Jim, but the obituary of Mary Jim appeared in the Vernon News in 1918 as a victim of the Spanish flu.

"Among the Head of the Lake victims was Mrs. Louie Jim who died on Saturday night at the age of over 90 years, although some of her relatives claim she is over 100 years. The old woman was remarkably smart for her years, and during the past summer planted and cared for a crop of potatoes, melons and other garden stuffs that put to shame both women and men of one-third her age. Her land which has been leased to the Dominion Canners for tomato-growing was yielding her a handsome competence, and for some months before her death she had become happy and contented, with all care for her future laid aside. She was only ill a few days."[14]

Ned Louis: *Louie Jim owned lots of land around here. They were rich people. They had lots of horses and cows. When Mary Ann got with Louie Marchand and came here with him, Louie Jim told them they could clear out the flour mill and live there. Mary Ann was Louie Jim's niece.*

LOUIE

ERNEST BREWER & EMILY JACKO

MILLIE MICHELE

JACKO CABIN - HIGHWAY 97

JACKO

(1) **LOUIE JACKO** 1862-1938 & Mary Anne Logan ?-1914

1888-1936	1889-1944	1900-1918	?-1913
(2) **Emily**	**Johnny (Amap)**	**Phillip**	**Celina**
E. Brewer	Sapelle		

If the Jacko surname, as portrayed in Mary Balf's documentation of place names, is indeed correct then the Jacko name could very well have been transported from Eastern Canada to the Columbia River and on into the Kamloops area through Jaco (Jacques Raphael) Finlay, the son of James Finlay and an Ojibwa woman. Balf suggests that the place names in the Kamloops area are derived from an individual named Alex Jacko.

> "Alex Jacko was a rather shadowy figure, a half breed who sometimes worked for the HBC, and was very probably descended from James Finlay (Jacques, or Jaco in later generations.) By 1855 he owned a considerable number of horses, and pastured them south of the river junction. He died in 1863, but his son Phillip pre-empted the family horse range in 1866 extending from the lake to the creek mouth. The lower portion was bought in 1875 by John Peterson, who married Alex's daughter Nellie, and eventually took over the name of the creek and... possibly lived in the Indian settlement northeast of the river junction. He [Alexander] died in 1863, but his son Phillip continued horse breeding, with occasional work for the H.B.C."[2]

The Jacko, or Finlay, family were major players in the fur trade. John Jackson author of *Children of the Fur Trade* states:

> "The name Finlay stands out because it spanned the entire history of the British North American fur trade. It was a lineage that stretched from the St. Lawrence and Saskatchewan rivers to the Columbian drainage. (The name) Jacques (Jacco) Raphael Finlay... was the invention of his Scots father, (James Finlay) who wintered in 1768 at bleak Nipowi on the middle Saskatchewan River. The baby's mother was an Ojibwa girl Finlay probably picked up at Sault Ste. Marie or Grand Portage as a temporary winter housemate."[3]

Jackson goes on to explain that in 1806 James Finlay's son, Jacques or Jacco, slashed and mapped the road from Rocky Mountain House over the mountains to the Kutenai country where David Thompson would later in 1807 "... follow the Columbia to the sea."[4] A year later, unsatisfied with Finlay's work of trail blazing, Thompson demoted Jacco. Undaunted by the humiliation, Jacco became a freeman and joined on with the Hudson's Bay Company to help support his growing family. In 1809 Thompson realized his mistake and in 1810 re-hired Finlay as clerk and interpreter. Eventually Finlay was put in charge of Spokane house which "... for the next fourteen years served as the main supply depot for the Salish, Kutenai, and lakes tribes." Johnson goes on to say that, "Few were more closely identified with Spokane House than Jacco Finlay and his lodge of growing children."[5] Apparently Jacco died in 1828 and left behind children who were scattered about in the Colville Spokane region.[6] It is very possible that one of his descendants came north to Fort Kamloops as an employee of the fur trade.

Jackson wrote that an 1860 census of Spokane County reveals twenty-seven-year-old Alex Finlay as just one individual in a long line of the Finlay family. However, it is unclear whether Balf's Alex Jacko and the twenty-six-year-old Finlay are the same person. The ages do not fit. Whatever the case, hospital records claim that Alex Jacko was an uncle to Louie Jacko. Neither Jenny Marchand or her brother Riley Brewer could determine who Alex was, or compile an exact family lineage other than the one seen here.

Louie Jacko married Mary Anne Logan and had four children. Their daughter, Emily, married Ernest Brewer and died in 1936. Emily's brother Phillip died at age eighteen in 1918 her sister Celina on July 15, 1913 and their mother, Mary Ann Logan, January 18, 1914. All are interred at the Head of the Lake cemetery.[7]

In addressing Balf's and Jackson's profiles of the Jacko family, Jenny explained:

Jenny Marchand: *I don't know who those people are there. Maybe that Alex was my grampa's brother. And that Phillip is too old to be my uncle Phillip. Anyway, my uncle Phillip died when he was young. What I understood is my grampa, Louie Jacko, owned all that land in Kamloops where the residential school is. And they let it go to the school and they were supposed to be able to get it back but they never bothered. I went to school at Kamloops for three years and got up to Grade Five. After that I stayed home and helped my mother 'cause she had so much work to do.*

Riley Brewer: *My grandfather, Louie Jacko, he was a man who always rode a horse. I think he was from Kamloops. I remember him quite well because he stayed with us one whole winter. He owned property and had a small log house on the north end of Madeline Lake. He owned that land too from the north side of O'Keefe store all the way up to Theresa Ashtons. He had a house and a big log barn there. So he had lots of land. I don't remember my grampa doing much of anything, just riding his horse. Maybe he was too old then, so I don't know what kind of work he did.*

Riley and William Brewer: *My uncle Amap was bent over to the front. One time my grampa left his horse in the field where Lyle's house is now. The horse still had his bridle and saddle on. Uncle Amap went over there and pulled on the stirrup. The horse kicked him in the chest. I guess they didn't believe in hospitals then, cause he must have broke some ribs or something 'cause he stayed like that for the rest of his life.*

Riley Brewer: *Uncle Amap lived with ol' Sapelle. She was from Lytton. She was supposed to be a Medicine Woman. Only thing I seen her do was at that place over by O'Keefe Station. Pierre Logan had something stuck in his chest and he could hardly breath. The doctors couldn't do nothing, so Pierre Logan came to see Amap and ol' Sapelle. I wouldn't believe it myself but I seen it with my own eyes. She laid ol' Pierre Logan on the floor there and worked on Chista. After he was feelin' around his ribs for a hole. Then he started breathing good again. I had to believe that. I seen it with my own eyes. I'm not much of a believer of them guys but I had to believe them. I* *remember her saying to Pierre Logan, "You're gonna live to be an ol' man," and he did, too! Since I can remember Amap and Sapelle they had an ol' T model Ford. They had a picture of them in Seattle pickin' strawberries. And they had a picture in the newspaper, I think it was in Vancouver, around there. The road in places was made out of iron and steel that was hooked up to the rocks. They went through that when they were driving that ol' car.*

Ned Louis: *Amap and Sapelle worked at the blaster mine up here on Six-Mile flat. They make about seven to eight hundred dollars every spring. Then they don't have to work. They just live. They had a cabin up there on the flat, on the point, where they stayed all summer then they go clean rock out at Lillooet for some more gold. Then they go to Aggazzi to pick hops.*

Riley Brewer: *Sapelle had two daughters and a son, but they weren't ol' Amap's. Ol' Tommy Jack was her son. He lived in Merritt. When Dickie Williams died in Kamloops they had those ol' Indians there. And they heard about Tommy Jack. They went an' got him and he walked up and down that river. He told them guys, "He's way over there along the log jam!" You could hear them hollering around there. They looked around and they found him. There was another guy in the river, supposed to be stuck in the mud around there. They had a motor boat and a bantam rooster. It's supposed to crow when you went over a dead person. Gus Gottfriedson had a rooster and it crowed and he slapped on it the side of the head and said, "You bullshitter!" Then they hooked that guy and pulled him out. The rooster was right!*

Jenny Marchand: *I must have been about nineteen when my grampa died. Vera was a baby then, I think. That time me and Louie were living across the lake. When winter came we came over here and lived with my dad. Grampa got sick late that fall and he died. He lived with my dad most of the time after my mother was gone. My mother died just before Vera was born. My grampa wasn't much of a storyteller but we would all beg Uncle Amap to tell us stories. He'd say to us, "Okay, but only if you will stay awake." Of course, we'd all fall asleep.*

MILLIE

PIERRE

EDWARD

SUSAN

HELENA

GEORGE

LOUIE & UNIDENTIFIED CHILD

JOE WILLIAMS

(1) **JOSEPH WILLIAMS** 1856-1926 & **Millie Paul** 1866-1955
　　　|
　　　1884-1931
(2) 　**Pierre Joe Williams**

(2) **PIERRE JOE WILLIAMS** 1884-1931 & **Mary Louise Alexander** 1895-1998

1917-57	1919-47	1920-47	1923-L	1924-L	1930-L	1934-85	1937-L
Edward	Abel	George	Louie	Susan	Helena	Moses	Roy
L.Kimbasket							

(3) appears before Edward row.

If current belief is indeed accurate then Joseph William is a descendant, possibly a son, of early Mission settlers William Peon and Julie Laroque. William, it seems, originated from the Peon family of Spokane Prairie in Washington, or what was later called Peon Prairie. Ruby and Brown include the following history in their book entitled *The Spokane Indians: Children of the Sun.*

> "A half-blood man named Peon... had lived among the Spokanes for a long time. They called him 'Sea-al' and gave him one of their women for a wife, by whom he had many children. Angus McDonald placed one of Peon's sons, Baptiste, in charge of a company trading post northeast of the falls on a direct route between Lake Coeur d'Alene and the Colville Valley. Baptiste too married an Indian woman... was head of the powerful Peon family, and became chief among the Upper Spokanes on the three thousand acre fertile prairie (formerly Spokane Prairie) bearing the family name."[2]

Before this time, "Louis Pion [sic] is reported to have wintered with Montegue of the NorthWest Company at the rendezvous near the head of Okanagan Lake, 1814-15. There he met and associated with the head Chief of the Okanagan Tribe, Huistesmetxe or Walking Grizzly Bear."[3]

Buckland inquired into the origin of the Peon name and came up with two possible accounts. The first theorizes that Peon was quite possibly just one of the Sandwich Islanders "lent out" to work as an employee of the fur companies. Another suggestion is that after the arrival of these Kanaka Islanders to Fort Okanagan, Peon took a Native wife and named his subsequent son Louis. But as for William Peon, notes Buckland, "In his early manhood, he worked for the Hudson's Bay Company as guide, packer and linguist. He married Julie, one of Chief Nicolas' many daughters, who was evidently a half-sister to Mary, one of his father's wives."[4] He was the same man who packed in Father Pandosy to Mission Creek. Baptism records, thereafter, serve to explain the relationship of William to the other Peons who were active in the infant settlement of Mission Creek. A descendant, Mickey Derickson, and a cousin from south of the border claimed to Buckland that their ancestor Peon was not French by origin, but "came to the Okanagan from a tropical country."[5]

Prior to his arrival in the Okanagan Father Pandosy stayed a while with the Jesuit Order of the Society of Jesus priests at Fort Colville to avoid retaliation from the American Army on the Yakima Indians. After being instructed by his Bishop, he came north and was packed in by William Peon. Thereafter, Peon remained at the Mission and "according to family tradition" was given a square mile of land at the Mission in recognition of his services of "supplying food and clothing to a village of starving Nicola Indians in the dead of winter."[6] In any case William Peon pre-empted in 1861 and built a large house. His sons, Gedeon, Bazil and Baptiste also pre-empted parcels of land near their father around the same time. Baptism and marriage records covering the period from 1860 to 1866 bring to light marriages, baptisms and deaths of the succeeding Peon families.[7]

The surnames Joe and Williams are referred to interchangeably to identify family members. The confusion with the surname, Joe Williams, lies in the retention of Pierre's father's full name.

Descendant Joseph William married Penticton's Millie Paul, the daughter of Dominic Paul. Through Dominic we wind our way back to Kalamalka, whom Buckland says was a name given to a Peon son by his father, a Kanaka fur trader. Joseph and Millie had one son Pierre, who was more commonly known as Pierre Joe Williams. Joseph apparently died a rather sudden and mysterious death, and Millie married Francois Gregoire. Subsequently, they had three children-Celestine, Mariette and Tommy Gregoire. Pierre married Mary Louise Alexander and had the children listed here.

Pierre Joe Williams: *After you told me that my grandfather Pierre Joe was killed by a horse, I asked my mom about it. I'd heard the story before but couldn't remember the details. Mom told me that Pierre and their son Edward were coming home after the race at Princeton when some guys from Merritt had a young boy with them who also had a racehorse. So they challenged Pierre's son Edward. They told Pierre our horse can beat yours. They made a wager and the boys went racing off. Then one of them whacked Pierre behind the head, took his money and left him with seven dollars. Them days even though they robbed and killed, they still had a little honour in them. That's, I think, how they made it look like the horse killed him. I don't think the authorities even questioned what happened to his prize money, so there was no inquiry or anything. Pierre was a good horseman, he broke horses and raced all his life, so how was he going to fall off his horse! My granny, of course, couldn't do anything about it. Women back then weren't considered powerful enough to do anything about such things. So she said it will look after itself. After that Granny married Speed Powers. Speed's father was Martin Powers from Kentucky and his mother was a sister to Ucutt and Christine Joseph who lived later in Penticton. So that made him related to Tommy Armstrong, too. Speed was born out near Lumby and was raised on the knob at Blue Nose Mountain. His first wife was Luc, or who we called Blind Lucy.*

Granny shot her last deer up at the old cabin beside where Harry Hayes had his place. She was in her seventies and it was probably 1968. My brother George went up and picked it up for her. She tied it up in a tree with a skinny little rope, up high enough so the coyotes and bears [skim-keest] couldn't get at it. How she did that is beyond me. She told George to go pick it up and she said, "I got to quit hunting now 'cause I can't carry my deer home any more." She used to walk up that mountain every day. She never hunted the deer, she said she'd wait for them to come along and just shoot them. She used a little single shot twenty-two. She killed a bear up here too, with that same gun. It was hanging around up here on the hill and she shot it with one shot. Who in their right mind would shoot a bear with a twenty-two, but she did, and killed it with one shot. Speed was still alive and a good rider, so he'd go and bring the deer back after she'd kill one. Speed was a good hunter, too. One time him and Edward Fred were hunting. Edward was out in front of him. They were walking along up here and Speed told him to get down. Edward ducked and Speed shot over him. Edward said he never even seen it, and Speed was farther away. Speed taught me something about hunting too. He said he was hunting and saw a big buck with five or six points. He shot it in the back and it fell down. So he walked over to it and pulled out his knife to cut its throat. After he stuck the knife in, that deer kicked like heck and managed to throw him about thirty to forty feet in the air. He told me, don't ever do that, kill it first, 'cause they can kill you! I remember that time pretty clear 'cause he came riding down the hill. He was still in his eighties and still riding. Granny finally sold his horse 'cause she got scared he'd get hurt. He looked pretty mad, but more sad than anything, 'cause he couldn't ride anymore.

Granny lived a long life and was pretty healthy and active till about five years before she died. She never used the sweat house very often. Only about three or maybe four times a year. She used to say you only use it when you have to. It's a personal, spiritual and a sacred thing. That's the purpose of it. And you never mix men and women in a sweat. Maybe, she said you could sweat with other people, but you go in with a different frame of mind like if you're going to work with other people or something like that.

She said the way you face the sweat house door was very important. People could tell what kind of a person you are by the way you face the door. They can see if you are mean, kind or mischievous. She said the door should be faced so you always greet the way the world turns. That's the way she said it, rather than saying face the door to the east. If you face it that way then people will know you are a kind person. But if you face it opposite to the way the world turns, then people will see you are a mean person; you are always looking back where you have gone. I don't remember the significance of south and north, but I do remember, she said you take bad energy from the past and good from where you are going. That's what she told me about the sweat house.

I remember long time ago when the people used to fish down here at Blacktown. Donald Abel came that time with a Model T or Model A car. He brought a big fishing net with him. It had to be maybe about thirty feet long. That time Speed rode his horse Shorty out in the lake pulling that net. The other end was attached to the shore. There was about thirty people there with galvanized tubs. Speed pulled the net into shore and all those people went and filled their tubs. Then they'd wait awhile and tell stories and visit. Then Speed would go for another round. They did that quite a few times throughout the day then they all went home. I remember that time because Donald Abel had his car there. I was impressed by that car.

I remember too, that Granny would fix the fish. I'd see rows and rows of fish hanging from the ceiling. The normal kickinee was about fifteen or sixteen inches long then. Anyway, you could see them turn nice and red when they were drying. Oh, I'd get hungry for some! I would look up at them and Granny would say, "No, don't do it, they are not ready yet." Finally, a week went by and she said before she went to bed, "You can try some." She went to bed and only me and Marina were there. I took a fish down, took the stake off and ate it. I remember we ate by that old coal oil lamp. I ate until I ate about half a dozen! Marina ate only about two. It got me so sick I threw up all night and was sick for a couple of days after. I learned my lesson, don't ever gorge yourself on dried fish. Granny never said nothing. She just told me late, "Wy-choo-chin," which means "I already told you, try only a little bit!"

According to family, Mary Louise was well over one hundred years old when she died in 1997. Speed also made the one hundred mark when he died in 1974. Both are interred at the Head

KOOSTEMEENA

SQWNIM-TE-NALQS

ALEX ANTOINE

GILBERT ANTOINE

HARRY ANTOINE

JIMMY ANTOINE

BAPTISTE NICHOLAS

KALAMALKA / NICHOLAS / ANTOINE / VERNON

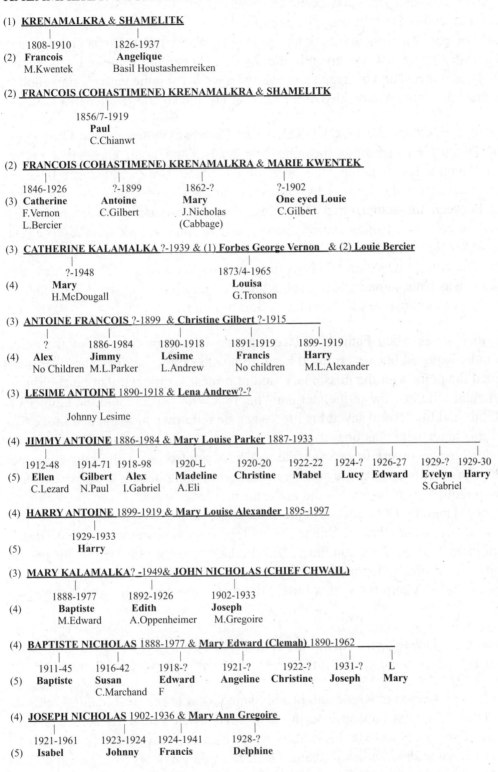

(1) **KRENAMALKRA & SHAMELITK**

1808-1910	1826-1937
(2) Francois	Angelique
M.Kwentek	Basil Houstashemreiken

(2) **FRANCOIS (COHASTIMENE) KRENAMALKRA & SHAMELITK**

1856/7-1919
Paul
C.Chianwt

(2) **FRANCOIS (COHASTIMENE) KRENAMALKRA & MARIE KWENTEK**

1846-1926	?-1899	1862-?	?-1902
(3) Catherine	Antoine	Mary	One eyed Louie
F.Vernon	C.Gilbert	J.Nicholas	C.Gilbert
L.Bercier		(Cabbage)	

(3) **CATHERINE KALAMALKA** ?-1939 & (1) **Forbes George Vernon** & (2) **Louie Bercier**

?-1948	1873/4-1965
(4) Mary	Louisa
H.McDougall	G.Tronson

(3) **ANTOINE FRANCOIS** ?-1899 **& Christine Gilbert** ?-1915

?	1886-1984	1890-1918	1891-1919	1899-1919
(4) Alex	Jimmy	Lesime	Francis	Harry
No Children	M.L.Parker	L.Andrew	No children	M.L.Alexander

(3) **LESIME ANTOINE** 1890-1918 **& Lena Andrew** ?-?

Johnny Lesime

(4) **JIMMY ANTOINE** 1886-1984 **& Mary Louise Parker** 1887-1933

1912-48	1914-71	1918-98	1920-L	1920-20	1922-22	1924-?	1926-27	1929-?	1929-30
(5) Ellen	Gilbert	Alex	Madeline	Christine	Mabel	Lucy	Edward	Evelyn	Harry
C.Lezard	N.Paul	I.Gabriel	A.Eli					S.Gabriel	

(4) **HARRY ANTOINE** 1899-1919 **& Mary Louise Alexander** 1895-1997

1929-1933
Harry

(3) **MARY KALAMALKA** ?-1949 **& JOHN NICHOLAS (CHIEF CHWAIL)**

1888-1977	1892-1926	1902-1933
(4) Baptiste	Edith	Joseph
M.Edward	A.Oppenheimer	M.Gregoire

(4) **BAPTISTE NICHOLAS** 1888-1977 **& Mary Edward (Clemah)** 1890-1962

1911-45	1916-42	1918-?	1921-?	1922-?	1931-?	L
(5) Baptiste	Susan	Edward	Angeline	Christine	Joseph	Mary
	C.Marchand	F				

(4) **JOSEPH NICHOLAS** 1902-1936 **& Mary Ann Gregoire**

1921-1961	1923-1924	1924-1941	1928-?
(5) Isabel	Johnny	Francis	Delphine

The name Kalamalka was a prominent surname of the Okanagan Band before the turn of the century. Although now extinct, the name is well recognized and remains at Head of the Lake through the present surnames Antoine, Nicholas, Oppenheimer and Qualtier.

Over the years, the Kalamalka name has been the subject of curiosity as to its origin. Early historian Frank Buckland inquired into its origin and reported his findings in the 14th report of the Okanagan Historical Society.[2] His research took him to Hawaii where the archivist claimed that Kalamalka was a Hawaiian name that was given to the son of a Hawaiian fur trader by the name of Peon. Apparently Peon married an Okanagan woman and gave his son the name Kalamalka. It is this same family that appear to have resided at the head of Okanagan and Kalamalka Lake.

Before the turn of the century the head of Kalamalka Lake was noted by the Okanagan, the Oblates and the DIA as N'Inkamuplux meaning "the head of the small lake." It is not to be confused with In-kama-pelks meaning "the head of the much larger Okanagan Lake."[3] N'Inkamuplux was reserved for the Indians by Governor James Douglas in 1864, but when conflict arose later between the settlers and Okanagan, the area around N'Inkamuplux was reduced and reserved, in part, as a fishing station. Surveyor John Jane included the reserve in a survey drawn up in 1867. He noted "the land at the mouth of Coldstream Creek is occupied by an old Indian named Francois,"[4] who farmed about forty to sixty acres. Research discloses that Francois was also known as Cohastimene. Kay Cronin included the following story in her book, *A Cross in the Wilderness* that illustrates Kalamalka's effort to join the church.

Kalamalka had four wives when Father Le Jacq was the Oblate missionary of the area. Kalamalka wanted to be baptized but was refused because he attested to having more than one wife. The chief argued the point with the missionary, and in protest, explained that he could not choose any one particular wife in view of the fact that "his first wife was old and the mother of his first born son, John" and the second saved his life "when he fell down a ravine and broke his leg." His loyalty to this latter wife was one of grateful concern, for in her effort to return him home after the accident, her feet were frozen and she was left crippled. So really how could he choose among them? The other two wives are not mentioned. After more debating, Father Le Jacq went to see the Bishop about Kalamalka's case and in the meantime the wives solved the problem. They themselves were old and tired, "So they told the chief to go out and find a young girl whom he could marry. They, in turn, would then be able to live on their own in retirement, with the chief supporting all five of them." As the story continues, Kalamalka met Father Le Jacq on his return from the Bishop and enthusiastically reported to the priest that "they all live together in a cabin I gave them, and they come and help my wife a little. So now we are ALL happy."[5] Kalamalka was thus baptized.

Sacramental records, in part, tell more about the Kalamalka line. They are in chronological order to keep some perspective on the growth and widespread relationships of the family.

First, four-year-old Paul, the son of Krenemalkra and Shamelitk was baptized March 17, 1861 by Father Pandosy, OMI. The next baptisms occurred in 1868 when Father Richard baptized Francois Krenemalka, aged sixty, Marie Kuintkou, forty-five, and Angelique Krenemalka, aged thirty-eight. On the same day, Father Richard, OMI, married Francois to Marie and also married Angelique, age thirty, to twenty-five-year-old Basil Houstashemreiken.[6] Basil, at the time, was a resident at Okanagan Lake, but was born at Adams Lake. His father is noted as Houstrashemreiken.

The next marriage record is that of Paul in which Father Richard records Paul as the son of Francois Kanmalka and Marie Kwentek. Father Pandosy married Paul to Catherine Chianwt in 1874. Her parents are listed as Chianwt of Head of the Lake and Louise Skwe-t-nalkrs of Penticton. Their witnesses are "Abel de Pentekten et de Paul-Ignace."[7] Paul, it seems, died in 1919. A later record reads, "Kalamalka Paul resident of Penticton Band, died April 18, 1919 at Penticton." He was sixty-four years old. His son Alex died the same day.[8]

In 1883 Jean Riliktza (probably Chilihitsa), aged thirty-eight years, son of Nicholas and of Krenkrenmalke, "indiens de la place," was baptized. His sponsor was Basile Horolsiken. This Jean, or Johnny, could very well be the John Nicholas who married Mary the daughter of Francois Kalamalka.[9]

In 1919 a meeting was held at the old council hall at In-kama-pelks to determine the right of Jimmy Antoine to lease his grandfather's property at N'Inkamuplux. It was determined by the people then that Jimmy was a direct descendant of Kalamalka, but so was Jimmy's nephew, Johnny Lesime of Enderby, and his half-sister Lizzie Stelkia of Inkameep Indian Band, at Osoyoos. To settle the matter, the local Indian Agent took a statement from Jimmy to clarify his ancestral roots.[10] Further research confirms the authenticity of Jimmy's statement.

Francois, or Cohastemene or Kalamalka, and Mary had four children: Catherine, Antoine, Mary and "One-eyed Louie." Catherine and Forbes George Vernon had two daughters, Mary and Louisa.[11] The Vernon brothers had come to the Valley with Charles Houghton. By 1871 the brothers owned four hundred acres in the Coldstream area and by 1883 leased three thousand two hundred sixty more acres[12] and stocked the Commonage Reserve with a large herd of cattle and sheep. Louisa was born in 1873 or 1874. Forbes George Vernon was elected to the Provincial Legislature later in 1875.[13] After he left, Catherine then thirty-eight, married forty-two year old Washington born, Louie Bercier in 1891.[14] The couple remained at Long Lake where they farmed before eventually settling at Whiteman's Creek with Catherine's daughter Louisa and husband, George Tronson. Mary married Henry McDougall, but had no children.

Antoine married Christine Gilbert and had five sons, Aleck, Jimmy, Lezime, Francis and Harry. Taking over for Cohastimene at N'Inkamuplux, Antoine and his brother Louie farmed what acreage they could in the natural clearing at Long Lake. Antoine died around 1899 and Christine became the wife of his brother, One-eyed Louie.

One-eyed Louie and Christine had one son. Louie looked after the place and supported his father Cohastimene and sent Jimmy and Lesime to school at Kamloops. Jimmy guessed One-eyed Louie died around 1903 and his son shortly after. His guess was pretty much correct. As seen in the Vernon News he died in February 1902.

"Several days ago an Indian known as 'One-eyed Louis' [sic] left for the hills on the east side of Long lake with the object of smoking out a cougar, the den of which he had discovered some time previously. As he did not return within a reasonable time his friends became anxious and a searching party was formed in order to ascertain what had become of him. After following his tracks for some considerable distance they found his body not far from camp, he having apparently taken sick and tried to get back to his cabin. There were no marks of violence on his body, and had thrown away his rifle some distance back from the place where he was found, which strengthens the belief that death was due to either sickness or fatigue."[15]

Cohastimene died about 1910. Christine, then twice widowed, married Johnny Stelkia of the Osoyoos Band about 1905. Later they moved to Inkameep Band. Christine and Francois' youngest son Francis went with them. Francis contacted tuberculosis and died August 16, 1919.[16] Before his death, however, he left his portion of property to his half-sister, Lizzie Stelkia, and it was within the context of Francis' will that the ownership of the land at Long Lake came into question and Jimmy's statement was requested. Jimmy's brother Lesime married Lena Andrew of Enderby and died in February 1913. A death record for Alex has not as of yet been located, but apparently Harry also went to Oliver as he died there in 1919. Christine McLeod, or Mourning Dove, was then the Osoyoos Reserve school teacher and reported the death.[17] Christine Kalamalka died around 1915. Again no record could be found for her birth, or death, or marriage to Antoine.

As noted in the Kalamalka family tree, the Nicholas surname is derived from Johnny Nicholas, the husband of Mary Kalamalka. However, being that Nicholas is also the name given to Chief N'Kwala by the Hudson's Bay Company, it is likely that Johnny was a descendant in the N'Kwala line. In fact, within the order of chiefs, Johnny appears to be known as Chief Chwail for he was on hand in 1903 as a witness to a criminal case involving a serious matter committed against a female band member.[18] He is again mentioned in the News as the father of Johnny Nicholas. "Johnny Nicholas, son of the chief of the reserve... died suddenly in the house of Isaac Harris, near Larkin, on the evening of the 17th of January, 1906 of heart disease."[19]

Johnny and Mary were also known as Johnny and Mary Cabbage, a nickname derived from the identification with their large cabbage garden at Head of the Lake. Unless Johnny was also known by another name, he cannot be found in records. Together Johnny and Mary had Baptiste, Joseph and Edith. Baptiste served as chief from 1919-1922. Later he married Mary Edward, or Clemah, of Spallumcheen and moved there and raised a family. Joseph married Mary Anne Gregoire, the daughter of Herman Gregoire and Angelique Ahoolah. Edith married Johnny Oppenheimer and had a handful of children. Fortunately, Eva Lawrence, nee Oppenheimer, remembers her grandmother, Mary Nicholas.

Nicholas

Eva Lawrence: *My grandmother, Mary Nicholas, was a traditional woman. Whatever she did she did the Indian way. She spoke mostly Okanagan and raised me and my sister and brothers until I was about four. Then I went to live with my grandmother's relation, Nancy Gregoire, and her mother, Sqwnim-te-nalqs.*

My mom Edith Nicholas died of tuberculosis in 1926 when I was just a year old. My sister Ella married Ben Louis and died just one year after her wedding. My grandmother Mary Nicholas lived across the lake, just this side of Jimmy Bonneau's. She had land there. It is called In-kama-pelks. It is all called that, right up to Jimmy Antoine's house, at Neehoot. They moved up to Salmon River after that.

Someone told my son Dave that we were Shuswap. But we're not. I happen to know why we have relatives in Enderby. My uncle Baptiste was the chief at In-kama-pelks. He was from the N'Kwala line because he is a descendant of Chwail and at that time they elected them according to Indian's bloodline. He wasn't chief for very long and he fell in love with a beautiful Enderby woman, so he quit and transferred to Enderby. But his mother stayed in Salmon River. So, my cousins there are raised the Enderby way because their mother is from there. Instead of her moving here, he moved to her reserve.

My grandmother, Mary Nicholas, didn't just raise my brothers, but also her other grandchildren, Isabelle Nicholas and her brother, because her son Joseph died of TB not too far apart from my mother Edith. They were brother and sister.

Antoine

Victor Antoine: *My grandfather Jimmy Antoine is a descendant of Kalamalka. His grandfather was Koostamena from the head of Kalamalka Lake. Kalamalka was Jimmy's great grandfather. Jimmy's father was Antoine Francois and his mother Christine Gilbert. If I understand it right, Christine was the daughter of a custom's officer who worked at the border crossing in the vicinity of Kettle Falls or Midway. Jimmy went to Kamloops Indian Residential School from the time he was eight until he was sixteen. The Kalamalka family had that land between the highway and the railroad track and straight back off the lake taking in the vicinity of the Kal Lake store. All of that land belonged to the family.*

The old man told me that when he was small his folks moved over across the lake beside where the Bonneaus now live. There was a spring there and that's where they got their water. He said his grandfather Koostamena used to come over there from Kalamalka Lake and take him back to his place alongside Coldstream Creek. That was a fishing ground for the people. He said in late February and March, his grandfather would come for him and on their way back would stop at that place where the Vernon city dump was later and they'd get some groundhogs. They'd stay there, I guess a couple days, and then go on to Kalamalka Lake. The old man said he stayed there awhile, then when he was about eight they took him to Kamloops Indian School. He went there every year until he was about sixteen. Then he came back here.

The old man said Mary Louise Parker came from Cheesaw, Washington. She came here to visit friends or maybe it was her relatives, and she saw him and after that she stuck to him. He said what else can you do when a lady sticks to you. Anyway, they got married and lived at Kalamalka Lake and he worked at Coldstream Ranch. After some business with developers, Indian Agents, and other people, all of that land exchanged hands and it became a cutoff. Jimmy, Mary Louise, and their three kids, Ellen, Gilbert and my dad, Alex, were evicted; they were homeless, so they came across the lake back to his folks' place.

After my grandmother Mary Louise died in 1933, Jimmy got to be good friends with Francois Gregoire. My grandmother Mariette was married to my maternal grandfather, Joe Abel, but after leaving him several times before, she finally left for good and went back to Francois'. In that time, Jimmy got with my grandmother Mariette and they left for Douglas Lake. They stayed up there and both worked for the Douglas Lake Cattle Company. Somehow, Mariette called Taby McRae her aunt. That's where they stayed, I guess, at Douglas Lake. They spent about two years there and after the tension died down here they came home with a string of about six horses and quite a bit of money. They got Frank Gottfriedson to build them a house across the lake and that's where they stayed.

I was born to Mary Abel and Alex Antoine in 1941. After I was born and was about six months old, I was given to my grandparents. I was pretty sickly, I guess, and must have been born breech because they used an instrument to haul me out. After that I had a curve in my spine. My grandmother was at the Empress Theater in town when my mother came in there and gave me to her mother, Mariette. I guess I was in poor shape because they took me into Wong's Restaurant and Wong warmed me some milk and cut a tablecloth to make me a dry diaper. After they got me home they took me to a doctor and I was put in a body cast. But it didn't work and I was getting sores from the cast and I wasn't picking up. They thought I was going to kick the can. So my grandmother took the cast off and ran her fingers down my spine and must have fluked it, because my spine straightened out. She used Indian medicine on my sores and bought a goat for its milk and I picked up. When I was older my mother wanted me back, but they took me to the Indian office to prove I was Alex Antoine's son and my grandparents were given custody over me. From that time on I was raised by my grandparents, Jimmy Antoine and Mariette.

When they came back from Douglas Lake they went into ranching. He had that place across the lake, and a rancher named Carswell, I think, wintered his cattle there and Jimmy took calves in trade. My grandmother helped to keep them going by growing a big garden, and in winter, tanning hides and sewing gloves. By the time I was about six years old they had quite a few cattle. The old man was good friends with Speed Powers and they more or less went in company together with the hay and stuff like that. Speed had no family; he was married but had no kids. He was a real good rancher. By 1947 the old man was very well off. But in 1949 he made a serious mistake, he sold a good bunch of horses and cattle and bought a tractor, a threshing machine and a binder. He thought he was going to do all the threshing out here. But at that same time the combine came out and he went broke. A couple of years later, I guess, they sold that equipment to Douglas Lake Cattle Company. So, all through the fifties we had some hard times. Failure affected him deeply and he went to drinking.

In 1955 my grandmother asked me if I would be interested in ranching and farming the land. So I agreed. The old lady was a really strong person. When she put her mind to something she did it. So that winter she started tanning hides and making gloves, moccasins and buckskin coats if she had an order for them. She got a dollar and a half for gloves, about three and a half for moccasins, and between fifty and sixty bucks for a coat. She'd take them to that second-hand store in Vernon and that guy would buy the whole thing.

The following Thursday we would go the auction sale at Larkin and buy mixed-breed day-old calves. First thing, she would give them two needles. Most of them were really weak. Anyway, we'd rush home with those calves on our laps and put them behind the stove, dry them up and give them special formula. She knew that if they survived the first few days without getting the scours they had a good chance of making it.

I was eighteen in 1958 and by that time we had a herd of about fourteen head. The older ones by that time had calves. We'd turn them out in the spring on the range and next spring they had calves. Some of the guys from here had bulls up there on the range and I remember those guys would stop at our place and tease my grandmother. They'd say, how are "our calves" doing? I thought to myself, what are they talking about, those are our calves. But Jimmy Bonneau and them other guys had bulls up there and that's where our calves came from.

The old man leased out that place across the lake in 1958 to that potato farmer. Then in 1959, leased it to Sakakibara. Sakakibara wanted to try the new hybrid tomatoes and would have to have enough ground for different varieties, so he had to have a long-term lease and said he would irrigate it by installing a pump and pipes. As soon as my grandmother heard the word irrigation, she told my grandfather, "Let's take only a little of the money and keep the irrigation equipment after his lease is up as part of the deal." She heard that after growing tomatoes on a part of the land it would be real good for grain and hay later. Jimmy agreed, and Sakakibara went to work. It provided us young guys with summer jobs too. Anyway, just before the lease was up she told that Japanese guy, "You rebuild that motor, it's five years old now and worn out, I can hear it." He balked at it though and my grandmother went into town and raised hell with Bulman's Cannery and the Indian Agency. That did it, and he had the pump re-built. She was quite satisfied with everything and we had enough irrigation equipment. In the spring of 1960, they bought this little tractor and the rest of the equipment we needed to produce our own hay.

During that time, they were pretty well-off and I continued to go to school and by 1956 I was tested for the university program and continued but failed Grade Twelve because of a problem with math. So they tested me for the trade program and I tested high for heavy duty mechanics and welding. To gain experience, we were placed among the certain businesses in Vernon. But my grandfather wanted me to become a lawyer and there was no way I could explain that I couldn't go to university because I had difficulty with math. Then in 1961 I came home from school and the cows and all the farm equipment Jimmy sold lock, stock and barrel. He didn't want me to farm.

Throughout his life Jimmy made use of his formal education and although he became a thorn in the side of both Indian Affairs and fellow band members he is known as one who never backed down from a challenge. From his own account he said:

> "I am of the chief's line and I am an individual. I still look after myself and still have my own ideas, which no one can change. Everything I believe in knows I am a descendant of 'Kalamalka.' Because of my Okanagan lineage, I can walk with my head held high."[20]

LAWRENCE

SUSAN

JOE, SUSAN & HENRY JR.

HARRIET & WILLIAM

AGNES

HELENE & SARAH

ANDREW THOMAS

LAWRENCE

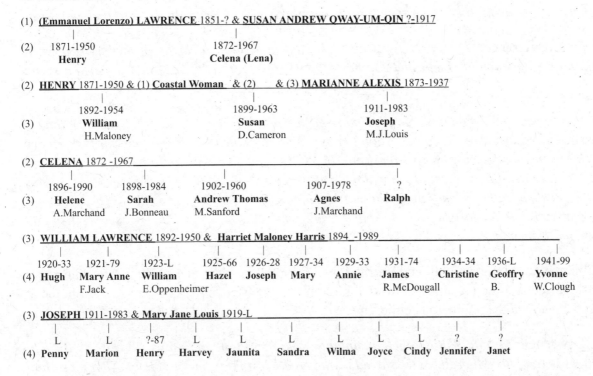

(1) **(Emmanuel Lorenzo) LAWRENCE** 1851-? & **SUSAN ANDREW QWAY-UM-QIN** ?-1917

(2) 1871-1950 — **Henry**
    1872-1967 — **Celena (Lena)**

(2) **HENRY** 1871-1950 & (1) **Coastal Woman** & (2) & (3) **MARIANNE ALEXIS** 1873-1937

(3)
- 1892-1954 **William** H.Maloney
- 1899-1963 **Susan** D.Cameron
- 1911-1983 **Joseph** M.J.Louis

(2) **CELENA** 1872 -1967

(3)
- 1896-1990 **Helene** A.Marchand
- 1898-1984 **Sarah** J.Bonneau
- 1902-1960 **Andrew Thomas** M.Sanford
- 1907-1978 **Agnes** J.Marchand
- ? **Ralph**

(3) **WILLIAM LAWRENCE** 1892-1950 & **Harriet Maloney Harris** 1894 -1989

(4)
1920-33	1921-79	1923-L	1925-66	1926-28	1927-34	1929-33	1931-74	1934-34	1936-L	1941-99
Hugh	**Mary Anne**	**William**	**Hazel**	**Joseph**	**Mary**	**Annie**	**James**	**Christine**	**Geoffry**	**Yvonne**
	F.Jack	E.Oppenheimer					R.McDougall		B.	W.Clough

(3) **JOSEPH** 1911-1983 & **Mary Jane Louis** 1919-L

(4)
L	L	?-87	L	L	L	L	L	L	?	?
Penny	**Marion**	**Henry**	**Harvey**	**Jaunita**	**Sandra**	**Wilma**	**Joyce**	**Cindy**	**Jennifer**	**Janet**

The Lawrence surname is a derivative of the Portuguese name Lorenzo. As noted in the Abel family tree, Suzanne Andrew (Qway-um-qin) married a white man "Emmanuel Lorenzo from Portugal." Within Father Baudre's census of 1877, twenty-five-year-old Suzanne "Quihammikin" is in the family group with parents Andre "Koiatumkan," fifty years old, and his wife, Bernadine, then forty-six.[2] Current family however, refer to Suzanne as a Ko-mas-ket. In any case, Emmanuel and Susan had two children-Henry Jr. and Celena, or more commonly known as Lena.

The marriage record of Henry and Marianne too lends some confusion concerning the couples parentage. If left as is, the record, typed later in 1942, would leave no window to the past. However, having been corrected by an unknown source, details as to the parentage, while still in question are clearer. First, Henry Lawrence (not an Indian) is listed as a bachelor, then corrected to read "widower." His age is corrected from forty-two to forty-five. The name of his father is corrected from just Lawrence to Manuel Lawrence. The space for his mother's name was left empty then "Susan Andrew." was added. Marianne's age too is corrected from fifty to twenty-five, and "widow" added later. Her parents too are later added as "Seymour and Annie Quihamplein." They were married by Father Le Jeune, February 23, 1920. Their witnesses were Joe Abel and Catherine.[3]

The comparison of Marrianne's parentage easily compares with her parentage from her first marriage to Alexis.

Ned Louis: *Henry Lawrence Jr. lived in the BX area [east of Vernon]. That place had quite a few non-status people living there long time ago. Some of our people went up there to pick potatoes.*

Mary Jane Lawrence: *Yeah, they lived up there and later he traded the property for a worn out, old threshing machine. Lena and Joe never could figure out why he would do such a dumb thing.*

Henry Jr. had three families. He first married a woman from around Chehalis and that is where ol' Willie Lawrence was born. I don't know what happened to his mother, but then Henry got with Susan's mother, a woman from Enderby. Susan had relatives there that she used to go visit. In fact, Manuel Bercie and Johnny James were Susan's half-brothers. So, whoever is their mother is Susan's mother. Henry then married Marianne Qway-um-qin. She wasn't Qway-um-qin then, she was Alexis because her first husband was Johnny Alexis' dad, ol' Alex Cise. He died and she married Henry.

William married Harriet Maloney Harris, July 27, 1930,[4] the daughter of Mary Ann Alexander and Irishman Jack Maloney and widow of Johnny Harris. Subsequently, they made their home at Six-Mile Creek and had numerous children.

Willie Lawrence: *My dad Willie joined the infantry and served in the first world war. We lived in two places here at Six-Mile. First, we stayed by the creek, just up from the school. That place had boards for the walls and a tent for the roof. We were living there when I woke up one morning and my brother and sister were dead. We moved after that and lived at Edward Bonneau's log house until they built that other house. That was my mom's house.*

Joe and Mary Jane made their home at Whiteman's Creek where the Lawrence farm is today.

Mary Jane Lawrence: *Joe bought this place by sealed bid from Louie Bercie and his woman Louise. That's how we got this place.*

When we were first together, Joe logged for Tom Morrison and Bell Pole out of Lumby. Our first house was built from the logs taken from the property, then shipped by barge to Kelowna and traded for lumber. I remember when the lumber was delivered right here on the beach! The mill sent everything Joe needed to build our house; all the nails and everything. In later years, Joe farmed about three hundred acres of vegetables here at Whiteman's Creek, at Harry Parker's and at Deep Creek. He liked to grow cabbage and other vegetables that could be dehydrated and used at the army camps for the soldiers.

The house burned down in November of 1949, and we moved in with Mom and Dad at Six-Mile. Joe was farming at Six-Mile and he went real early in the morning to see someone up that way. I saw that the house was in flames and knew I couldn't do anything. So, I loaded Joe's dad and the kids in the car and tried to get help. I just got to the Whiteman's Creek bridge and saw him talking to Harry Parker. By the time they went back to the house, it was too late. That was a real horrible winter. Dad was building that new house from scratch when we moved in with them.

It was a just a shell when we lived in there. Their log house burned down two years before that and they lived in a tent with board walls for practically two winters. It was really crowded in their little house and the winter was really cold. And to make it worse, by the time we came back in April we found that the young fruit trees had froze out.

By June, Joe was working for Bell Pole and I packed up the kids, the food and the blankets into the car. I was going to Oroville to thin apples. Joe was out at Lumby hauling logs for Bell Pole. When we got to town I met up with Brown. There was a little park where Eaton's is today and it was there that Brown confiscated our car and dumped me and the kids on the street. I didn't know what to do. All of our food and blankets were in the car and the nights were still cold. So I left the kids in the park and hitch-hiked to Lumby to find Joe. I couldn't find him and hitch-hiked back to town and went to the police station. There I found Constable Ellington, an RCMP, and told him what happened. He told Brown to bring the car back and take us home. Brown said he couldn't get into the car until next day because it was locked up. Ellington told him to just get it and bring it. Finally he showed up and drove us home. He took the car with him. I didn't know till later that he had no right to take the van because Joe put it in my name. Joe didn't find out for days what happened.

When Joe got older he retired from gardening, but after his death in 1983 his son Henry took to the plow and restarted the business. Unfortunately Henry died in a tragic car accident in 1987 and thereafter the farm was taken over by a son-in-law. In retrospect, the Lawrence family have their roots in the farming industry beginning with Emmanuel Lorenzo and Susan Andrew (Ko-mas-ket). Their time goes back to the days when Moise was Chief, Father Baudre was the missionary and the Royal Commission of 1877 began.

Rosie Williams: *Henry [Emmanuel Lorenzo] and Susan travelled a lot. Tuma, Lena their daughter, got a toothache when she was around seven years old. At the time, the family was at the coast somewhere and Tuma was brought back here to live with her grandparents. The infected tooth left Lena's face disfigured and so there are no pictures of her. Our two grandmothers were Margaret Bonneau and Lena Lawrence. We didn't know Margaret very well, and the only thing I remember is that she used to come visit Mom and Dad when we lived down there by old Alexis. We knew Tuma better because she lived with us. She was Mom's mother. The thing about Tuma was she was real patient with her grandchildren. It's not like now, we get frustrated with our grandchildren, but Tuma never did. I remember she would be playing cards by herself at the table and we'd go over there with our little hands and mess them all up. She never got mad, she'd wait until we had enough then lay her cards out again.*

LOGAN FAMILY

MARY LOGAN

ALEX DUBRETT

BAPTISTE LOGAN

ABRAHAM DUBRETT

JOSEPHINE, ANNIE, MARY & LIZZIE

JOSEPHINE LOGAN

CHARLIE EDWARDS

WILLIAM SWALWELL

ANNIE DUBRETT

CHRISTINE

LOGAN / DUBRETT / SWALWELL / EDWARDS

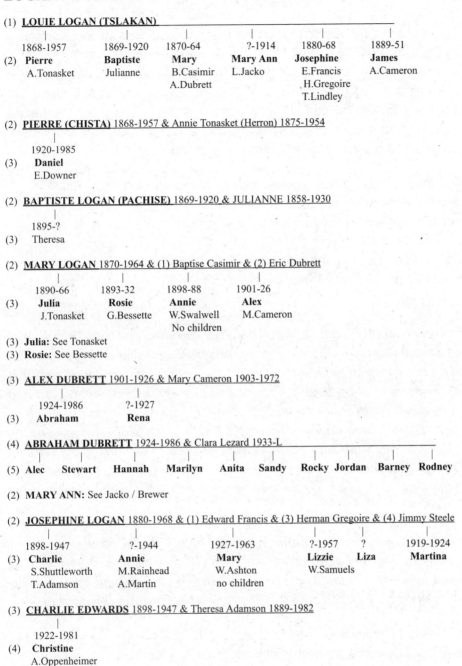

(1) LOUIE LOGAN (TSLAKAN)

1868-1957	1869-1920	1870-64	?-1914	1880-68	1889-51
(2) Pierre	**Baptiste**	**Mary**	**Mary Ann**	**Josephine**	**James**
A.Tonasket	Julianne	B.Casimir	L.Jacko	E.Francis	A.Cameron
		A.Dubrett		H.Gregoire	
				T.Lindley	

(2) PIERRE (CHISTA) 1868-1957 & Annie Tonasket (Herron) 1875-1954

1920-1985
(3) Daniel
E.Downer

(2) BAPTISTE LOGAN (PACHISE) 1869-1920 & JULIANNE 1858-1930

1895-?
(3) Theresa

(2) MARY LOGAN 1870-1964 & (1) Baptise Casimir & (2) Eric Dubrett

1890-66	1893-32	1898-88	1901-26
(3) Julia	**Rosie**	**Annie**	**Alex**
J.Tonasket	G.Bessette	W.Swalwell	M.Cameron
		No children	

(3) Julia: See Tonasket
(3) Rosie: See Bessette

(3) ALEX DUBRETT 1901-1926 & Mary Cameron 1903-1972

1924-1986	?-1927
(3) Abraham	**Rena**

(4) ABRAHAM DUBRETT 1924-1986 & Clara Lezard 1933-L

(5) Alec	**Stewart**	**Hannah**	**Marilyn**	**Anita**	**Sandy**	**Rocky**	**Jordan**	**Barney**	**Rodney**

(2) MARY ANN: See Jacko / Brewer

(2) JOSEPHINE LOGAN 1880-1968 & (1) Edward Francis & (3) Herman Gregoire & (4) Jimmy Steele

1898-1947	?-1944	1927-1963	?-1957	?	1919-1924
(3) Charlie	**Annie**	**Mary**	**Lizzie**	**Liza**	**Martina**
S.Shuttleworth	M.Rainhead	W.Ashton	W.Samuels		
T.Adamson	A.Martin	no children			

(3) CHARLIE EDWARDS 1898-1947 & Theresa Adamson 1889-1982

1922-1981
(4) Christine
A.Oppenheimer

The family tree above is a concerted effort on the part of current people to join together four prominent family histories. Some are descendants while the remainder are related through marriage.

Logan

As noted by James Teit and later by Carstens, "Logan was the grandson of the Kamloops chief, Telaka'n, (Male Grizzly Bear) who had succeeded the Kamloops chief Kwolila. Kwolila, it will be remembered, was N'kwala's Shuswap uncle, the son of his grandfather's Shuswap wife."[2] The above Logan family descend from the Telaka'n line at Savona and area. Logan Lake is historically named for the same family. Second eldest, Mary Logan, used to say that she wasn't just anyone, but someone important because they named a lake after her family.[3] Mary Balf, writer of the history of Kamloops gives credence to Mary's statement.

"Tslakan, corrupted into Logan by the traders, was a 'Boute du Lac' (Savona) Indian who traded many furs during the 1880's, and established a good horse farm. He apparently intensely disliked the white influx and maintained great pride in being Indian, even insisting on the prefix "Mr." as for white men. His daughter is remembered in Mount Anne nearby; she too was a skilled trapper until her death in 1934. Her husband Gabriel had been killed in an accident in 1905 and she raised the children single handed."[4]

Millie Steele: *Old Logan wasn't a chief. He only assisted the Shuswap chief and travelled all over the country with him. Mary Logan was my mom's mother; my maternal grandmother. She said she had a half-sister over around Invermere in the Kootenays that she never ever met. One time I met a woman who said she was the niece of Mary Logan. She was from the Kootenays and was moving to Revelstoke. She must have been part of that family. Old Logan, I guess, fathered a bunch of kids and some of those in this family tree had different mothers. In one family there would be a couple of kids with the same name. Mom said Father Le Jeune used to do that. If the parents couldn't think of an English name for their daughters, Father Le Jeune would just call them Mary. It looks like that's what happened with Mary Logan and her sister Jenny's grandmother, Mary Ann Logan.*

Lavina Lum: *Pierre, or Chista Logan, married Annie Tonasket, or Big Annie. She was married before to Johnny Herron. They are Danny Logan's mom and dad. Chista used to have that land at Irish Creek where Jenny and Louie Marchand live. They had real big gardens and hay fields up there. Mary Logan had her place above Irish Creek. The house and barns are all gone now.*

The second eldest son, Baptiste, better known as Pachise Logan, held the chief's seat at Head of the Lake from 1909 to 1912. Baptiste's term in office occurred at a rather difficult period in Okanagan history when fruit farming became the leading industry and grain farming took a back seat. Without the means to build an irrigation system, the Okanagan were ill equipped to compete. Finally, because Chief Logan would not conform to demands of the Inspector of Indian Affairs he was deposed for allegations of "intemperance and incompetence."[5] Baptiste died in 1920 and his wife Julienne died in 1930. There is no record of the death of their daughter Theresa.

Dubrett

Mary Logan had four children – Julia, Rosie, Annie and Alex. Julia married Johnny Tonasket. Rosie married George Bessette and Annie married Billy Swalwell. Annie and Billy had no children but raised Billy's niece, Lavina McDougall, and Annie's niece, Marguerite Bessette, after Rosie died. Alex Dubrett, aka Logan, died in 1926 of tuberculosis at Round Lake at the early age of twenty-seven years. Two years before his death his son Abraham was born. A daughter Rena was also born but died in 1927. Apparently, Alex and Charlie Lezard were good friends and it was later that Charlie's step-daughter Clara married Alex's son, Abraham. The marriage produced ten children. Abraham died in 1986. Lavina Lum, Millie Steele and Marguerite Marchand tell the stories of their extended family.

Millie Steele: *Mom, Aunt Rosie and Aunt Annie were old Dubrett's children. They were supposed to have been born at Deadman's Creek or Kamloops before Mary Logan came here.*

Lavina Lum: *There used to be an ol' pine tree over here by ol' Jacko's place, where that little log house that's still standin'. I see it every time I come through there. That's where Dubrett and Mary Logan's youngest one was born. That day, Mary Logan went to gather some sticks for a fire and had Alex under that tree. In them days, the ladies used to wear two skirts at one time and she wrapped him up and took him back to camp. That's when Alex's dad knocked on my mother's door and told her that Mary Logan had her baby. My mother used to tell me, right at the base of the tree, that's where, Tslakan, or Alex Dubrett, was born. When he grew up he got with Mary Cameron, and Abraham was born. Alex and Mary had two other kids, too, but they both died when they were young.*

Swalwell

To date there is no absolute evidence of the history of the Swalwell surname within the membership of the Okanagan Band. However, an excerpt from the Okanagan Historical Society Report that documents the Swalwell name bears mention here. It reads "Swalwell Lake (Beaver Lake) expansion of Vernon Creek: is named after William Swalwell, settler in the Shuswap Valley in the 1870's. William Swalwell moved near Kelowna in the 1890's."[6] Eliza Jane Simpson of the Duck Lake Simpson family married also one William Pellister Swalwell in May of 1895.[7] Whether they are one in the same person, as well as the father of Billy Swalwell, is still unclear. The Oblates recorded the marriage of Billy Swalwell and Annie Dubrett. It reads Billy "Swaloal," was a bachelor, born at "Head of the Lake" and his parents were "Saul and Magam." On July 29, 1913, he married Annie "Duprat" of the Head of the Lake. Her parents are included as Eric Duprat and "Loogan." Again, Father Le Jeune officiated at the marriage and Pierre Michel and Susan were witnesses.[8] No age is included on the record. It is amazing how accurately the record confirms the story by their adopted daughter, Lavina Lum.

Lavina Lum: *When I first remember, my dad had a two-story house there where the go-carts are now. Billy Swalwell, my dad, owned that land. In them days you could trade your property without papers. Everybody did that. They used to haul water, but my dad wanted that place at Deep Creek, so he traded his sister, my aunt Mary Louise Powers, for that place. That's why Susan Joe owns that now. She got it from her mother.*

At Little Rope Ranch, Deep Creek, there was a little creek that come down at Allen Edward's place. That ol' lady Mary Edwards had lots of flowers; she was always into flowers. They lived in that log house. The spring was where Pete and Josephine Gregoire lived down at the mill. There was two log houses below the road. One was Sqwil-pelks' house and other, this way, was her daughter Nancy's. We were in her house. Sqwil-pelks raised Mary Louise. When the ol' man died that place belonged to Mary Louise.

At Little Rope Ranch Dad built a little one-room cabin. It was a long cabin. He was gonna' build a house up there on that other part. He started to build a house at the foot of the hill, when I was a teenager, and of course, I'm all over there, and all over Irish Creek. So, one spring I was out there about this time of the year and Dad started to build that house. He had the walls up but not the roof. I was lookin' around there and I seen a spring comin' out from underneath the house. I tol' my mom, "You better come see, our house has a spring under it." She said, "I tol' your dad there's a spring there, but he just said it was the runoff." So after that Dad saw it. They built that house at Irish Creek and stayed there till they passed away.

Buckskin Susan was Chief Pierre Michele's wife. My dad and Theresa called her auntie. My mom stayed with them, 'cause you know, my mom and dad eloped! The people had their own police and they went and got my mom and took her over to the chief's place. She sat right there! My mom said they had a great big log house with an upstairs. Mom said there was a few of them stayed there. The chief told my dad, who was quite a bit older than Mom, to go to work. Dad had his own horses and his own place, so the chief put him to work puttin' up hay and stuff like that and my mom stayed there at the chief's place. So they kept them there and you know the priest don't come around every week or even every month. So when they do they have to mention [banns] so many times before they can get married. It was only after that that they got married. Other people got married that same day 'cause the priest was there. Later when I needed my birth certificate they had trouble finding it. I told them I was the daughter of Billy and Annie Swalwell and believe it or not they found Mom and Dad's marriage certificate in Wenatchee. That same time they found Auntie Virginia's birth certificate in Spokane. My grandmother, ol' Mary Logan, would tease Mom in Indian. She'd say she was just twelve years old when she got married! Mom would say back in Indian, "I wasn't twelve years old!"

My dad was handsome. Even when he got old he was still a handsome lookin' man. You know, he'd take off any ol' time. One time we were doin' hay. I was about thirteen years old and I always drove the small team. The thing I'd have was like a slew, but it had sides and that's what I'd drive to pick up the hay. Mom and Dad drove the wagon. They'd unload my hay first then the wagon. That time we were just at the top of the load when something hit my dad. He just stuck his fork into the hay and started singin' his song. I don't always remember his song, only sometimes it will come to me. My dad sang, looked around, and I was standin' there watchin' him. My mom said something in Indian. She knew he was gonna take off. My dad had a Model T Ford. He put his fork down and told my mom, "You and the daughter, you finish this and then you let the horses go." Those horses were a big, big team. We had a hard time getting those harness off those Oheecan. [Clydesdale horses] Mom's not too tall and the harnesses are heavy. My mom said, "I'm not gonna turn those horses loose and I'm not gonna bother with them!" That ol' man would leave and not be back for a long time. He went in and changed his clothes and we watched him while he took off. He was gone for two or three weeks that time. Anyway, we finished the hay with the small team and I asked my mom, "Why does he just take off like that, he didn't even help us finish the hay!" Well, Mom would get lonesome for him and worry about him and when she does that, she takes out her flute. She'd play the flute when she was lonesome or worried, but only for me, not when Dad was around.

Marguerite Marchand: *Our dad wasn't around very much. So when we wanted to go into town we would walk from Deep Creek over to the corner of Westside Road and the highway to catch the Greyhound Bus. It cost thirty-five cents from the corner, but if we walked to the top of O'Keefe hill, then it cost only twenty-five cents. It was nothing in those days, really, to walk over that far. Anyway, one day we were walking with our mom and I remember her asking us, what are you going to do when you get as old as me. Then she starting jumping around to show us how young she felt. Then she jumped again and twisted her ankle. We didn't go to town because we had to carry her home. Like Lavina said, our mom liked to sing and dance. After Lavina mentioned it I remember her playing the flute, but what I remember most is how much she liked to sing and dance.*

Jenny Marchand: *My grandmother, Mary Ann Logan, died the same year my mother Emily married my dad, Ernest Brewer. My grandmother's sister, Mary Logan, tol' me she will never ever forget what happened here. She remembered since she was a teenage sixteen years old.*

What happened was, there was these strong winds, a tornado. She said they were out in the field gathering up potatoes. The wind came through that field where they were workin' and she said they could see it. It was a real strong wind. So they all ran and put their hands around the trees and hung on. That wind went through and picked up those hundred pound bags of potatoes and it went up in the air and they never seen it again. She said it just picked up anything in the way and they never seen it again. I think it was up at O'Keefe Station where that happened. She said after that, she has never seen that happen again.

Josephine Logan was the last to survive of the original Logan family. She died in 1968 at the age of eighty-nine. Josephine was very proud of her connections to her grandfather N'Kwala and in a mark of respect unveiled a monument in his memory at Head of the Lake in 1960.[9] The event was captured in the news and was attended by notable people from the Okanagan, Shuswap and Thompson Bands, as well as the general public.

Edwards

The Edwards surname is most likely just one of the several given names that evolved into a surname. Some say Edward Francis came from Kamloops. Charlie, the son of Josephine Logan and Edward, was born approximately 1898. He first married Susan Shuttleworth, the daughter of George Shuttleworth and Mary Kruger. Before having any children they parted company, and he later had a daughter with Theresa Adamson and named her Christine.

While serving in World War I, Charlie kept in touch with his mother, Josephine, through letters and picture postcards from overseas. Next to his war buddies, Charlie has the appearance of being a full blood, and from his lineage it appears that he was. He died in 1947 and is buried at Head of the Lake cemetery.

Edward and Josephine's eldest daughter, Annie, first married a man with the surname Rainhead, then married a second time to Alex Martin of Colville Indian Agency in Omak, Washington. Annie was twenty-one at the time and Alex forty-two.[10] Annie remained at Omak for the duration of her life. They have children, but none are known by name at this time. Mary Edwards married William Ashton, and after separating went to Washington where she lived out the rest of her life. Annie and Mary had three maternal half-sisters. Lizzie's father was Thomas Lindley. Lisa's father was Herman Gregoire and Martina's father was Jimmy Steele. Lizzie married W. Samuels in 1945,[11] while Liza and Martina died as young children.

Corrine Marchand: *I spent a lot of time with my great grandmother, Josephine, in the later years of her life. She is the one who had a main hand in my learning our language. Between her and Big Annie and Gramma Theresa, I learned to tell time by saying the words after Mom saying the words and me repeating them. She was very smart for no schooling and speaking hardly any English. She and my Gramma Theresa gave my two girls their Indian names. Thanks to Great Gramma I am who I am today.*

I remember very little about Grampa Charlie Edwards. But what I do remember, I cherish as my favourite memories of him. I remember one of the things he used to do with me as a little girl. He was trying to teach me how to say turkey in Okanagan.

Another time I remember is when we were down the States. Dad and Grampa were working there. When Grampa wasn't working he would go up town to Oroville to visit his friends and I'd tag along even over Mom's protest that he might lose me when he got with his friends. But, no, I got my way. I liked to eat Mom's lipstick so when Grampa took me with him he would buy me some lipstick. There I'd be with lipstick all over my face and me hanging on to his back pocket. We'd go all over Oroville and I'd go home all dirty faced.

I remember living in a log cabin at Salmon River. Johnny Jones bought the place from Mom. Grampa and ol' Jimmy Logan logged together there, and I remember the horses in the barn. Uncle Ernest and Auntie Dorothy lived with us, where Kenny Williams lives now. What beautiful memories!

Mary Jane Lawrence: *I remember Mrs. Jimmy Logan [Slim Annie Cameron] mostly as riding her horse. She used to ride that horse that she brought back from Douglas Lake, all the time. She'd ride that good lookin' bay horse down to her sister Ella Alexis' place. She wore a divided skirt and always with a nice blouse to go with it. She did a lot of riding. I remember it was after she left Jimmy Logan, and before she got with ol' Jock, a Scotsman from Merritt, that she rode that bay horse. She went back and forth to Merritt when she met ol' Jock, but by then he had a car. Then they'd drive down here to visit.*

LOUIE / LAMPROW / TRONSON

CELINA

AGNES

MANUEL

ALEX

WILLIAM, ESTHER & ANDREW LAMPROW

ELIZABETH   LOUISA   DAVE   GEORGE   LOUIE
CAMERON   TRONSON   CAMERON   TRONSON   BERCIE

LOUIE / LAMPROW / TRONSON

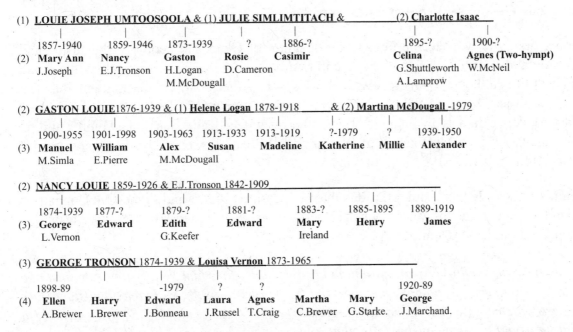

(1) **LOUIE JOSEPH UMTOOSOOLA** & (1) **JULIE SIMLIMTITACH** &   **(2) Charlotte Isaac**

1857-1940	1859-1946	1873-1939	?	1886-?	1895-?	1900-?
(2) **Mary Ann**	**Nancy**	**Gaston**	**Rosie**	**Casimir**	**Celina**	**Agnes (Two-hympt)**
J.Joseph	E.J.Tronson	H.Logan	D.Cameron		G.Shuttleworth	W.McNeil
		M.McDougall			A.Lamprow	

(2) **GASTON LOUIE** 1876-1939 & (1) **Helene Logan** 1878-1918   & (2) **Martina McDougall** -1979

1900-1955	1901-1998	1903-1963	1913-1933	1913-1919	?-1979	?	1939-1950
(3) **Manuel**	**William**	**Alex**	**Susan**	**Madeline**	**Katherine**	**Millie**	**Alexander**
M.Simla	E.Pierre	M.McDougall					

(2) **NANCY LOUIE** 1859-1926 & **E.J.Tronson** 1842-1909

1874-1939	1877-?	1879-?	1881-?	1883-?	1885-1895	1889-1919
(3) **George**	**Edward**	**Edith**	**Edward**	**Mary**	**Henry**	**James**
L.Vernon		G.Keefer		Ireland		

(3) **GEORGE TRONSON** 1874-1939 & **Louisa Vernon** 1873-1965

1898-89		-1979	?	?			1920-89
(4) **Ellen**	**Harry**	**Edward**	**Laura**	**Agnes**	**Martha**	**Mary**	**George**
A.Brewer	I.Brewer	J.Bonneau	J.Russel	T.Craig	C.Brewer	G.Starke	.J.Marchand.

The Louie family has a very interesting history. Given the time element and scope of research a full story cannot be told here. None the less Esther Louie provides many details of her association with her father-in-law Gaston Louie. The Tronson history is also interesting, and is included here as a means to identify current family relationships and history. The Louie family also has roots in the Shuttleworth family through the marriage of first, Andrew Lamprow, and then George Shuttleworth to Celina Louie, and the marriage of Agnes Louie to William McNeil.

The family surname, not surprisingly, takes its roots from Louis Umtoosoola, the father of Gaston Louie and grandfather of William Louie. The old barn south of Irish Creek, was built in the late 1890's was built by Umtoosoola, "one of the first Indians to take up farming in the region."[2] Umtoosoola and Julie's son, Gaston Louie, also known as Gasto, was a player in the agricultural arena of the early century. He played a significant dual role in the economic and political scheme of things at a time when Indian Affairs and Indian Agents were enforcing authority over band leadership and band business. Much of Gaston's struggle as leader and chief has already been covered by historians, however, a recap of some of these events can be retold here as a means to provide a short vague description of his character for the reader who is unaware of the rich Louie family history. Fortunately Gaston's daughter-in-law, Esther Louie, nee Pierre, is able to provide us with a much different perspective of Gaston Louie.

Gaston was elected as Chief at Head of the Lake sometime in 1915. It is still unclear what actual date, or on whose authority he became leader, but he did govern until 1918. Gaston was of strong character and followed his own convictions. At the cost of his freedom, he and fellow band member Ko-mas-ket opposed the rule to register, baptism and the leasing and sale of lands.[3] Gaston also refused to lease land for the war effort or to any non-band member.[4] As a result, both

Gaston and Ko-mas-ket were jailed for a period of time when their crops were ready to harvest. As it turned out, Gaston was deposed for intemperance.[5]

Gaston's first wife was Helene Logan, the daughter of Okanagan people, "Shuyalsht" and Julie.[6] Gaston and Helene had five or more children but only three sons, Manuel, William and Alex survived to adulthood. William was the only son to father children. Gaston and Helene's daughters, Susan and Mary Madeline were twins. Susan, unmarried, died at twenty years old while Mary Madeline died as a young girl. Long after his wife's death, Gaston had more children with Martina, aka ol' Lala McDougall, of Westbank.[7] William, however, lived to enjoy ninety-seven years. He was born in 1901 and died in March of 1998.

William's widow, Esther Louie, the daughter of Casimir Pierre and Agnes McDougall of Summerland, is thoughtful and sincere when remembering her father-in-law. Her story is unique in its colourful mode of storytelling.

Esther Louie: *My father-in-law was more than my own dad. I love him. Really love him, just like my own dad. Sometimes my dad gave me heck, but Gaston, no way! When I make a mistake, he's standin' there watchin'. He smiles and turn around. He wouldn't say nothin'. So after awhile I'd think what he would do, and say, by golly, that's my mistake. I shouldn't be doing such a thing. The next time I'll do better.*

I was sad when he passed away. It took three years. I really missed him that long. He lived in Westbank. All of a sudden when he passed away, he was staying all alone in that house. Ol' Lala was workin' in the garden. All of a sudden that day he took all his clean clothes and he went down the creek. He took a swim, have a bath, and he fell down and couldn't get up. He passed away. So Peter San Pierre found him. He missed him and he took a walk down the creek. He wants to know what's goin' on. He miss him. He got down there. Sure enough he was layin' on the ground. He was dead. Something break inside. That killed him.

Me and the ol' man was home. Someone told us he passed away. My ol' man hooked up the wagon and we went down. We went through Westside Road. We don't take that other road. It's too far, so we go through here. In that day the road was through here. That's not too good, but it's all right for a wagon. A car can't go through there. Through here, it don't take too long to get there.

So we went down there. I sure took it bad 'cause I love him. I sure took it hard. I did every thing I could afford to do, cause he likes me and I like him. But ol' Lala, sometimes we fight. She was stubborn; stubborn in the wrong way!

When Gaston left to go to Westbank, he tol' William, "When I'm gone you take over the farm. You stay and you talk to your wife real good. Tell her what to do so she won't be stuck anywhere." Course, my ol' man he advises me sometime. When I'm hard up for everything and I don't know what to do. I lost my way sometimes so I'd tell him and he'd be thinkin' and thinkin' and thinkin'. Next couple days he'd say, "Here's where you got lost. Your standin' right here and here's all that hard work you bin doin' and this is where you got stuck. You got into the wrong road." He said, don't accept that thing. You turn this way, really carefully too." He's really smart. 'cause his dad tol' him, "You treat your wife good. Treat her right, she'll take care of you." His dad said, "There is no one to come up here to take care of you. She's the only one. No one else will do that for you. No way!" He said, "Look at Manuel. He got married and the next day they got separated."

Manuel and Tootsie got married in the old church at Head of the Lake. Me and William got married in town. I didn't want to go to the church. I didn't want to accept that. I tol' my ol' man, I'm not honest. I can't take that Communion. You never know what's gonna happen! I don't trust it! I don't trust myself 'cause I'm too young. I still want a good time. He said, "It's up to you, I'm not gonna force you." He said, "It's just the same if we get married in town. They're both the same." But I know, there is one that is very strict. I know one but I don't know which one. So we got married in the court room.

Our preacher was Judge McGustie. I was scared, shakin'. He said, "I know Esther, you are very worried." So we got married by the judge. He wasn't just a small judge. He was a criminal judge. We came back and we stayed home. The ol' man Gaston, stayed three years. He tol' me, "Esther I'm movin' out. I've been stayin' here long enough. I can't stay any longer. Cause if I stay any longer you never know what's gonna happen." And I don't know what that means. And later on he died and I was thinkin' about it. So I find out what it means. I sure like my father-in-law. I sure take care of him good. The best way I know how. I didn't hurt him, or anything bad, I didn't do that. He said, "I got to get out of here. Leave you guys alone." So he moved down Westbank.

One time I was over there at the gathering [meaning Corpus Christi and Head of the Lake]. Oh my goodness, sure was lots of people. People come from everywhere, Kamloops, Douglas Lake, Merritt, Vancouver, down the States. Some of them come from Oregon. People camp over there. They put up their tents. They stayed about a week and go back home. Some people came from the north. You see all kinds of things. People tan hides around here. A lot of old ladies, back then, they tan hides and they take their hides over there and they sell them. They give a good price for them. Some people give blankets. Those Indian blankets were pretty. The people from down the States, their blankets were the best. I don't tan hides, I got no buckskin. I got mad. Gee, I wish I could tan hides and I could get one of those blankets. 'cause if I paid for them with cash, it would cost me a lot of money. I never got one.

My mom passed away when I was about four years old, then my gramma [Julie Pierre, nee McDougall] took over and looked after me. I wasn't with her right away, I was everywhere. I was down Penticton staying with other people. I got tired of that 'cause I couldn't take it. So my dad bring me back to his house and my brother, Andrew Pierre, stayed home and look after me cause I was too young. We stayed there a long time. Andrew tol' my dad, "you better look for someone else to look after your daughter, I want to leave, I'm gettin' poor all the time and I need clothes. I gotta work and buy clothes for myself." So my dad tol' my gramma, "You better look after her, my son is gonna leave me. He's gonna go out to work." So my gramma took me back home.

Oh, I got sick lots of times. I was so sick, I just about pass away. I got a pain all over. My gramma gave me Indian tea. That medicine seem to work. I kept on takin' it and takin' it. But then I got another trouble, I gotta go to the washroom. I drink too much of that medicine. But I got better. Those old people, those ol' timers, they sure know how to make Indian tea. They know what kind of tea be good for a sick person.

My gramma was mean sometimes. So my dad got mad and tol' me, "You better leave. Go stay somewhere. You get a lickin' too much. You gonna turn out crazy if you stay with them. You gotta be on your own." Finally I made it up here. I was thirteen years old then. So I came up here and stay with ol' Lola. She was Gaston's second wife and my aunt. Well, I know how to look after her 'cause I'm used to that.

I came up here with ol' Lola. She came down to Summerland to visit. My dad tol' her, "You take her. If anybody accept her you let her go. She's gotta have a home 'cause she can't be like this all the time. Somebody's got to take over and look after her. She's old enough for that." So ol' Lola said, "All right, your gonna come home with me." I didn't know nobody 'round here. I didn't even know ol' Bessette. He's my relation. George Bessette's mother. That's my gramma Sulie's [Julie] half-sister. I think her name is Mary Anne. That's why I'm related to the Bessettes, on the mother's side. George's father was X-coo-scasa. I know him only by his Indian name.

Out of all my kids, it was only James and Madeline that was born in hospital. Ol' Lola was here with my first baby, Tooley. She said, "Now don't depend on me too much 'cause I'm not gonna do everything for you. You do it yourself. No one tol' you to come and have a man and raise kids. You're on your own." That's what she tol' me, so I never say a word. That woman, Theresa Pierre, Matilda's mother from Six-Mile, she came up here and helped me when my baby got sick. She bath him and look after me and my baby. Then she said, "You're safe, I'm glad the baby's safe an' happy, and you're safe an' happy, now I'm goin' home." That really hurt me. 'cause she was goin' home. I was too young then.

Gladys Bonneau: *Esther married William when she was really young. I got to know her when we worked together in the gardens across the lake. You know she was so young that we'd play together out there in the fields. William was so good to her. He'd help her with the babies and feed the babies and take her something to eat out in the field. He never did neglect her.*

Lamprow

Andrew Lamprow, nicknamed Swibo because he excelled at the card game, five card monty, came from Douglas Lake. Similar to others the record shows he was allowed entrance to the band by early Indian Agent Irwin in 1903.[8] Since the surname is undoubtedly French, and also a prime name entered in Hudson's Bay Company journals, it appears likely that Andrew was a descendant of a fur trader. His certificate of marriage to Catherine, or Celina, the daughter of Louie and Julie, in 1901,[9] reveals only that his parents' names were Andre and Mary.

Andrew and Celina had two children but both died as infants. Celina died at the age of thirty-eight in 1933. Andrew lived out his last years as a widower on the side hill above the Brewer Ranch on Irish Creek Road.

Mary Jane Lawrence: *I remember Celina, Andrew Lamprow's wife. There was a room at the back of the old church at Head of the Lake. I remember going back there. That is where the priest used to stay when he came here. Celina cooked for him. She was there cooking and had her apron on. So she must have helped out quite a bit. I don't remember her any other time.*

Edward Fred: *One time Swibo filled his pockets with eggs from ol' Brewer's hen house. He was sneakin' away from the yard when ol' Brewer called him. He said to Swibo, "What you got in your pockets?" Swibo said, "Just rocks!" Ol' Brewer had a stick in his hand and he hit the rocks. Swibo muttered and got ashamed that time, but he did it again. He stealed real quiet into ol' Brewer's hen house and gathered up the eggs he wanted for that day. Then laid down and was gonna squeeze himself through under the wall. Just as he did, he saw two great big feet there. He looked up and saw ol' Brewer standin' there with a stick. Ol' Brewer knew that Swibo always helped himself, but still he helped Swibo out a lot. Swibo was just that way. I guess he believed in getting things for nothin'.*

Another time I saw Swibo set his traps out in Irish Creek. I had traps too. We were trappin' for beaver. Anyway, I watched him from behind a tree and after he left I went over there and put my traps there and moved his way down the creek. Then later I was watchin' him and he came back to check his on his traps. He was walkin' along singin' that ol' Roy Roger's song, "You can't break my heart, it's been broken before." He kept asingin' till he got to his traps. Well, then he stopped his singin' and started to holler 'round there. He was so mad and I kept a watchin'. Finally, he found his traps and took off back home. He was mutterin' and swearin' to himself as he went up the road. He sure wasn't singin' no more Roy Rogers, that's for sure.

Tronson

Nancy Louie, the half-sister to Gaston Louie, married Edward J. Tronson, July 27, 1873.[10] By 1891, census records reveal that Edward and Nancy had six children. James, the youngest, was then four years old. In May 1895, at age thirteen, Henry was thrown from a horse and died.[11] James died at twelve years old, leaving only four surviving children George, Edith, Alfred and Mary. The couple also raised Charles Houghton and Sophie N'Kwala's son, Edward, after Sophie died.

Edward J. Tronson was Irish born. He sailed from Ireland around the horn of South America to Victoria in 1864. Later he was invited by his friend Charles Houghton to come to the Okanagan. After living for a time with the Vernon brothers at Coldstream, Tronson took up land, formerly Indian land, between Priest's Valley and the arm of Okanagan Lake in 1867, and began his ranching business. Later he and Charles Brewer formed a partnership and built a sawmill. He laid out the townsite at Priest's Valley in 1885, and also in the same year constructed the Victoria Hotel. In 1895 he was made Justice of the Peace and served on the Vernon Hospital Board from 1895 to 1906. He sold his Okanagan Landing property to Samuel Polson in 1908. In all, Edward J. Tronson acquired large holdings of property at Priest's Valley, the Commonage and at Armstrong. He died at sixty-seven years old in Victoria in 1909.[12]

After Edward's death Nancy took on the duties as family head. Some say she cared for the ranch, the cattle and the kids despite her age. Little is remembered about Nancy, however, being that she was a descendant of the Louie family, she must have had the fortitude of an Okanagan woman faced with societal changes of the times. Nancy did not die from disease but lost her life in a buggy accident in 1926.[13] Some say both she and E.J. Tronson were interred at the Pioneer cemetery, but were later moved to the Pleasant Valley cemetery, however, a cemetery list held at the Vernon Archives, does not show a Nancy Tronson.

The couple's eldest son George married Louisa Vernon. As we have already seen in the Kalamalka line Louisa was the youngest of two daughters of Catherine Kalamalka and Charles Vernon. The present city of Vernon was named for Charles George Vernon in 1887, in honour of the younger Vernon brother who in the end acquired twenty-five thousand acres of land and many head of cattle. The property was later sold to Lord and Lady Aberdeen.[14] The Aberdeen's planted hops and provided wage labour for many including the Nez Perce Indians of Washington State.

Thomas Tronson: *When we lived at Grampa George and Louisa's place, above Whiteman's Creek, my dad and I went across the lake to Okanagan Landing to go fishing. You could see the old house from the lake and there was a light on over there. Dad said someone must be stayin' in that old house. When we got across the lake, Dad walked up to the house and I stayed there fishing. He came back after, walking to beat hell and didn't have his hat on. I didn't pay too much attention because I was only interested in fishing. He didn't tell me until next day, until after he went looking for his hat. He said when he got to the house he went in and the lights went out. He said he got scared and walked really fast back to camp. That's when he lost his hat and didn't stop long enough to get it. He said away back, a whole bunch died there from that influenza. He said there were four in just one week. I guess he got spooked. I think they sold that house later to Thorlakson.*

Our grandmother, Louisa, was the daughter of Katherine Kalamalka and Charles George Vernon. She married my grandfather, George, who was the son of E.J. Tronson and Nancy Louie.

Gramma was real good to us. She used to pick berries all over there, and I used to go with her. We'd both ride our horses and camp out sometimes. But when she got mad, she wouldn't talk to us. I remember one summer I was haying with my dad at Whiteman's Creek and I must have did something wrong, because Gramma wasn't talking to me. Gee, that used to hurt me inside; when she'd clam up like that. Anyway, we hauled the hay to the barn and I jumped off the wagon to bring down the derrick forks. When I jumped I bent my ankle and it hurt like the dickens. They took me to the house and Gramma put me in the car and was taking me down the hill to the doctor in town. When we got back I told my dad, I should get hurt more often, because Gramma was just a talking to me all the way to town and back.

Gramma Louisa went to the Mission School at Kelowna until she was twenty-one years old. Hans Richter and Maria Brent went there too. Nancy Tronson went there too. My gramma said Nancy left when she got there.

There were five Tronsons in WW II. Four of my uncles joined in on the second war. My grandmother was so worried that they'd never come back. They said she died of a broken heart and worry, four months before the war ended, and all her sons did come back. It took a long time to get Dad's pension straightened out because he lied about his age to get into the army. He was only fourteen. He was kept back though 'cause he was so young. Only after a lot of guys got killed was he was sent to the front lines.

I went to school at Ewing's Landing and at Lumby. I hated to go to white school. All they did was fight and call us Siwashes. To be a half-breed you didn't belong anywhere. We used to go early to the Lumby school and build fire. But there was this one time I remember. Three of us boys went to the church early to make fire and we got into the wine. By the time Father came, we were all drunk and the heater was just white. Father didn't say too much to us but he told us to go home and tell our parents ourselves. That was worse than getting a whipping.

Grampa George used to work for Hoover's sawmill. He worked with horses and logged about three thousand acres above Whiteman's Creek. He died when I was nine years old of high blood pressure and diabetes at Vernon. Of his kids, Ella was the oldest and lived the longest. Both her and Grampa died when they were ninety-two years old.

Ella married Alfred Brewer. He was the son of Charles Brewer and Jenny and an uncle to Ernest Brewer. We used to go visit Ernest. He'd tell real good stories. One time when I was six years old we were there. It was after Ernest's wife died and Jenny and Louie were living there. Anyway, I saw my first negro man there. He was there cooking and I kept staring at him. Finally, he looked at me and said, "What's the matter, you never seen a black man before." Well, I didn't! He was the first one I seen.

Ernest told me a story of long time ago. He said when the gold rush was over sometimes guys would pass through Head of the Lake. Of course, at that time they carried everything with them on their good looking horses. They'd be wearing silver spurs, nice clothes and gauntlets, a nice saddle and sometimes a bag of gold in their saddlebags. Anyway, Ernest said next time you seen that horse it would have a different rider. So you know what happened!

Gramma was related to George Simpson too. One time I was going with their daughter Isabelle and my grandmother said, "What are you doing? That's your relation!" I never went out with her again and I didn't bother to ask how we were related. I met Bernice too. She was my mother's sister, Agnes' daughter. I was going to take her to the show and she said come home and meet my mother first. So I went along and when her mother found out I was from Vernon she asked if I knew the Tronsons. I said yes, I'm one of them. That was the first time I met my Aunt Agnes.

On May 19, 1919, eighteen-year-old Agnes Louie married thirty-year-old William McNeil. [15] The marriage record shows that Agnes was the daughter of Louie and Charlotte. They lived at Head of the Lake. The couple had no children. William's parents were William McNeil and Harriet Johnny.

William's sister, Emily McNeil, and Alexander Christian were both twenty years old when they were married by Father Le Jeune, at Salmon River, in 1923. [16] Alexander's parents were Christian Dominic and Annie Thoma. They were born at Enderby. The descendants of Alexander Christian are now the Christian family at Enderby.

LOUIS

MARY ANN

PIERRE LOUIS

ALEX MARCHAND

FRANCOIS, SOPHIE, MARY JANE, NED, RITA,
MARTHA, BEN, KATHERINE, PIERRE, EMERY & SALLY

MARGOIRE, KATIE, LOUISA, HELENE & SHIRLEY

RUDY LEON, ROBERT, JOHN,
HELENE, ARTHUR, BOB PENNING & RALPH

COLDSTREAM HOPYARDS

KATHERINE & PIERRE LOUIS
QUEEN ELIZABETH II & PRINCE PHILLIP

LOUIS

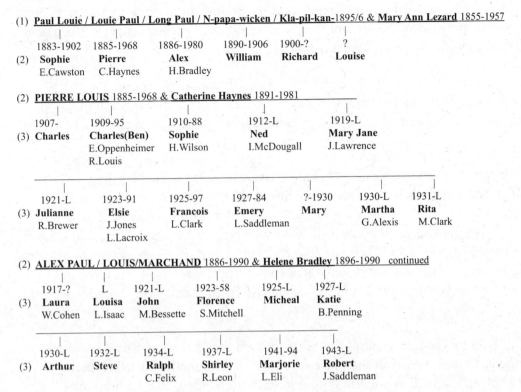

(1) **Paul Louie / Louie Paul / Long Paul / N-papa-wicken / Kla-pil-kan** 1895/6 & **Mary Ann Lezard** 1855-1957

1883-1902	1885-1968	1886-1980	1890-1906	1900-?	?
(2) **Sophie**	**Pierre**	**Alex**	**William**	**Richard**	**Louise**
E.Cawston	C.Haynes	H.Bradley			

(2) **PIERRE LOUIS** 1885-1968 & **Catherine Haynes** 1891-1981

1907-	1909-95	1910-88	1912-L	1919-L
(3) **Charles**	**Charles(Ben)**	**Sophie**	**Ned**	**Mary Jane**
	E.Oppenheimer	H.Wilson	I.McDougall	J.Lawrence
	R.Louis			

1921-L	1923-91	1925-97	1927-84	?-1930	1930-L	1931-L
(3) **Julianne**	**Elsie**	**Francois**	**Emery**	**Mary**	**Martha**	**Rita**
R.Brewer	J.Jones	L.Clark	L.Saddleman		G.Alexis	M.Clark
	L.Lacroix					

(2) **ALEX PAUL / LOUIS/MARCHAND** 1886-1990 & **Helene Bradley** 1896-1990   continued

1917-?	L	1921-L	1923-58	1925-L	1927-L
(3) **Laura**	**Louisa**	**John**	**Florence**	**Micheal**	**Katie**
W.Cohen	L.Isaac	M.Bessette	S.Mitchell		B.Penning

1930-L	1932-L	1934-L	1937-L	1941-94	1943-L
(3) **Arthur**	**Steve**	**Ralph**	**Shirley**	**Marjorie**	**Robert**
		C.Felix	R.Leon	L.Eli	J.Saddleman

Pierre Louis and Alex Marchand were the two eldest sons of Mary Ann Lezard. She was a niece to Louie Jim (Kemitiken). From his own account, Pierre kept his father's surname while Alex became known by his stepfather's name Marchand. Throughout the years many descendants have endeavoured to compile an accurate family tree but in most cases were unable to follow any direct line back to the family head. Recent findings by Alex's family[2] helps to clarify kinship ties of Mary Ann while further research initiated by grandson, Leonard Marchand, furnishes deeper understanding of the Marchand kinship line.[3] But it is the written information included in the 1952 Indian Affairs Inquiry into band membership, that began in Vernon in 1952 and ended in Colville Washington in 1954, that brings to light the relationships of the Louis line.

Evidently ancestral roots of the Louis family extend back to Kinkinahwa,[4] the Salmon Chief at Kettle Falls. Gauging from present knowledge Kinkinahwa was part Iroquois. He had four sons. One was Pierre and Alex's grandfather by the name of Grandlouis.[5] Grandlouis' son was also known as Louie Paul Louie, or Louie Paul or Long Paul. They were Arrow Lakes people.[6] Paul was also known by two Okanagan names Kla-pil-kan and N-papa-wicken.[7]

The following information is given in question and answer format by Pierre Louis at the inquiry. Rather than quote the whole of the inquisition the following is presented in story form using Pierre's evidence and adding the present family names. Pierre gave his mother Mary Ann's age at the time of the inquiry as ninety-seven or ninety-eight.[8]

"My mother's mother was the daughter of Quihammikem (now Pierre). Quihammikem's sister was married to Kalamalka. The mother of Mary Ann and Louis Jim were brother and sister."[9] Pierre Jack backed up this statement.[10]

"My father was born on the Inninakaneep Reserve near Oliver, B.C. My grandfather married Newiliskut (same surname as Nancy Newslaket Gregoire). They had two children by their marriage here, Victor and Susan. My patron grandmother died here on this Reserve and she was a full member of the Okanagan Band No. 1. So were my two aunts and an uncle.[11] My grandfather's name was Grandlouis and my Christian name all my life was Pierre Louis.[12] My father's occupation kept him moving, he did not work out for a living, (but) went from Reserve to Reserve and wherever there was nothing doing. (It is) different now, they have potlatches.'[13]

"We stayed with my grandmother at Siwash Creek on the Okanagan Reserve No. 1.[14] I came to Canada before at the place on Anarchist Mountain. I worked there as a chore boy and as mail boy hauling mail to Captain Kinney, who had the mail line.[15] That is all since I come up here in 1900. I was nine years old. My father died at the little Mission down at Ellison's."[16]

Chief Basil Williams (William Wohollesicle also known as Chief Basil, 1878-1898) was a relation.... In the Kalamalkan and Kemitiken (Louie Jim line) we have one married to two sisters. It is an awful big family. Before that it was the same, so this who is all related from one side to the other off every Reserve from here to the States.[17] We have the Tonaskets they are relatives of ours all the way to the States. Chief Logan is not related."[18]

Pierre testified that he was born August 15, 1885, at Colville, and left there at age fifteen. He attended Tonasket School for five years from 1891 to 1896, Saint Mary's Mission at Omak from 1898 to 1899 and Oroville public school for the following year.[19]

Ned Louis: *My grandfather was known by two names, Kla-pil-kan and N-papa-wicken. He and my grandmother Mary Ann were my dad's and Alex Marchand's parents. They were full brothers. Mary Ann had more children with Louis Marchand after Kla-pil-kan died. Alex took ol' Louie Marchand's name and my dad stayed as Louis. Alex is known by N-papa-wicken too.*

I don't know too much about my grandfather. Dad never talked too much about him because he wasn't with his family very much. Dad only told me little stories about when he was a little fella and a teenager. I remember what he told me though. He told me Kla-pil-kan was itchy-footed. They'd be up here in Vernon in the summer and they'd put in a winter at Oliver, or sometimes further down south, and sometimes over the mountain in the Kootenays, up the Columbia River and other parts of BC. Then when spring come, and the weather got good up here, they'd come again. Later on, I got some rumours that he did some guidin' and he got itchy-footed and went up north. Some say he had another family in Williams Lake. I don't know how true that is. We don't know nothing about it. That was way, way before I was born.

The people used to go back and forth to the States. My grandfather Kla-pil-kan met Mary Ann here. She was born at Polson Park. The people were like the snowbirds they come here, and they'd go back and forth. Mary Ann went with him. That's what Dad said.

When he was a little fella, one year they went from where they were stayin' on the Kal Lake side, and wintered at Oliver. They left Dad and Alex there at Oliver and they went down and never came back till the weather was good in the spring. He came up with the birds. He was drivin' about seventy-five head of cows and a herd of horses. He'd been gamblin' all winter, and he went down south to these weddings, and what-not and when he got back to Oliver he rested up then drove the herds up here. The next fall they went back down with just the horses they was ridin'. He got rid of the cows and horses while they were here. Dad used to say when the old fella was winnin' [at gambling] we lived like kings, and when he was down under we were all in the dumps.

Mary Jane Lawrence: *Mom and Dad met at the hop yards in Coldstream. Dad was a ranch hand there and Mom worked picking hops. My mom's sister, Mary Eli, tried to play match-maker with Mom and Isaac Harris. She sent Mom on the boat to Okanagan Landing where Isaac was supposed to meet her. But Dad was already in love with her and intercepted the boat at Kelowna. He took her from there and went back to Penticton and married her at the Corpus Christi celebration in June of 1907. I guess lots of people got married that same day. Mom said George and Celina Wilson got married that same day and remembered, because Celina wore a wedding veil.[20] I guess that is when the priest made his rounds and that year Corpus Christi was held at Penticton. They came back up here and Ben and Sophie were born at the hop yards.*

Pierre was elected chief in 1932 on the recommendation and approval of Indian Agent Ball. He was considered honest, educated, industrious and loyal. He held office until 1959 when he was defeated by Jimmy Bonneau. Pierre's son Ned speaks of some of his father's achievements.

Ned Louis: *Dad never went completely by the book. He used to tell us guys don't go deep into the Indian Act, just go around the edges. That way we will still be within the law and if you use only the edge then we can have both the provincial and federal law. We will always be protected. But, if you go deep into the Indian Act we'll get locked in. That's why we have to write all the newborns' names and the families once a year. We have to stay ahead of the government and keep our own records. Those kids are our weight later.*

Every year, about this time [April], Dad would set aside one week to register in his little black book all the births and deaths of the year. He'd tell his councillors, "We will be talking only about the newborns and their parents. I will be writing their names and birthdays in my book." He did, too! There were pages and pages of names and dates and everything he needed to write. That book went with the house when it burned.

At the time Dad was writin' names in his book the Indian Department was keepin' records too. And the Department was kickin' a lot of people off the Reserve. So that's why Dad registered them in his book. He knew that we'd need them later when they tried to make the reserve smaller. Them guys [Chief and Council] tried to put families on all of our boundaries. That way they couldn't close in on us and take our land. They tried that over there across the lake. They thought that if they put families on those benches over there it would protect that property from being taken away. The people ended up coming over here on this side of the lake when the school opened, though, and some of them moved to Salmon River and Round Lake.

While Pierre worked around the Reserve community, Katherine attended to the family needs and during the summer worked in the Chinese gardens. Besides their large family of ten children they also made room for Walter Williams, the orphaned son of Maria Williams. The couple maintained a few head of cattle and grew hay at Six-Mile Creek. Pierre worked in cooperation with his brother, Alex, and half-brothers, Joe and Willie Marchand, his nephews and fellow band members. Among his accomplishments as father, husband and chief are the opening of Six-Mile Creek School, the construction of the much needed irrigation ditches, road building and the attainment of logging permits. His efforts at education for the young brought changes whereby the children were no longer separated from family. His efforts as leader saw productive changes to the once limited farming endeavours. Housing was also an issue of the times and by issuing logging permits the people acquired the material to construct their own homes.

Ned Louis: *Dad had three teams. He had two teams working when they were building Westside Road going south. He was on the grader with his teams and had the other teams working in the garden over there. They split one team for cultivating all summer. Ol' Jack Alex from Penticton and William Victor were the two drivers for the cultivating teams and ol' Alphonse Louie drove the team for the delivery wagon. When the stuff was ready ol' Alphonse would help with taking it to town and loading it into box cars on the boats at the wharf. So Dad had four teams. That's all the work the old people had especially the women folks. They were in the garden, either pulling weeds or picking all summer. I used to drive him to meetings and sit in while the different bands had meetings.*

Taken from the files of the Colville Confederated Tribes at Nespelem, Washington, is the heritage and particulars of Pierre, Alex and their siblings. The evidence given by Alex states he was born September 15, 1886 and lived on the north half of the Colville Reserve until he was thirteen years old. He attended Tonasket Indian School in 1896, and thereafter, attended school at the Colville Mission of St. Mary's in 1899. Scant evidence as to the other children of Mary Ann is also given in that record but as the information is rather confusing it has been omitted except for the two children in the family tree.

Alex married Helene Bradley. Helene was the daughter of Lena Lawrence. They had ten children. Their son Ralph leaves the following history of the family.

Ralph Marchand: *My dad Alex wasn't really a Marchand. He took his stepfather Louie Marchand's name. He was Pierre Louis' brother. We lived here at Siwash Creek in that log house that burned down a few years ago. Dad built the first part and the second part belonged to George Smith. They attached the second part to the first part and that's where we lived. It's that same place, beside William Wilson's, that Billy Cohen lived in. Billy was married to my sister Laura. Our barns were up there where Sophie Wilson's old house is. Dad had a little shed a ways from the house and that's where he kept his horse equipment and those trophy things that you see in that picture. Someone burned that shed, and all his stuff burned.*

When I was young I used to go with my dad to other reserves. We'd go to potlatches and gatherings. We were at Enderby one time and my dad went to the other side where all the people were sittin'. He introduced himself to the people, one by one, and told them who he was and who his family was. Then he called me over there and introduced me to the people. The people called their kids over and introduced them to us. That's the way it was. The people say as long as these people are in our territory you don't hurt them. We know who they are and they are our friends. No one ever bothered me and sometimes I even used that rule to my own advantage. I met a lot of people like that.

I lived alone here at Siwash Creek when I was real young. My dad would be off rodeoin' and my mom would make me go to Salmon River to live with her. I'd go when I got a whippin', but I'd be back here in the mornin'. Ol' Johnny Alexis would try to make me go stay with them, but I said, "No, I'm okay here, I got lots to eat." It sure isn't like it is now.

My dad wasn't around much when I was growing up. He was gone most of the time following rodeos. He had a car, but he travelled a lot with Billy Kruger from Penticton and with Hans Richter. It was in 1912 that he rode in Calgary. He made his last ride in the late forties, early fifties, at Falkland. He also won first in 1914 at the Vancouver Exhibition. A lot of those guys wouldn't ride in the same rodeo as my dad 'cause he used to take off his hat and fan the horse's face. You weren't supposed to touch the horse at all, but he always did. Those other guys would ride at a different rodeo on the same day.

During the war Dad gathered horses for the army. They wanted green broke horses. Dad said he jobbed them. I asked what jobbed meant and he told me that he would put a rock between the cinch and the horses chest. When those horses tried to buck, the rock would dig into their chest and the horses would quieten down. That's what you call jobbin' them.

My dad used to round up wild horses off the range for fox meat too. They were all over here and in Westbank and Penticton. I used to go with them. There was my Dad, Johnny Robins, Cougar Bill McDougall, Boss McDougall and Billy and Joe Kruger from Penticton. Even Harry Robinson came along one time. He said he was writing a book and wanted to get some more experience.

Some people used to come there when we would have the horses corralled and ready to sell. They'd say a particular horse was from their mare, or something like that, and just take the horse. I told my dad, "Why do you let them get away with that." He said, "It goes back to their word. If he said it was his then you believe him." So that's how people lived, by their word. That's how I met all those ol' timers.

I used to stay with Billy Kruger in Penticton. Ol' Joe Kruger would tell me, "Quit stayin' over there and come give me a visit. Spend some time with me." He was runnin' a riding stable. He had a barn and the stalls all neat in a row. All the horses were in their own stalls and all the reins and saddles and things were hung up there, so you could go ridin' anytime you want. There was a sign there, too, that said the name of the horse and described the horse's disposition. So you come in and read that picked out your horse and went over there by the barn and put your money in that box. There was nobody there to collect it. You couldn't do that nowadays.

I used to go with my dad and Johnny Robins and his family up to the Bald Range in Westbank. Those people used to have great big baskets made out of wood slats. They lined those baskets with cloth then took the branches of the husem bushes and hit it with a stick until the berries all fell onto a tarp under the bush. Those baskets would be just full of husem. They made home-brew out of those berries, enough to last them for a long time.

We used to go up here above Six-Mile to go huntin' and fishin'. We caught fish out of Pinaus Lake and my dad showed me how to fix them. All we took with us was salt and tea. That time we found some grouse eggs and my dad tol' me to cook them. I wondered how we were gonna do that. He told me make a fire, so I did, then tol' me to dig a little hole and put the eggs in. Then he tol' me to scrape the coals over the eggs. He said when you hear them crack then you will know they were cooked. Then he showed me how to fix the fish and the deer meat.

One time this man who owned a lodge back in the bush at Bear Creek told us that he needed a couple of horses to pack in the supplies. In trade he would give us this great big Indian motorcycle. So my dad had a couple of horses that we kept from that wild bunch on that range. By that time they were kind of spoiled. Didn't matter what you did to them they'd always pull back and break the ropes then take off. Anyway, we traded him and later we ran into him and he said, "You know those horses you guys traded for, I put the saddles on them and filled them with flour and started to pack into the lodge. At first those horses did all right, but after a while they just sat back and broke the ropes. I had flour scattered all over Bald Range." He said, "Them horses never came back." I told him, "Well you know I have a similar problem, except this ol' Indian won't run."

Alex is often remembered for his stories of horses, riding, rodeos and horse sense. One niece however remembers him for his affection for her. He often picked her up, threw her into the saddle behind him and took her fishing. "Of all my uncles," said Debra Marchand Nicholas, "Alex was my favourite."

MARCHAND

JOACHIM

CHRISTINE & FRANK   LOUIE   JOE

CHARLIE   WILLIE   SARAH

VICTORIA   PETE & TOPSY   LOUIE

MARCHAND

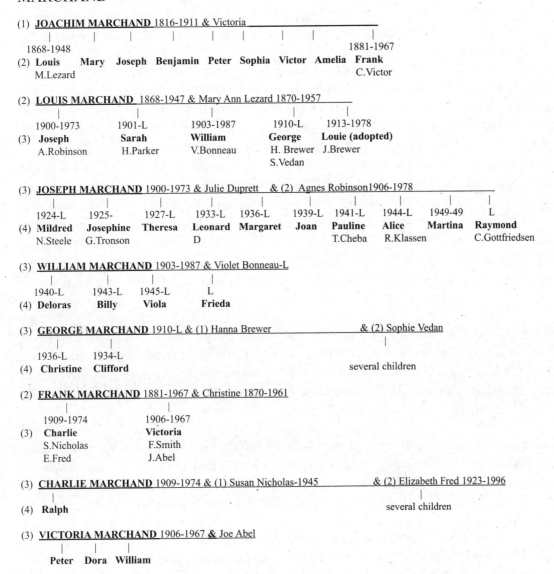

(1) **JOACHIM MARCHAND** 1816-1911 & Victoria _____

1868-1948								1881-1967
(2) **Louis**	**Mary**	**Joseph**	**Benjamin**	**Peter**	**Sophia**	**Victor**	**Amelia**	**Frank**
M.Lezard								C.Victor

(2) **LOUIS MARCHAND** 1868-1947 & Mary Ann Lezard 1870-1957 _____

1900-1973	1901-L	1903-1987	1910-L	1913-1978
(3) **Joseph**	**Sarah**	**William**	**George**	**Louie (adopted)**
A.Robinson	H.Parker	V.Bonneau	H. Brewer	J.Brewer
			S.Vedan	

(3) **JOSEPH MARCHAND** 1900-1973 & Julie Duprett & (2) Agnes Robinson 1906-1978

1924-L	1925-	1927-L	1933-L	1936-L	1939-L	1941-L	1944-L	1949-49	L
(4) **Mildred**	**Josephine**	**Theresa**	**Leonard**	**Margaret**	**Joan**	**Pauline**	**Alice**	**Martina**	**Raymond**
N.Steele	G.Tronson		D			T.Cheba	R.Klassen		C.Gottfriedsen

(3) **WILLIAM MARCHAND** 1903-1987 & Violet Bonneau-L

1940-L	1943-L	1945-L	L
(4) **Deloras**	**Billy**	**Viola**	**Frieda**

(3) **GEORGE MARCHAND** 1910-L & (1) Hanna Brewer & (2) Sophie Vedan

1936-L	1934-L	
(4) **Christine**	**Clifford**	several children

(2) **FRANK MARCHAND** 1881-1967 & Christine 1870-1961

1909-1974	1906-1967
(3) **Charlie**	**Victoria**
S.Nicholas	F.Smith
E.Fred	J.Abel

(3) **CHARLIE MARCHAND** 1909-1974 & (1) Susan Nicholas-1945 & (2) Elizabeth Fred 1923-1996

(4) **Ralph**	several children

(3) **VICTORIA MARCHAND** 1906-1967 & Joe Abel

Peter	**Dora**	**William**

Curious about his paternal background Leonard Marchand asked J. Jacques Seguin to research the history of the Marchand family. With the use of census and sacramental records Seguin came up with the following family history.

Joachim Marchand was born at Batiscan, Quebec on February 29, 1816. He left Quebec at age twenty-four in the summer of 1840. He made his way west to seek his fortune. He arrived in St. Louis, Missouri in 1850, where it is likely he worked for a time for the fur company out of Fort Benson. In 1854 he and a companion left Fort Benson with three horses and three dogs and made their way through Indian country to the Hudson's Bay Fort near Kettle Falls in 1855. By 1856, Joachim was married to a fourteen-year-old Indian woman, Victoria, and settled at Rickey Rapids in the Colville Valley. Joachim died at ninety-eight years old in 1911. Altogether they had nine children. The eldest Louis and youngest Frank made their way north to the Okanagan Valley, and the Coldstream Ranch, in the ensuing years.[2]

Millie Steele: *Joachim was supposed to have met Victoria at Colville. Her mother was married to a white Hudson's Bay Company man, and their four daughters worked at the Company store at Fort Colville. Victoria married my great grandfather Joachim; her sister Josette married a Tooloo; Susette married a La Fleur and the other sister married a man by the name of Bergeau.*

Ned Louis: *Dad said ol' Louie Marchand wasn't much of a cowboy. They were comin' this way from further down, around the flats, around Oliver. Louie was feelin' pretty good and he was ridin' this nice lookin' baldy horse. The ol' fella [Louie] got on the horse and one thing led to another. The horse went to buckin'. He bucked like hell and the ol' fella fell off. He took another drink and got back on again. It bucked again, and as he was goin' down the horse kicked out and into his ribs where he had his flask. When the horse kicked out, it smashed the bottle, but it didn't hurt Louie. Dad said that's a cowboy right there! He wouldn't get back on. Dad said he was just a teenage then and ol' Louie said, You get on! Dad mentioned another fella, an Indian, who was comin' along with them. Dad put the spurs on and he got on. The horse went to buckin' and he was a clinchin'. He was out of the saddle and in the saddle. When the horse quit buckin' he said he was still on but didn't know how he stayed on. The other Indian that was along was praisin' him for being a hell of a cowboy. It looks like ol' Louie lost his cowboyin' when the horse broke the bottle.*

Dad said that when Louie and my grandmother, Mary Ann, got together, they came up here. She was Louie Jim's niece and had no place to live. So, Louie Jim gave them the flour mill which was along the ditch here at Six-Mile Creek to live in. They cleaned it up and moved in there. That place burned down. And after that Dad built a new place here. The ol' fella died later when he was living with Uncle Willie.

Leonard Marchand: *Grampa Louie and my grandmother had four kids who were born here. They are my dad Joe, Willie, Sarah and George. Gramma always led the prayers in church and when my dad got older, people from all over even down the States, called on him and my mother to lead the prayers and hymns at funerals. They reluctantly agreed to lead, but, really they didn't want to.*

The women in them days really worked hard. They had big gardens, apple trees and even worked out for the Chinese who had gardens in the area. Gramma Marchand used to can all the fruit and vegetables and wash clothes sometimes all day. It was a hard life but they saw it through.

Dad bought Christine Brewer's house at Six-Mile and we all lived there. I remember the day it burned up. Grampa Louie stayed in a room at the back of the house. One day we called him in for supper and I guess he filled his fire before he came in. Then all of a sudden the house was on fire. Pauline was a just little then, and we couldn't find her. We thought she was trapped inside, but then she appeared.

Pete Marchand: *My grandmother's parents were killed by small pox and that left her and her other three sisters orphaned. They got separated then and got raised by different people. Gramma tol' me that the people she lived with here at Six-Mile [likely Louie and Mary Jim] owned all this land around here. They owned all that property over there where Edward Bonneau lived. She tol' me that they had lots of cows and it was her and that ol' lady's job to look after those cows.*

Sometimes there was blizzards. It was real cold in them days and lots of snow. They had only moccasins so they tied gunny sacks on they feet to keep them warm.

Mary Jane Lawrence: *Christine was a tiny woman and kept her home really clean. The floor boards and the table top were just white from scrubbing and she always had coffee on the stove.*

Pete Marchand: *Yeah, Grampa liked coffee, strong and black. That was in that old house, down there. The snow finally pushed it down. That old house was built over there where George Louis' place is now. Then the ol' lady had some land here and Grampa traded his team of horses and a mower, I think, for this place. Then they brought that ol' house over here on skids.*

This house was built on a permit called improvements. Ol' Pierre Louis gave them out when he was chief. So if you needed, say twenty thousand feet of lumber to improve your house or to build a house, then you got that. Maybe Gramma would get five thousand and Grampa would get five thousand and I'd get five thousand. You got it all in lumber. The logs go to Kelowna and they know how much you need. It all came back by boat to Pierre Jack's wharf and my grampa hauled it back here and we built the house. Everything came on the boat; the nails and windows and boards. You can finish your house that way. This house was built in 1938.

My grampa farmed this place, all down to the lake. He always worked. He had a few head of cows and some horses named Duck, Nellie and Prince. Well, that's what kept them going during the depression. They didn't get very much for them. Maybe a hundred dollars for a cow and maybe twenty-five or thirty dollars for a calf. That's what they lived on when he wasn't working.

He did a lots of logging too for other people like maybe ol' Jones, a white man, and with Felix Gregoire. In them days there weren't no chainsaws, just cross-cut saws. He'd get a partner and away he'd go. He did a lot of falling. They worked above Siwash Creek on the flat. They bring the logs down by wagon or sleigh and dump them into the lake down at Alexis beach or maybe the pole wharf. Sometimes they only got two or three logs on the sleigh, that's how big the logs were. They weren't lodge pine, like now, they were big logs. Them ol' loggers depended on their horses for hauling and skidding. If your horses were small then you haul only a small load. Then those ol' trucks come in and that's what they call cross-hauling.

Years before, I wasn't born yet, Grampa and Lesime McDougall had a trapline way up there above Six-Mile. Way up there above Pinuas Lake. They trapped lynx, mink, martin and weasels and stuff like that. Years ago a fire went through there and burned Grampa's trapline and cabin.

When I was small I wasn't allowed to go near the lake. They scared me and said you might see something come out of that lake: They scared me in every way. "Don't go too far, the sneena might bite you." When I was thirteen or fourteen years old I sneak down the creek to catch kikinees after school. Sometimes I'd be there till dark. Oh and they'd go and look for me. They'd pack up my kikinees and give me heck 'cause I stayed there too late. Them days there was bears and cougars all through here. And them days there was hardly anybody around here, you know? Just here and there. Well, we got a house here and Johnny Pants over there [Alfred Bonneau] and ol' Qway-um-qin at Blacktown and the Jacks over here across the creek.

Mary Jane Lawrence: *Ol' Frank never went anywhere without his horses fixed up. They were all tied up real nice with their tails tied up and braided. He kept his horses like show horses.*

BUCKSKIN SUSAN

MICHEL

(1) **<u>PIERRE MICHEL (KLASAKEE/ HLAKAY)</u>** <u>1864-1918 & Buckskin Susan 1855-1940</u>

|

1904-1918
Jenny

Pierre and his wife, nicknamed Buckskin Susan, left no children to pass on the family name. Pierre and his fourteen-year-old daughter, Jennie, fell victim to the Spanish flu in 1918.[2] Of Pierre Michel, the news wrote:

> "A prominent figure among the Head of the Lake victims was ex-chief Pierre Michele, often known as 'lame Pierre' who died on Sunday night. He had not enjoyed robust health for several years, and these are the ones who most easily succumb to the malady. Few Indians of the reserve enjoyed the confidence of his fellow-men, whether Indian or white, as fully as did 'lame Pierre' He had a high sense of honor and justice and his word could be relied upon."[3]

After Gaston Louie was ousted in 1912, Pierre was again appointed Chief and served until 1917.

Jenny Marchand: *It was too cold to stay outside to visit in the winter, so we all went to the Michel's where we visited and shared lunch. Of course, in the other seasons we visited at the church where there we had foot races, horse races, baseball and card games.*

Ned Louis: *He died long time ago, but I do remember when ol' Michel went by buggy to Spences Bridge for meetings with the North American Indian Brotherhood. His one leg was crippled and that's why he was known as Lame Pierre.*

Pierre Michel and his ol' lady, Buckskin Susan, lived in a log house at Head of the Lake, on the bench above the rodeo grounds. After Pierre died their house burned down. At that time we were living in Baptiste Nicholas' house, there by the Gregoire's and while we were there, Buckskin Susan bought it and moved in with us. But she asked Dad to move to where it is now by Leonard Gregoire's. I remembered we were in there when Dad moved it. He went to the Coldstream Ranch and borrowed a stump puller. I remember he used a chain and hooked it around a post and inched it up over the bank and on to where it is now. That is one of the oldest houses left standing out here now. Susan was related to my mother.

Victor Antoine: *Uncle Gilbert told me that when he was old enough he stayed with his great aunt Buckskin Susan Nicholas. She was the widow of Pierre Michel and had that land at Head of the Lake across the bridge. She wasn't infirmed or anything she just needed someone to stay with her and do the heavy work. Uncle Gilbert said she was a hardworking, religious woman with a real sense of humour. She made buckskin and grew a big garden and went to church from daylight to dawn. She never missed the services. Anyway, he said that when he took her to town, she'd pick up some wine. Sure enough they'd come home and pour themselves a drink in a cup and she'd bless it and pray over it and have a drink. Pretty soon she'd go to sleep and after he made sure she was okay then he'd take off and have some fun of his own. He always said, though, that she had a real good sense of humour and was really pious.*

JOHNNY

ANGUS, EDITH & ELLA

ERNEST

ANGUS

OPPENHEIMER WEDDING

EVA

ERNEST'S CHILDREN

CORRINE

OPPENHEIMER

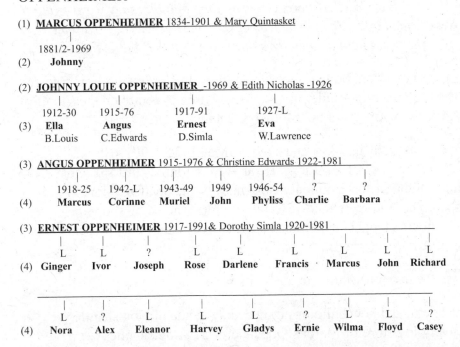

(1) **MARCUS OPPENHEIMER** 1834-1901 & Mary Quintasket
|
1881/2-1969
(2) **Johnny**

(2) **JOHNNY LOUIE OPPENHEIMER** -1969 & Edith Nicholas -1926

1912-30	1915-76	1917-91	1927-L
Ella	**Angus**	**Ernest**	**Eva**
B.Louis	C.Edwards	D.Simla	W.Lawrence

(3) **ANGUS OPPENHEIMER** 1915-1976 & Christine Edwards 1922-1981

1918-25	1942-L	1943-49	1949	1946-54	?	?
Marcus	**Corinne**	**Muriel**	**John**	**Phyliss**	**Charlie**	**Barbara**

(3) **ERNEST OPPENHEIMER** 1917-1991 & Dorothy Simla 1920-1981

L	L	?	L	L	L	L	L	L
Ginger	**Ivor**	**Joseph**	**Rose**	**Darlene**	**Francis**	**Marcus**	**John**	**Richard**

L	?	L	L	L	?	L	L	?
Nora	**Alex**	**Eleanor**	**Harvey**	**Gladys**	**Ernie**	**Wilma**	**Floyd**	**Casey**

The Oppenheimer name comes to the Head of the Lake Band through Johnny Oppenheimer. Stories agree that Johnny came from the Colville area after an incident that caused the three brothers to flee to British Columbia. After arriving at Inkameep, two of the brothers changed their names. Manuel retained the Louie name, Joseph changed his to Kenoras[2] and Johnny took the Oppenheimer name. Manuel remained at Inkameep and raised his family there. Joseph went to the Invermere area in the Kootenays and Johnny came to Head of the Lake. His four children were already born. Their mother was Edith Nicholas. Johnny told his brief story in 1967 to a professor from Victoria.[3] He does not mention his father or mother's names, but his daughter Eva Lawrence notes his mother as Mary Quintasket and his father as Marcus Oppenheimer. We also explore the history of the Quintasket line through Mourning Dove.

Johnny Oppenheimer: *I went to school at St. Mary's Mission Indian School at Colville. Quite a few Indians went there to learn. It was a big school. I was there when I was only seven years old. I was born down the States, right there at Colville. My father died when I was six months old. After my mother remarried I came to Canada when I was six or seven months old. I've been in Canada pretty near all my life. I only came out of school at vacation time and go back to school until I was about sixteen or seventeen years old. I quit school then. I thought I had enough. I wanted to get out in the world and do something. I was raised at Oliver. That's where I grew up, most of my life and when I was twenty-four years old I came up here to Vernon. I've been here over sixty-three years. I'm now eighty-seven.*

Eva Lawrence: *In the States, my dad, Johnny, was known as Johnny Louie. He had a brother Manuel Louie and a sister, who is Charlie Quintasket's mother.[4] So most of my relations on my dad's side are down in Oliver and Colville. Lilly Armstrong at Penticton is my cousin, too.*

My dad and his brother Manuel got into some trouble in the States, and to avoid arrest, they came north across the border. At Osoyoos they decided to separate. Manuel stayed in Oliver and my dad came here, because of us kids, we were already born. He was an American, Colville Indian and at that time they didn't allow Colvilles here. It wasn't long ago that they were trying to even make Pierre Louis go back to the States. So my dad was never a member here. He is a member of the Colville Tribe. We got on the Band here as members through our mom, Edith Nicholas.

The settlement of Marcus, Washington, on the opposite shore from Kettle Falls was founded by Marcus Oppenheimer, who took the opportunity to establish a business centre on the shores of the busy Columbia River. An early report gives the following details.

> "Marcus Oppenheimer was born in 1834 and died in March 31, 1901. He was naturalized on Oct. 27, in the State of Kentucky. He arrived in Marcus in 1862 and purchased the buildings of the British Boundary Commission and opened a store in a log cabin.... In his store he sold merchandise to prospectors who came shopping down the Columbia by boat.... Oppenheimer used these barracks until 1881, when, after the withdrawal of American troops, the buildings were removed."[5]

Mourning Dove describes the boom town of Marcus at its peak.

> "Marcus enjoyed the boom, and new buildings crowded away the old log shanties of pioneers and the early log store of Marcus Oppenheimer.... Log shanties were replaced by fine homes, hotels and restaurants. Both Marcus and Republic ended up with dozens of square-front saloons. The church bells on the Sabbath were drowned out by the laughter of the men in bars, dives and brothels."[6]

Mourning Dove wrote that her father's name was Joseph Quintasket, a Nicola Indian with a strain of Canadian Okanagan on his maternal side. His traditional name was T-quin-tasket, which means "Dark Cloud." He was born about "1864 in the upper or Lake Okanagan community of En-hwx-kwas-t'nun (Arrow Scraper), located a short distance south of present Kelowna, British Columbia on the east side of Lake Okanagan."[7] The footnote, however, refutes Mourning Dove's statement by saying that other evidence places her father's birth place at Penticton.[8] In any case, Mourning Dove goes on to explain that her father's mother died while visiting an Indian encampment at Colville and was orphaned after his stepfather's death. He never returned to the Okanagan Valley. Although Mourning Dove does not include her paternal grandmother's name, she does go on to include a story of her father's maternal grandmother, Pah-tah-heet-sa.

Pah-tah-heet-sa was a famous Nicola Medicine Woman who came out the winner after being challenged by a grizzly bear on the Nicola Trail. As the story goes, Pah-tah-heet-sa fought the bear over a berry patch and when the warriors saw what was happening threatened to shoot the grizzly but lowered their arrows when she said, "Wait! We are fighting this to the finish. He is a mean animal and I am a mean woman. We will see who is the strongest and conqueror in this battle." With these words she drove a stick into the bear's mouth several times. In fact, they fought "... until the sun lay low in the western sky. Only then did the grizzly walk away, broken and bleeding."[9]

Eva Lawrence: *When my mother died, my real grandmother, Mary Nicholas, took me. I went back and forth between who I called Granny Nancy and my grandmother, Mary. Nancy then lived at Deep Creek. She took me to the Indian office in town and told me to say I wanted to live with her. I guess I liked her 'cause that's what I said when they asked me. I liked my Tupa, Nancy's mother,*

Sqwnim-te-nalqs more, but I went and stayed with Nancy. So I think how Granny succeeded with me is because she went with the church while my grandmother, Mary Nicholas, was not a church goer, she was more traditional.

I was really close to the Westbank, Penticton and Kamloops people 'cause they used to come around. I was just a little kid and Antoine Eli, he was a Chief at Westbank, he was the one who named me Sqy-alqs. It means "blue dress." It was his mother or his grandmother's name. I learned all this from Tommy Gregoire. He said that name is not from around here. In them days you not only got names from family, but from friends too. I gave it to my grandson, Dwayne. He wanted his daughter to have an Indian name. He had Dave Parker pronounce it and write it on her certificate. So, it's good; an Indian name that is registered!

My granny, Nancy, taught me honesty. She did it with a stick though; a different form. She'd give me the stick and tell me to remember the things she taught me, I guess the things her mother taught her. Like always be good to old people and always offer your visitors something. So those things she really drilled into me. I grew up with that sort of thing. The way Tupa and Granny raised me is the way I raised my kids and they seem to be doing okay.

Granny Nancy sacrificed some of her land and her little house at Neehoot so I could go to school. They told her she had too. So it was sold to the Tonaskets then they sold it to the Logans. Anyway, at the time we lived at Neehoot it was too far for me to go to Six-Mile to go to school everyday. Granny Nancy didn't want me to go to Kamloops, either. She didn't want me to go away. So her and I moved into a house here at Six-Mile. Not this house, but the first one. It was originally owned by Julie Tonasket. I remember that house. It had only the outside walls and Julia, I guess, put some cardboard and cloth on the inside to keep the wind out. Granny added more through the years, but one winter it was so cold, about forty or fifty below, and Granny set up a tent over our upstairs bed. In the morning we had to shake the frost off our blankets and hit the tent from the inside to get the frost off. That's how cold the house was.

While Eva remained with Nancy and Sqwnim-te-nalqs, her brothers Angus and Ernest went to Kamloops Indian Residential School. When they returned to Head of the Lake they furthered their education at the Six-Mile Creek Day School. Later they found jobs and married local women. Angus married Christine Edwards and had seven children. Ernest married Dorothy Simla and had the grand total of eighteen children. Their sister Ella married Ben Louis, but died just a year after their marriage. Eva married William Lawrence Jr.

Besides working in the logging business cutting cordwood at Hoover's sawmill at Deep Creek, Ernest and Angus played ball. The brothers played key roles on the Six-Mile Creek baseball team. Ernest was catcher while Angus played relief pitcher for Charlie Bessette. Casimir Tonasket relieved Ernest as catcher for Head of Lake Bluebird team. From experience many speak of the rough and ready games fought for the coveted Bluebird trophy that was donated by Isaac Harris. Others also speak of the distance travelled to various local reserves in the spring and summer seasons. When the Blue Bird trophy was not up for grabs, trophies such as black eyes, skinned shins and broken arms were displayed as the best prize. Ernest and Angus were part of this era and left more trophies elsewhere than were taken home. Most speak of these days as the best in their lives.

PARKER

JOSEPH

ANNIE JOSEPH PARKER

CHARLIE

LOUIE CHRISTIE

HARRY

MARY LOUISE

GEORGE

EDNA

CAROLINE

BERTHA

ROSIE

PARKER

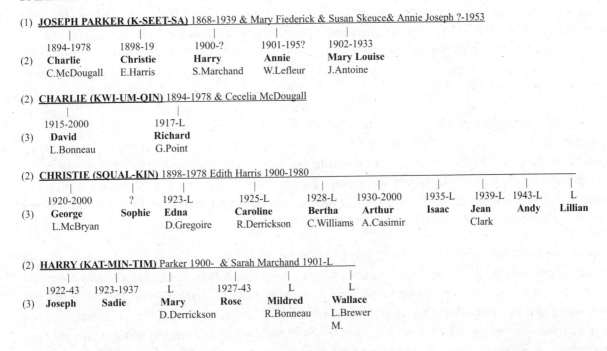

(1) **JOSEPH PARKER (K-SEET-SA)** 1868-1939 & Mary Fiederick & Susan Skeuce& Annie Joseph ?-1953

1894-1978	1898-19	1900-?	1901-195?	1902-1933
(2) **Charlie**	**Christie**	**Harry**	**Annie**	**Mary Louise**
C.McDougall	E.Harris	S.Marchand	W.Lefleur	J.Antoine

(2) **CHARLIE (KWI-UM-QIN)** 1894-1978 & Cecelia McDougall

1915-2000	1917-L
(3) **David**	**Richard**
L.Bonneau	G.Point

(2) **CHRISTIE (SQUAL-KIN)** 1898-1978 Edith Harris 1900-1980

1920-2000	?	1923-L	1925-L	1928-L	1930-2000	1935-L	1939-L	1943-L	L
(3) **George**	**Sophie**	**Edna**	**Caroline**	**Bertha**	**Arthur**	**Isaac**	**Jean**	**Andy**	**Lillian**
L.McBryan		D.Gregoire	R.Derrickson	C.Williams	A.Casimir		Clark		

(2) **HARRY (KAT-MIN-TIM)** Parker 1900- & Sarah Marchand 1901-L

1922-43	1923-1937	L	1927-43	L	L
(3) **Joseph**	**Sadie**	**Mary**	**Rose**	**Mildred**	**Wallace**
		D.Derrickson		R.Bonneau	L.Brewer
					M.

The Parker name came into the Band through Joseph Parker. After discussing the family with descendant Edna Gregoire, nee Parker, it is clear that the first two wives of her paternal grandfather Joseph Parker, may be lost somewhere in the memories of past generations. Edna did recall, however that Joseph's first wife was an Arrow Lakes woman, while descendant charts reveal Joseph's first wife's name to be Mary Fredericks.[2] Christie and Harry's marriage record confirms their mother's name as Mary. However, Harry's records reads he was born at Oroville. Christie was twenty when he married twenty-year-old Edith Harris in 1919. Their witnesses were Joseph Jimmy, probably Jimmy Joseph, and "Lucy Shinlow."[3] Harry then twenty-one married nineteen-year-old Sarah Marchand January 3, 1921. Jimmy and Sarah Bonneau witnessed their marriage.[4] Both couples were married by Father Le Jeune, OMI.

The art of storytelling is very visible in the stories told by recently deceased David Parker. Unfortunately David passed away on his birthday, February 28, 2000. He was eighty-five years old and the father of six children. David took an active role in many service groups such as the Friendship Centre, Alcohol and Drug Treatment Program and the Aboriginal Disabled Society of British Columbia. Dave not only served in the army, but served his community well through interpreting and translating the Okanagan language. His most favoured occupation led him on the trail of cougars and other game animals in the Okanagan and Lillooet district. Most of all his gift of music and song, a trademark of the McDougall and Parker families, was a very large part of Dave's life. His contribution to this study illustrates both his talent for translation and his fondness for storytelling. His cousins, Arthur and George Parker, also died the same year.

David Parker: *My grandfather, Joe Parker, told me that his dad was known as James Parker. James was a wandering white man. My great grandmother took up with him. When James Parker*

got into Spokane from the Kalispell country, the sheriff gave him twenty-four hours to get out of town, not because he was a crook or anything, but because he liked to fight and fightin' brought trouble. My grandfather, Joseph Parker too, was a fightin' man. Of course, that was in his drinkin' days! Now, that's all the history that I know of James Parker. My brother, Richard, is doin' some diggin' into the Parker history, but, I never heard that James Parker was from the same line as the Comanche, Quanah Parker.

My grandfather, Joseph Parker was known as K-seet-sa. That means to singe the hair off a groundhog. He used to do that and the burning of the hair also lent a flavour to the meat. Groundhogs have a lot of fat on them, so burning the hair made the meat real tender and tasty. My dad Charlie Parker's Okanagan name was Kwi-um-qin which means "frost on top of the mountain." Uncle Christie's name was Squalt-kin. Uncle Harry's name was Kat-min-tim. I don't remember Mary Louise or Annie having an Okanagan name.

From what my grandfather told me, my grandmother, Annie Joseph, married Pierre Joseph who was from around Chesaw, Washington. When my grandfather Joe came around there he got with her, and my father, Charlie, was born when she was still with Pierre Joseph. After my father was born my grandfather and grandmother took off together and came to Canada. That was a way for them to get away from the law. When they came, they brought along Caroline, the two-year-old daughter of my grandmother and Pierre Joseph, with them. She left the two older children Katherine and Alex, with Pierre and came to the Arrow Lakes. Later, my grandfather rejected Caroline and they eventually took her back to Cheesaw. My grandmother died there, at the Arrow Lakes, then my grandfather came here to the Okanagan.

Here at Westbank he got with a woman called Two Bit Susan. At least that is what I assume. Her grave is at Westbank. On the grave is written Susan Parker. So I assumed that was her. I'm not sure when that happened though.

After that he wound up with a woman called Anyes. She was the first grandmother I knew. At first, I got there and had one grandmother, then the next time I got there I had another grandmother. What happened was, I was only three and the Spanish flu epidemic was here. Anyes died of that flu epidemic in 1918. That's when Annie Joseph came an' took over. I say she was waitin' in the wings.

Next he got with Annie Klome Joseph. I remember Baptiste Klome. He was the brother to Annie. It was 1919, and I was four years old. I remember him lying on the ground in front of the house and Annie, his sister, was blasting the disease out of him. I mean by that, she had balsam pitch and she put it on his chest and lit it. My mother said the ol' man was pretty sick with tuberculosis and he tol' her that in his dreams he was chasing his body and couldn't catch up to it. He said to her, "I'm gonna die, I was chasin' my body and couldn't catch up to it." He died too!

Around the time I was born, 1915, my grandfather came to in Penticton. He'd been on a drunk. When he came to, he was ashamed of himself. You see, he tells me this story himself. He quit drinkin', but I guess he thought a little cider won't hurt. One time before Anyes died she was mashing elderberries in a little wooden keg. I asked what that was. She said it was for the chickens, but actually she was mashing it to make wine. She wouldn't tell me that, though, 'cause when I was a kid I was observant, and a talker, and if they said anything, I was just liable to repeat it. So they were careful about what they said around me. After Annie Joseph got there, that put an end to the wine. She'd go meet the row boat and when my grandfather landed there with his friends, and if there was any bottles, she took them and dumped them all out. That was the end of his drinking.

My grandfather said when he first came to, he was an orphan in the Kalispell country. He was around as a kid, and pretty hungry, and he said when he got older and big enough, he decided to be an outlaw. He strapped on a gun and was out stealing horses, and what not. Along the way, he met up and associated with good people. They changed him. They talked him into becoming a working man. He learned to trap and was a market hunter. He shot deer and sold the meat to the stores in the Arrow Lakes. He set his trap line up from the Arrow Lakes, all the way here into the Okanagan. Then he'd go back and unload his traps. He made traps out of deadfalls-any wood that was laying around at the time. One time he told me he built a trap to catch a bear and a grizzly came along and tore it all apart.

When my grandfather came over here, after my grandmother died, he came with his children. My dad was about nine, Christie about seven, Harry about four, and Annie was the youngest. When he got here he couldn't just sit around and watch the kids, so he farmed them out. Old Semo Paul and his wife Susan took uncle Harry. They were really kind people. Christie, I think, stayed at Okanagan Landing with Suk-ukulawh meaning "got set on the ground" and my dad stayed with Skees-is-lahw, meaning "sticks all over the ground." He lived at the Landing, too. I don't know those people by any English name. Anyes took Annie, and eventually when my grandfather came down from the mountains, where he was trapping and hunting, he got with Anyes. Then Christie and my dad came back from where they were staying, and stayed with Anyes. Semo kept Harry and wouldn't let him come back.

When I first came to Whiteman's Creek, I didn't know that Harry was my uncle. I thought he was Semo's kid, 'cause he lived there. So anyway, I used to stay with Semo, and his wife Susan quite often myself. My dad and them would take a trip down across the line or just be away somewhere, and they'd leave me with Semo. And that's how I got to Six-Mile on Sundays. We'd go in the buggy up to Johnny Pant's place there by Six-Mile Creek. That was the nearest place to the church. That's how I got to see ol' Spe-pa-cheen blow that horn.

My dad's sister, Annie, married Bill Le Fleur and went and lived around Brewster, Washington. When she tried to come back to Canada they wouldn't let her cross the border 'cause she had no papers of any kind. So she stayed down there.

My dad Charlie had an allotment down the States. Pierre Joseph said that my dad should have a little ground to work when he got older, so he registered him under his name down the States, near Cheesaw. Only the southern part of the Colville Nation remained reserve. The northern part has only small reserves now, I think. That's where Pierre Joseph had his place. And that's where my dad had his allotment. He relinquished his place, and his American citizenship, when he joined the Canadian Army.

My mother's people come from Penticton. My maternal grandfather was David McDougall Jr. He married Nancy, who was the daughter of Anatasia. What happened was the Chief at Penticton used to have lots of wives and fathered a bunch of children. So he had different families. I know I am related to the Gabriels, Phillips and, of course, the youngest brother, Atmin. Mary Theresa was the first original Gabriel at Penticton. She was married to Capprian [Cyprian Lawrence]. He was the half-brother to my great grandmother Sylhimpt. Phillip or Pleep was a full-brother to Anastasia. People thought Atmin was crazy, but he wasn't really. He was just odd.

One time I was in Vancouver. I was there to try to transfer from the Army to the Air Force. To do this I had to take an IQ test. I only had a Grade Six Indian School education and wasn't sure if I could do well on the test. I ended up getting the highest mark out of the three of us who wrote the test. Anyway, before I wrote the test, I was asked by the senior officer if there was any insanity in my family. My mom was living down there, then, and I went back and asked her, "Well, what about Atmin?" My mother said, he wasn't crazy, it was just that Indian doctor bit. It made him odd. Well, people didn't understand him, didn't understand his oddity. So I relaxed at bit. But he was odd. He did things differently than most others.

One time my dad was going up to Douglas Lake. He had a slow horse 'cause at that time he was breaking horses for the people at Douglas Lake. All of a sudden the horse shied and my dad looked up and here was this apparition coming down the road, like it had wings. My dad yelled, "hello, hello," and no answer came back. My dad had a thirty-two revolver in his chaps pocket and he pulled that out and went up close and Atmin laughed. Then my dad really gave him the dickens. He said to Atmin, "Just a little more and I would have shot you!"

You see what that was, when he was around the different places where the people spoke the language, he would tie a rope around his waist and tie fir boughs onto it. Then he dragged the boughs along behind him to hide his tracks. He always went barefooted and so he'd hide his tracks, then nobody would know it was him. Then when he got tired of pulling those boughs, he'd put them up on his shoulders and carry them. As he trotted along it looked like wings, and in the dark you just didn't know what you were lookin' at. My dad told me those things about Atmin. I still remember him, too. He tried to teach me to count in English. He had the words like six and eleven, but he had them all screwed up and in the wrong places. Atman used to stay with us at Whiteman's Creek, but when they told him to go pack wood he'd have it in his arms and he'd jump and kick like a horse and scatter the wood all over. He didn't like to do chores or help in any way. People still tell stories of him and his odd ways.

My first Indian name was given to me by Mary Theresa. She called me after my grandfather Nthel-thle-mils, little David McDougall Jr. He was a very kind hearted man, and that's what the name means "kind hearted." Then. when I came up here to Vernon and people got to know who I was a descendant of, they called me Kam-schu-chulst which means, "breeze from the heart." When I was about seven years old, my father Charlie Parker, called me Tsalipa which means "solid or pine-pitch stump." When I was growing up and just about a man, I was the biggest in the family, I wore the biggest clothes and could lift heavy things, and such, then he called me Tskoos-koos-xin which means "big toes." I used to like it when he called me that name 'cause I knew he was appreciating me for who I was.

Isaac Parker: *Joe Parker had two wives, maybe three. My dad [Christie] wasn't too clear on that. But he tol' me that his first wife, who is Charlie, Harry and my dad's mother, come here from the States somewhere. Of course, you heard of Quanah Parker, well from what I heard, that's who Joe Parker is related to. Back in them days if your name was Parker, the Army was lookin' for you. That's how come Joe Parker headed north to Montana, then to the Kootenays. They settled there and that's where my uncles and my dad were born. After that, evidently, is where my grandmother died, in the Kootenays somewhere. Then from there, Joe Parker moved to Vernon, and that's how he got with Annie Joseph.*

I can remember when my grandfather, Joe Parker, was still alive. He was bed-ridden, then. I run into the house and there was a flat rock there that made a step into the house. The other door was open and I tripped on that rock and I skinned my knees. I can still remember this. I started cryin' and went to his bedroom. He put his arm around me and patted me. I never forgot that. That was around 1939. I was about four or five years old then.

Grandfather died of a heart attack. I remember one evening my dad was gone, loggin' down in the Kelowna area. At home his two dogs were really barkin' around there and I happened to look out to the south, where Theresa's house is now. Along the bank there was a gate and it was closed. I was lookin' over there and there was my grandfather. He was walkin' up to the gate and I noticed somethin'. He got to the gate and walked right through it. He came about halfway between that gate, and where I was standin', and waved at me. He turned around and walked back through that closed gate and disappeared over the hill. I ran after him but he was no where around. After I couldn't see him, I remember, I ran up and told my mother that I saw grandfather. She just said, "Your grandfather's dead!" After I became a teenager, I questioned her about that again. She said, "He liked you and he just wanted to say bye."

My grandmother [Annie] was always givin' me huckleberry jam 'cause they always went to Silver Star. In fact, where George [Parker] lives now they had a root cellar. There used to be, just down the bank there, two old houses. One was used for food storage and the other was my grandmother's hide tanning house. Those two houses are gone now but that one house was filled with berries and fruit and vegetables.

I went to school at Cranbrook. My dad didn't like that school in Kamloops for some reason or another. Anyway, when he finally relented, there was no room for me at Kamloops, so I went to Cranbrook.

Ben Louis: *They used to have baseball games at In-kama-pelks and racing and wrestling. I remember when they used to say Christie Parker was a good wrestler, but the only one he couldn't handle was William Louie. William Louie always beat him. He couldn't pin William.*

Like his brothers and cousins Harry Parker is remembered not only for his carpentry skills, but also his musical talent. Throughout the years, and well into the seventies, he held his home at Whiteman's Creek open for dances. As told by his wife, Sarah, and John Marchand, the music would go on and on throughout the night and well into the next day. Many good times were hosted by Harry and his wife Sarah.

CATHERINE

SOPHIE & MICHELE JACK

PETER

MARY

SEMO PAUL

PAUL HOUSE

JIMMY, MARY & SHIRLEY

PAUL

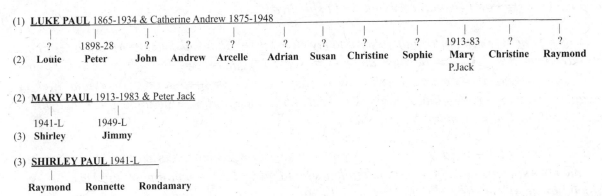

(1) **LUKE PAUL** 1865-1934 & Catherine Andrew 1875-1948

(2) Louie	Peter 1898-28	John	Andrew	Arcelle	Adrian	Susan	Christine	Sophie	Mary 1913-83 P.Jack	Christine	Raymond
?		?	?	?	?	?	?	?		?	?

(2) **MARY PAUL** 1913-1983 & Peter Jack

(3) Shirley 1941-L	Jimmy 1949-L

(3) **SHIRLEY PAUL** 1941-L

Raymond	Ronnette	Rondamary

The Paul surname originates with Arrow Lakes-born Luke Paul. Some believe that he was related to Annie Joseph, the common-law wife of Joseph Parker, and also a relative of the Adolph family of Colville, Washington.[2] Luke's wife, Catherine, is the daughter of Spallumcheen's Chief Andrew and his wife Arcut (1850-1930). Catherine's half-sister, Charlotte Isaac, whom records say was born in Washington,[3] first married widower Louie Umtoosoolow, and after he passed away she married George Shuttleworth. Apparently, after Andrew died Arcut remained at Irish Creek with little Harry Joe.

One brief glance at the family tree shows how the ravages of accidents and disease took a devastating toll on the Paul family. Vital records do not include the names or cause of death of these ten children, but fortunately, while still alive, Mary Paul located the names of her brothers and sisters among sacramental records at Kamloops.

Ned Louis: *At one time there was a little village on the bench above Mary Paul's place. That's where ol' Harry Antoine and Arcut lived. They were little short people. Antoine Eli lived in that little village, too. All of those people were related. Luke Paul died up there at the Paul place and they buried him at Head of the Lake. Antoine and his family moved over to Westbank after that. My mother's sister Mary Schwartz married Antoine Eli. They had quite a few kids. Alex married Mary who is Maggie Bessette's daughter. Archie married Madeline who was Jimmie Antoine's daughter. Then there is Thomas and some other sisters. They all lived at Westbank.*

Shirley Paul: *If I remember right, my gramma's grandmother on her mother's side, her name was Supee. My grampa, Luke, and grandmother, Catherine, had twelve kids. They were all born on the hill up here. Mom's brothers and sisters all died long before they had any kids. Mom was the only one to have kids. Me and Jimmy. My uncle Louie and uncle Peter lived until they were young men, but they died.*

My grandmother died when I was about seven years old. It was on November 23, 1948. We lived up here and my grandmother needed her stumpage cheque. So she walked from here all the way to Hoover's sawmill and back again. It was raining and snowing that day. She got back home and later that night she got sick. They took her to the hospital and told her she had double pneumonia. She wouldn't stay there though because she believed in Indian doctors and herbal medicine. We came home and they took us up to Enderby to the woman Indian doctor's house. The doctor worked on her and later that night she died.

I was laying between my grandmother and my mom when Mom woke me up. She said Gramma was leaving us. She knew that because an owl was scratching his claws down the roof of the house and Coyote was howling outside the window. It was so close and so loud that you would think he was going to come through the window. All I remember after that was the undertaker measuring my grandmother and my mom dressing her.

When I was little I used to think my grandmother was my mom. I called her Mom. Anyway, one time my real mom came to my grandmother's and I guess I did something wrong because I got whipped for it. When she did that, I cried and I ran to my grandmother and put my arms around her legs. But she took me and put me out in front of her and told me that she wasn't my mom, she was my gramma and I was to listen to my real mom. That really hurt me, but that's how it was in those days. My mom wasn't around much because she was always away working. She even stayed with her relatives, the Eli's in Westbank, for quite awhile. She was working down there in the gardens.

My mom was pregnant with Jimmy when my grandmother died. We were living at our house and Jimmy Antoine and Mariette found out we were there by ourselves, and Mom was ready to have Jimmy. So they took us over to their place across the lake and we stayed in a little cabin that they had there. When Mom went in to have Jimmy, she signed me over to Jimmy and Mariette in case she didn't come home. But she did come back and we went back home.

We didn't have wood so Sa-sa-peen, that's Josephine Edwards' son, Charlie Edwards, brought us some wood on his buckboard, then later brought some logs on a bigger wagon. He sawed and split it for my mother. Annie Joseph saw we were alone and her and George Parker came and got us and took us to George's place. We stayed the summer there and that's when I remember George Wilson. I didn't like him because him and his grandson [Lawrence Wilson] used to come to George's and they would tease the heck out of me.

Jimmy Antoine had two gardens. One was over there on the highway where the Tonasket's live now. The other was across the lake where that big wheat field was then. He had a little log house there and a little shack. That's where my mom and I stayed in 1950. My mom worked there all summer long. She worked for Ernest Brewer too. That place where William Brewer lives now was all garden too. I remember Big Annie [Logan] worked there with my mom.

I went to residential school, maybe in 1951 or '52. I know that because at that time my mom worked over there at Jimmy Antoine's. In later years, after I came back from there, I went to Irish Creek School. My mom kept me home because she needed me to look after Jimmy. We stayed over at Josephine Edward's that summer. Just why, I don't know. Around October when the garden was finished I went to school at Irish Creek. But she didn't let me go to school in the winter because then this whole place at Irish Creek had blizzards and, I guess, I wasn't dressed for that kind of weather. It was really cold. So I guess she kept me home too much. Anyway, the Indian Agent came out and I had to go back to residential school.

The first time I went there I couldn't speak English. And didn't learn anything. I didn't know what I was being told. I don't know how long I was there, I just know I was being strapped all the time. They finally got Theresa Lewis, who is a Dennis now, to teach me to speak English. The other kids at residential school tried to help me but they got in trouble too. I was always in the corner. I was trying to forget my language. For many years I was ashamed of being Indian. Even after my mom died you couldn't get me to talk to people. I was ashamed and I had the fear of being strapped. So I crawled into a shell and wouldn't open my mouth. And a lot of things that people told me I couldn't absorb it. But now I'm coming out of it. I teach at the kindergarten and really love my work. I teach too, one hour a week, at Head of the Lake hall.

Mary Paul died in 1983. She was a significant person in preserving Okanagan culture and traditions. She served as a good teacher, guiding others through the steps of tanning and beading, all of which she learned from her mother Catherine. Like so many others, Catherine and Mary embroidered and beaded gloves, moccasins, vests and jackets and sold them at the Hudson's Bay store in Vernon. Mary's voice, too, has been captured on tape and serves as good reference for Okanagan hymns and songs. Shirley, Mary's daughter, is also a valued teacher of the language. She teaches at Sn-c-ca-mala-tn Kindergarten and Day Care at Blacktown. Her knowledge of the Okanagan names of animals, birds and different forms of greetings and words is a gift to her students. The future success of preserving the language is embodied in the knowledge and gift of sharing, through the daughter of Mary Paul and Peter Jack and the granddaughter of Luke Paul and Catherine Andrew.

Ned Louis: *At Dirty Lake, Little Harry lived just below ol' Shuttleworth's. And below that was Luke Paul. Ol' Eli was there too. They are the same family as Luke Paul. Little Harry was in between there. Little Harry and his small little woman. Ol' Antoine lived there too, with his wife and my aunt Mary Shwartz. They were originally from here. Ol' Eli's Indian name was Sn-sn-kanult.*

Semo Paul and his wife Susan were also band members in the early history of the band. Their origin however cannot be positively established. Semo, or Seymour, and Luke Paul's names appear on the list as present at the meeting held at the Head of the Lake in August 1909 to protest the sale of Long Lake Reserve.[4]

Ned Louis: *Seymour Paul raised Harry Parker. At one time our people were up and down the Kettle and Columbia River. That is where I heard Semo Paul comes from. I remember him, so he came here many, many years ago. His old lady died and he was still livin' there, where Sarah Parker lives now, and I used to see him ridin' up the road on weekends. He was a short little fella, if I remember right, and he was old and his hair was real black, curly and cut to his shoulders; kinda squared off around his face. It was when the first Stetsons came in. He had a hat on like that. He died when I was a little fella.*

PIERRE

ANNE

NARCISSE & TERESE

PIERRE HOUSE

MATILDA

ELIZABETH

HENRY

PIERRE

(1) **PIERRE QWAY-UM-QIN** 1848-1929 & Christique 1858-1927

1862-1949	1870-1939	1875-1937
(2) **Anne**	**Marianne**	**Narcisse**
G.Smith	Alexis	T.Hewitum
J.Williams	H.Lawrence	

(2) **NARCISSE PIERRE (SKOO-PUCKS)** 1875-1957 & Theresa Hewitum 1878-1957

1904-80	1906-75	1908-72	1910-?	1911-19	1912-74
(3) **Matilda**	**Elizabeth**	**Henry**	**Kamticha**	**Leo**	**Angus**
G.Bessette	A.Louie	Maggie		A.Jack	
E.Wilson					
M.Lezard					

(2) **Marianne:** See Alexis and Lawrence
(2) **Anne:** See Shuttleworth/Smith

The name Qway-um-qin means "wealthy head" and is a story continued from the Abel and Ko-mas-ket history.[2] Pierre Qway-um-qin and Christique were the parents of Blind Narcisse, Marianne and Anne Qway-um-qin. The descendants of Blind Narcisse are now known as Pierre. Pierre Qway-um-qin died at eighty-seven on May 11, 1929. His death record maintains, however, that he could have been well over one hundred years old when he died. His wife Christique died two years before at age sixty-eight, January 8, 1927.[3]

Once again records reveal names and relationships in the Pierre family, while oral history provides the links to present day. According to the records, Theresa Hewitum, the wife of Narcisse, was a sister to Mary Tomat. Mary was the daughter of Chief Tomat of Westbank.[4] She made the news in 1913 during the Royal Commission when she cut off the irrigation water from gardener, David Gellately, at Westbank.[5] Grandson, Martin Wilson, also claims a relationship between the two women, but admits to being unsure of a positive tie.

Theresa's specialty seems to be that of midwife. Neighbours attest to her being there when siblings were born. As noted, she assisted Esther Louie in the delivery of her babies and helped to deliver Charlie and Ellen Lezard's children at Six-Mile Creek.[6]

Martin Wilson: *I don't know who my great grandmother was. My mom and them never tell me who was my relations from away back. They just tell me that, that one is your relation, and that one is your relation, but they never tell me how I am related. But my great grampa was Qway-um-qin just like my grampa.*

My grampa, Narcisse, was blind, I think from a gun that exploded in his eyes. He had two Okanagan names. They called him Qway-um-qin like his dad and Skoo-pucks. Skoo-pucks means "hair on the chest." Even though he was blind he knew me by the touch of my hand.

Grampa's sister, Marianne, had two husbands, ol' Alexis, Johnny Alexis' dad, and then Henry Lawrence. Johnny Alexis' dad died and Marianne married Henry. My grandmother, Theresa, was, I think, a sister to ol' Lola in Westbank.

My grampa and gramma and Uncle Angus and me used to go by buggy all the time down to Westbank. Uncle Angus drove the buggy 'cause my grampa was blind. But me, I'm always ridin'! We used to stay with that ol' lady [ol' Lola] and go all the way down to the lake in Westbank and that's where I learned to play ball. The ball ground was down by the lake. And we used to go to funerals down there, too. We would go down this way on the Westside and camp at that little spring there at Bear Creek. Early the next morning, them older guys would go up the mountain and get a deer. They'd skin it and take the whole thing to the funeral. That's when everybody helped each other. On the way home we would go across the ferry and come back on the other road past Duck Lake. We'd stop at Wood's Lake and camp maybe three days, and salt and dry fish. We used to go up Silver Star too. I remember one time we got a white horse from Westbank and I rode him up to Silver Star. I couldn't understand that horse's name so I called him nulp. That means "bologna."

My grampa was real tall in one of those pictures that got scorched when my house burned. He had on those fur chaps and a hat. When he got old he shrunk. My gramma, though, was just little and real quiet. She never said too much.

I remember all around our house there used to be tents set up all summer. People used to come from Westbank and Penticton and stay in those tents. Those tents were there for anybody to camp, for as long as they wanted.

We used to go to visit Narcisse Jack and my grampa and Narcisse used to tell Chaptilk stories. Sometimes till three o'clock in the morning. Then they'd wake me up and tell me to go feed the horses. I had nobody to tell those stories to, so I forget them. That's too bad 'cause they always told me Chaptilk. My grampa was related to the Jacks, but I don't know how.

My auntie Elizabeth, or Qwintk, that means a kind of "blue and green colour," stayed with Alphonse Louie, but they never had kids. Everybody knows my auntie by Qwintk, just like me, they call me Nahoscoos. That means "stump." I got that name when I was little, about this high!

I heard my Grampa Narcisse say one time that he wanted to go visit Pierre Jack. I knew they'd tell me to take him, so I ran outside. Pretty soon my mom called me and said ,"You take Grampa to Pierre Jacks!" I got mad 'cause it will take all morning to go only that far and he was blind and slow. So I started to take him. When we got about here [meaning around Six-Mile ball ground] there was lots of stumps; it wasn't cleared yet, only the road was here. Ol' Grampa was moanin' and complainin'. He was gettin' mad at me 'cause he kept trippin' over stuff on the ground. Then I got mad and took him over to a stump. He fell right over the top of the stump and scraped his face and his stomach and arms. Boy, did he ever swear at me in our language. I helped him up and took him home. When my uncles and Mom saw us they took Grampa in the *house and fixed him up. He tol' them what happened. After that my uncles would laugh and laugh when we were far enough away from the house. And they called me Stump, Nahoscoos, and I still got that name.*

I remember ol' Frank Marchand. He was just a short fella. He was kinda smarty but he had good horses. And clean too. Them work horses were real tall too and had wide rumps. Oh, they were good horses. I remember Christine, too.

JOHNNY

HARRIET

ROY

EMERY

TOMMY ARMSTRONG & JOSEPHINE MCDOUGALL

IRENE MCDOUGALL

DELLA ARMSTRONG

ROBINS / ARMSTRONG

(1) **NANCY WILLIAMS** & John Robins
       |
       1906-1971
(2)   Johnny
       H.McDougall

(2) **JOHNNY ROBINS** (**Tekil-maka**)1906-1971 & Harriet McDougall 1906-1974
     | | | | |
     1925-1956   Baby   1943-1962   1949-L   1951-L
(3) **Roy**   **Johnny**   **William**   **Ranger**   **Emery**
                              D.Spaham   M.Snow
                                          M.Maxim

The Robins surname is represented today at Okanagan No. 1 and Okanagan No. 6 at Duck Lake by brothers Ranger and Emery. Their father, Johnny Robins, married Westbank's Harriet McDougall. Harriet and her sister Josephine were daughters of Amab and Louise McDougall. Josephine married Tommy Armstrong. Johnny and Harriet lived at Duck Lake while Josephine and Tommy lived near Whiteman's Creek. Ranger was raised by his parents; Emery was raised by his aunt Josephine and Tommy Armstrong. Another brother William Robins drowned in Duck Lake in 1962 as a result of an epileptic seizure. He was just nineteen years old.

Ranger Robins: *Dad said that when he about ten, his grampa, who was a powerful Medicine Man, told him that it was time for him to get his sumich. Doctor William lived at Whiteman's Creek then and Dad said you could just feel the power both inside and outside the house. Anyway, Dad laid on the floor on one of Doctor William's hides, and all around, hanging up, were hides of all of Doctor William's animal spirits. As he was laying there, he said he saw all those animals come to life and they danced all around the room. And the noises of the animals were clearly heard, too. He said he heard growling and other noises and he got scared. It was just too powerful. Anyway, he got up and told his grampa he didn't want it. His grampa told him it was okay. They could try again another time. But my dad never did. After that time though, he said he was never afraid. So that was one thing that he got because of his grampa. Anyway, his grampa died and after that he looked after himself. He said he stayed at Alexis', Cameron's, Pierre's and Abel's. They were all related to him. I remember he used to call Matilda Pierre's mom, Auntie.*

From what my dad told me, his mother Nancy, was married to a man named John Robins. Nobody knows who he was, or where he came from, but Maurice Lezard told my mom that John Robins was killed in a logging accident at Kelowna somewhere. Anyway, he was dead by the time my dad was born two years later. Then she died when my dad was born. After that he was raised by his grandfather, Doctor William.

He told me that he was about twelve years old when his grampa died and after that he just went all over the place and stayed with people who he said were his relations. Mom already had my brother Roy by the time Dad met her. Her and Roy were living in a tent at Westbank. After that Dad adopted Roy and registered him under his name, Robins. After that, we were born. There was William, me and Emery. Uncle Ben told me that he used to play with my dad when they were young. This one time, they were together up on the hill by Abel's. Ben laid down and told my dad to lay on his back and they would slide on the snow down that hill. Like I said, Dad wasn't scared to do anything. Anyway, he did, and they came flying down that steep hill and hit the fence. Dad's face got all cut up from the fence and he hit the fence post with his nose. Ben said he just got up and squeezed and pulled his nose back in place and they went on playing. Seems he always was getting hurt but he never stopped doing what he liked to do.

He said when he was about twelve he met up with a French man and went to work for him on a thrashing crew above Kalamalka Lake. There was a grain field there, where H&P Sausage was later, and that's where he said he learned to sew sacks, through that threshing crew that he worked with. After that he left and came back to the Reserve to the Abel's, the Pierre's and the Alexis' and Cameron's. He'd go over the hill from the Cameron's to Abel's. He'd stay there a while then go over to Matilda Pierre's place and stay there awhile too. That's where he found out that Frank Gottfriedson was his dad. He said he never bothered to talk to Frank about it though, he just carried on with his life and after a while he seemed to be accepted by Frank and Emma's family as a brother. In fact, he logged with his team for Frank and worked along with his brothers, Gus and them.

That time he was working for his dad he said Frank came over to the landing where all the boys were working. He said he was up on the hillside and could hear Frank yelling and hollering at his sons. He was giving them heck about something and asked where their oldest brother was. They told him he was up on top skidding. My dad said he looked down there and saw Frank climbing up the skid trail and he hooked up the chains to the logs and yelled at the horses. He said down the hill went the horses and Frank saw what was happening and turned around and ran back to the landing and into his truck. The boys were watching and told him aren't you gonna give that boy shit, too. He said, "Nope, that oldest boy wants to kill me!" He logged, mostly, though, for Johnny Alexis.

From an early age Dad taught me that horses were to be respected. They were his love and he spent his lifetime either on the back of a horse or driving a team. He made it his life's work. What he'd do is, when he heard that someone wanted a horse broke, he'd ride his saddle horse to their place and leave it there and take their green horse. He never left anyone without a horse to ride. Then he'd ride that horse till it was broke and ready to go back home. From there he'd pick up another one and do the same thing.

My dad was hurt from the time his horse flipped over and rolled on him. He told Pete Jones that it was before he married my mom. He was staying at Sarah and Victor Borrie's place, here at Winfield. He called Sarah his aunt. Victor's horse wandered away and my dad found it with some wild horses. He was riding bareback chasin' those wild horses off the mountain when his horse rolled on him. They took him to Victor's and he healed up there. Them days they didn't believe in doctors and he walked bent over after. A bone, I guess broke, in his chest and healed like that. You could see that bone there for the rest of his life.

From what my dad told me, there was a lot of wild horses in his days. He loved to chase them and when he corralled them he'd take them to the fox farm. The RCMP were always on his case over little things like poaching and things like that. He said one time he spooked an officer's horse off and took him and rubbed him down with black stove polish. From there he was taking the horse across the ferry and the horse spooked. The same officer was there on the ferry and offered to help Dad board the horse. It was the officer's horse, but he didn't even recognize him. He said he was scared, but if they caught on, he would have jumped the horse off the ferry and swam to shore.

Mom told me things about Dad and his horses too. She said when they were living at Westbank, where Willie Wilson's place is now, they had lots of goats that would run wild on Boucherie Mountain. She said she would see Dad through the window chasing those darn goats. Those things you know can get through anything and Dad wouldn't stop. Him and his horse would plow through that thick brush, go up and around, running all over that mountain till they caught the goat. Mom said too that one time she heard Dad yell on the mountain. She looked out the window and there he come straight down that mountain. She watched, she said, till his horse stumbled and Dad went head over heels and was rolling down that hill. He just wasn't afraid of anything it seems.

He told me he used to ride in the suicide race in Omak too back then when it was real dangerous. There is a way that you can do up the cinch on the saddles so that if you were falling off you just had to pull the cinch strap and saddle would come off. That's what he said them guys in the race did. When they raced there was a lot of pushin' and scramblin'. Dad said he did a lot of that himself and he'd stay ahead by pullin' their cinch straps. At that time, the river had lots of water, not like now where they use a lot of that water for irrigation, but really high, and when you hit the river the horses had to actually swim.

Dad and Pete Jones used to reminisce about their early days in Winfield. Pete Jones told me of how they used to race their buckboards into Kelowna. They would race from the end of Duck Lake to Dry Creek Road over to Glenmore and into Kelowna. They had rules too, no running. The horses had to just trot.

Uncle Gus told me, too, that one day he and Dad saw George Smith and Alex Marchand at Smith's place there trying break a horse to pull a buggy. Alex must have beat the horse or something 'cause they couldn't get it hooked up to the riggin'. Anyway, Dad and Gus thought they could help and they blindfolded the wild horse and Dad hooked him up, while Gus hooked up Alex's horse, Tiger. Alex climbed into the buggy and they asked him if he was ready. Alex said yep and they took off the blindfold, spooked the team and they took off around Francis Smith's field. They went 'round that whole field once, and then 'round twice, and took off across the ditch. Alex flew up off the wagon and fell hard on the ground. The horses kepta goin' and ran into the open door. They didn't stop until the wheels straddled the doorway. Gus said we better go back and see how Alex is. They asked him, "You okay?" He said, "You guys get the hell out of here, you just about killed me!" It was things like that my dad was known for. He was always pulling practical jokes on people and then set back and laugh his guts out.

I guess Dad and Uncle Gus were pretty close. Dad used to take Mom's buckskin up to Kamloops to sell. He'd stay up there for about a week and Gus said he'd stay with him and they'd ride all over up at Kamloops.

Mom was Amab McDougall's daughter, her sister was Josephine. Josephine married Tommy Armstrong and they lived down near Whiteman's Creek. My brother Emery was raised by Tommy and Auntie Josephine.

Pete Marchand: *I remember when ol' Johnny Robins used to come around. You could hear him coming all the way from Whiteman's Creek. It was in the winter and he had bells on his horse too, like Narcisse Jack and them. My grampa would say, "Listen that's Johnny Robins." I'd say, "Ah!" and Grampa would say, "Listen!" Then I learned what Johnny Robins' bells sounds like.*

Ralph Marchand: *The last time I was up Bald Range was with Johnny Robins. Ranger was a baby. They put a wooden box between the things on the pack saddle and put Ranger in there. Tied on that way it was like a cradle. They put him in there and went all over Bald Range huntin' and fishin'. That same horse that packed Ranger was a gelding, a blue horse and they called it the Old Blue Mare. Yet it was gentle, young and hard to spook and it was a gelding. They said one time they were back from somewhere and that horse went berserk and killed somebody. They had to get rid of it.*

At one of those places there, William who wasn't very big, got wanderin' around there and got standin' over these gopher holes. Those bees made their nests in them. The bees were comin' up and stingin' him. He was hollerin' and hollerin' and cryin'. I tol' him, "run, run!" He just stayed there. It took him quite a while before I guess he convinced himself to listen. Lucky he wasn't allergic to bee stings cause he got quite a few.

Josephine Armstrong had two daughters, Irene and Della. Both married at Okanagan No. 1. Irene married Ned Louis and had numerous children while Della married Albert Saddleman. Their son Albert Jr. was elected Chief and served a two-year term from 1991 to 1992 and again from 1994 to 1996.

The Armstrong name survives in Okanagan history through the family of Willie Armstrong at Penticton. Although Willie's brother Tommy resided at Whiteman's Creek with his spouse Josephine, Tommy did not have children. Another brother, Charlie however, relayed some family background to Doug Cox in 1981.[2]

Charlie remembered when his parents, Tommy Armstrong and Christine Joseph brought him from Vernon to Marron Valley, near Penticton, at the turn of the century. He said he was then just a boy of about ten years old. Thereafter, Charlie lived and worked with his uncle Enneas Sussap clearing land and building up the homestead from logs taken from the property. Stock was added to Charlie's holdings later in life and eventually produced at least 200 head of cattle marked with the "Half diamond-thirty six" brand. He made horses also a part of his life and at the time of the interview, told Cox, "I was just a kid when I was breaking horses, herding cattle and driving teams for some of the ranchers.... I could break a wild horse in the morning and be mowing hay with him in the afternoon."[3]

Willie and Lillian raised their children on the present ranch at Shingle Creek Road, just below the original homestead at Penticton. The Armstrong son's maternal ancestors are believed to originate in the Arrow Lakes with the eldest being Chermenchoot. Delphine Armstrong explains the rest of her lineage.

Delphine Armstrong: *My mother died when I was five years old. I was raised by my father Willie Armstrong and his wife, Lilly. Later I did a lot of research on my mother's side and when I discovered that Christine Quintasket, or Mourning Dove was my grandaunt, I was so proud. Christine Quintasket's paternal grandmother was of Thompson origin. She was known by the name of Soma-how-ataqha. Her great grandmother was Ha-ah-pecha. Ha-ah-pecha killed a grizzly bear with her digging stick while picking huckleberries on the trail near Merritt.[4]*

My paternal grandmother Christine Joseph recalled her family history to me. She said her family came from the Arrow Lakes. She said the eldest in her family was Cheremenchoot – which means "rattles himself." His son was Astist and his son was Knwm-sit-tc'a?. Knwm-sit-tc'a?'s son had four sons – Sussap, the Smitken brothers, McLeod and Tomat, and another son. Squmwhnelks had four children – Enneas, Cecilia, Agatha and my grandmother Christine Joseph.

My father had two brothers, Charlie and Tommy. Willie was known as Willie Armstrong Enneas, after my grandmother's brother Enneas. Willie's Okanagan name was K'wimlhilmixwn which means "Little Chief." His nickname was Makwalla which means some kind of weapon – like a tomahawk.

As a child I remember spending a lot of time with my grandmother, Christine. She would tell me the history of our people – how they lived, what they did and how they survived the wars between the tribes. There were wars among the Okanagan, Blackfoot and Secwepemc. My grandmother, Qaqna? [father's mother], passed on to me a lot of information like learning the proper way of speaking the language and the proper way of conducting myself as a proud Okanagan person.

Mourning Dove did research among her Elders, similar to what I did among my people. Finally, with the great influence of both sides of my family I feel honoured and am dedicated to teach and pass on the knowledge which was passed on to me by my ancestors. As I teach the language and tell of our great history, I feel I am a vessel through which our ancestors still speak.

LORD SHUTTLEWORTH

CHARLOTTE & GEORGE SHUTTLEWORTH

GEORGE SMITH

FRANCIS & SUSAN

MARIA

NORMAN

REGGIE

MARY

JOHNNY

ISABELLE

SHUTTLEWORTH / SMITH

(1) **HENRY DIGBY SHUTTLEWORTH** 1830-1870 & **Isobelle**

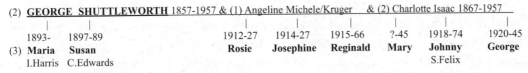

1855-1957	?-1826	1871-1896
(2) **George**	**Henry**	**Charles**
A.Michele	Josephine	
C.Isaac		

(2) **GEORGE SHUTTLEWORTH** 1857-1957 & (1) Angeline Michele/Kruger   & (2) Charlotte Isaac 1867-1957

1893-	1897-89	1912-27	1914-27	1915-66	?-45	1918-74	1920-45
(3) **Maria**	**Susan**	**Rosie**	**Josephine**	**Reginald**	**Mary**	**Johnny**	**George**
I.Harris	C.Edwards					S.Felix	

(3) **SUSAN SHUTTLEWORTH** 1897-1989 & **FRANCIS SMITH (SAWANA)** 1900-1971

L	L
Isabelle	**Norman**
R.Burgmaster	M.Kenoras

The Shuttleworth and Smith families are connected through the marriage of Susan Shuttleworth and Francis Smith. Francis' mother was Anne Pierre or Onn as people called her. Twenty years after Francis was born, Onn married fifty-five-year-old Joe Williams February 23, 1920.[2] His father was Williams and his mother Catherine.[3] Onn's father is listed as Pierre Andre and her mother Annie Joseph.[4] Henry and Marianne Lawrence witnessed the marriage.[5] As it is difficult to uncover any vital information pertaining to the origin of George Smith, the two families are combined under the two surnames.

There are several members of the Shuttleworth family listed in the census records of 1881 and 1891 who were scattered about the province acting as guides and packers. Henry Bigby Shuttleworth was a member of this large family. From Sismey we read that Henry was,

> "the youngest son of Lord Shuttleworth of Lancaster, England. He emigrated to the US in the early 1850's and served as a bookkeeper in the US Army at Colville where he married Isobel, the daughter of a sub-chief. He joined the Hudson's Bay Company on May 22, 1859 at Fort Kamloops and died at Hope in January 1900, at seventy years old."[6]

Still from Sismey we read that Harry, Henry's son, married Josephine, the youngest daughter of Chief Francois, at Okanagan Mission in 1883. Chief Francois packed for Tom Ellis of Penticton and Frank Richter of Keremeos from Hope over the Dewdney Trail. When Chief Francois retired the pack train was taken over by Harry, and Josephine went along as cook. Josephine was born at Penticton in 1867 and was the great granddaughter of the famous chieftainess of the Tonasket, Washington people. She died at eighty-three in November 1950 and at her request was buried alongside the graves of her people in Penticton.[7] George's daughter-in-law Mildred Leon Smith, who married Norman Smith, follows later with her memories.

The following biography was presented to the Vernon News in August of 1956 by George Shuttleworth's daughter, Susan Smith. George was born at Osoyoos, July 1, 1856 and died at 101 years old at Vernon. He began working with his father when he was fourteen years old.

"For a time he worked on a tug-boat, travelling down the Fraser River from Yale to New Westminster... he worked for Tom Ellis, training horses, bronco busting, herding, driving and branding long-horn cattle. Some of the drives were made from Penticton to Grand Prairie now called Westwold, for wintering and back in the spring to Penticton down the west side of Okanagan Lake. Mr. Shuttleworth remembers working on the main street of Penticton when it was nothing but boulders and stumps... and on the Summerland-Peachland highway with two teams of horses."[8]

Later he bought a farm at Westbank and farmed there until 1910 and later seven years for the Coldstream Ranch and then the O'Keefe Ranch. About this time he married his third wife. He spent his later years teaching the Okanagan language in Penticton.

Mildred Smith: *George Shuttleworth's mother was Maria Joseph, the eldest daughter of Chief Joseph from the States. They never stayed in the States for very long though because they were afraid that the army would come after Chief Joseph's family. They had to keep moving. At one point they lived down towards Langley. While he was at Fort Langley, he said his dad, Henry Digby Shuttleworth, was known as the hanging judge. George married Billy Kruger's sister Angeline Michele and had Susan and Maria. Susan was just a toddler when her mother died. Then George ended up with Charlotte Isaac, his second wife, and the two girls came up here to live at Head of the Lake. Susan first married Charlie Edwards. They lived in a little house above Irish Creek. After a while they parted and she married Francis Smith and had the two kids, Isabelle and Norman. Maria married Isaac Harris and had lots of kids.*

Ol' George was taped by one of the priests that used to come around here. I think it was Father Kane. The priest used to bring George communion and it was just after he received communion that George started to tell Father about his younger days. I was here at that time and I remember I was washing clothes on the scrub board and in between I served them tea and food. So, I was in hearing distance when they were visiting. George was telling Father about this time when he used to help his dad Henry.

When George was twelve he started to help his dad with the mail train from Spokane to Vancouver. The trip took three months by horseback. He said there was a trip he'll never forget. He had about seven little boxes that were going to China and he was given charge of those boxes. He said they went through here, over that way, and then through the Fraser Canyon because sometimes they had mail for people at Lillooet. Then sometimes they went down through the Coquihalla. One time when he was going through the Coquihalla one of the pack horses carrying those boxes slipped and fell down the canyon. He rushed down the canyon, unloaded the boxes and had to shoot the horse. He packed the saddle and everything back up the canyon to the trail.

It took him the better part of the day to do that. Then he loaded all that stuff onto his saddle horse. When they got to Vancouver with those boxes he asked what was in them. They told him it was ashes, the ashes of Chinese that died around Spokane or Idaho. He said he sure was mad. If he knew there were human ashes in those boxes he would have thrown them over the canyon himself.

Smith

Ned Louis: *What ol' George Smith tol' me when he was fifteen he came from Montreal to the California gold fields. Then he came up here through the Redwoods. When he landed here he met Dave Cameron and Thomas B. Struthers. They got together and lived up Six-Mile, on the fringes of the Reserve. Dave Cameron and Thomas B. Struthers married the Wilson girls [Edwards] and George got with ol' Onn. She is the daughter of ol' Qway-um-qin. She was deaf and mute. She was married first to Joe Williams. Charlie Williams, his brother, was my grandmother Teresa Qualtier's husband. Onn and George had Francis. Francis first married Victoria Marchand, but didn't have kids. Then they broke up and he married Susan Shuttleworth. She was the daughter of George Shuttleworth.*

George Smith was one of those guys that came here and homesteaded on the fringe of the Reserve at Six-Mile flat. That was more near the end of the gold rush period. Of course, them guys all did a bit of mining up on the flat and in the area. But there was another rush at Summerland, Peachland and here that brought pure English people to settle on the boundaries of the Reserve and all down Westside Road. They were all pure English and must have had money 'cause there were no roads out here only this narrow buggy road that is now Westside Road that went into Vernon.

John Marchand: *George Smith, a pure Englishman, lived up Six-Mile alongside Dave Cameron. My dad bought his log house and they moved it log by log down the hill and connected it to my dad's house there where my sister Laura and Billy Cohen lived later. From the look of it, George was a retired officer, and an engineer or something, because he worked on the creek up there at the hydraulic mine. He diverted that creek quite a few times, and that is Siwash Creek now. George ended up living with Dave Cameron and served as a butler to him. He cooked, cleaned and drove for Dave. He also looked after Dave's horses. It seems he did all the things a woman could do. So Mary Anne had it pretty easy. Anyway, I think George must have been a retired military man because he had a couple of the German helmets and a sword at his house. Then when Jimmy Cameron was about three or four I remember George getting him to march and turn and march back. Jimmy seemed to like it.*

Pete Marchand and Martin Wilson: *Francis Smith had his place down here at Siwash Creek. He had a barn and a team of bay horses that he used for farming and logging cordwood. Later he went to Chase to go logging. He lived with another Indian guy there in a cabin. One night he was walking to the store and he was hit by a truck and killed.*

SIMPSON / BORRIE / STRUTHERS

G. W. SIMPSON

ELIZA JANE

SARAH BORRIE

CHARLIE

ANNIE & GEORGE

GEORGE

CLARA

THOMAS B.

MARTHA & ALICE

SIMPSON / BORRIE / STRUTHERS

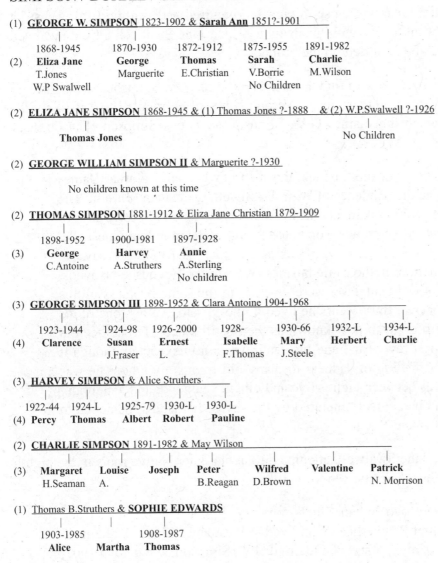

(1) **GEORGE W. SIMPSON** 1823-1902 & **Sarah Ann** 1851?-1901

1868-1945	1870-1930	1872-1912	1875-1955	1891-1982
(2) **Eliza Jane**	**George**	**Thomas**	**Sarah**	**Charlie**
T.Jones	Marguerite	E.Christian	V.Borrie	M.Wilson
W.P Swalwell			No Children	

(2) **ELIZA JANE SIMPSON** 1868-1945 & (1) Thomas Jones ?-1888 & (2) W.P.Swalwell ?-1926

Thomas Jones   No Children

(2) **GEORGE WILLIAM SIMPSON II** & Marguerite ?-1930

No children known at this time

(2) **THOMAS SIMPSON** 1881-1912 & Eliza Jane Christian 1879-1909

1898-1952	1900-1981	1897-1928
(3) **George**	**Harvey**	**Annie**
C.Antoine	A.Struthers	A.Sterling
		No children

(3) **GEORGE SIMPSON III** 1898-1952 & Clara Antoine 1904-1968

1923-1944	1924-98	1926-2000	1928-	1930-66	1932-L	1934-L
(4) **Clarence**	**Susan**	**Ernest**	**Isabelle**	**Mary**	**Herbert**	**Charlie**
	J.Fraser	L.	F.Thomas	J.Steele		

(3) **HARVEY SIMPSON** & Alice Struthers

1922-44	1924-L	1925-79	1930-L	1930-L
(4) **Percy**	**Thomas**	**Albert**	**Robert**	**Pauline**

(2) **CHARLIE SIMPSON** 1891-1982 & May Wilson

(3) **Margaret**	**Louise**	**Joseph**	**Peter**	**Wilfred**	**Valentine**	**Patrick**
H.Seaman	A.		B.Reagan	D.Brown		N. Morrison

(1) Thomas B.Struthers & **SOPHIE EDWARDS**

1903-1985		1908-1987
Alice	**Martha**	**Thomas**

The present Simpson family at Duck Lake Indian Reserve are fourth generation descendants of G.W. Simpson and his Aboriginal wife Sarah. Many have endeavoured to piece together a story of this mixed-blood family as a means of clarifying bloodlines, kinship ties and local history. As reference here, historians and interested parties such as Frank Buckland, Eliza Jane Swalwell, Mrs. Powley of Winfield and Mrs. Tutt of Kelowna and finally the Vernon Newspaper of 1902 have been consulted. Oral history is given through third generation Herb Simpson of Winfield and photographs supplied by Peter Simpson of Kelowna and Gail McAllister of Kamloops. It is a story worth putting together to be left as a legacy of the Simpson family.

George William Simpson was the son of a Presbyterian minister who immigrated to Philadelphia from Scotland. George was lured to the California gold fields and then north to British Columbia following a cattle herd owned by the Harper Brothers.[2] In 1868 his daughter Eliza Jane was born while he was managing the Haughton[3] Ranch in the Coldstream district near Vernon.[4] In 1870 he bought the Postill Ranch and the family moved there.[5] Later he bought

Frederick Brent's property at Okanagan Mission and was the first to introduce domestic cattle to the Okanagan Valley.[6] After amassing close to eighteen hundred acres in the Ellison district he sold to Price Ellison and went to live with his daughter Eliza Jane Swalwell on the Swalwell Ranch. He died there in 1902 and is buried on the property.[7]

Considerable research has been done to find the death record of G.W. Simpson, but apparently none could be found. However, an obituary in the Vernon News of February 1902, is likely the death record of the same person, but names G.W. Simpson as James Simpson. The obituary reads:

> "Death removed another of the old timers of this district when last Saturday, James Simpson passed away at the residence of W.m. Swallwell, Okanagan Mission. The deceased was a native of Wisconsin, and came to this province in the early days of the Cariboo excitement. At one time he operated a ferry at the mouth of Quesnelle, where at one time, he was credited with making as much as $3000 per day. He afterwards became a partner in the cattle business with Judge Haynes at Osoyoos, after which he and Colonel Haughton were together in the same business in this part of the district. For over thirty years he lived in the Mission valley, one of his farms there being the fine ranch now known as the Postill place. He had been in feeble health for the past few years, and his death was not unexpected, though it will cause a shock and feeling of sadness to many old friends by whom he was much esteemed. He was between eighty-five and ninety years old, and a naturally robust constitution had been much impaired by the severe hardships incidental to pioneer life in this province."[8]

The eldest daughter, Eliza Jane Swalwell, attempted to explain her Native roots in the eighth report of the Okanagan Historical Society Report in 1939.

> "At one time there were two Indian Chiefs, one was Enoch who lived at Duck Lake, and the other Chief Pantherhead who lived at Westbank. Chief Pantherhead had two sisters, one was my mother who married G.W. Simpson, and died in 1901, one year before my father. The other sister married a Frenchman named Boriot, who had a cattle ranch near Kamloops. He went on a visit to France, and while there was conscripted and killed in the Franco-Prussian war. His son, Victor Boriot, and his wife are now living on the Duck Lake Reserve. After her husband's death, my aunt came to live with her brother, Chief Pantherhead, and later she married Chief Enoch. These two chiefs, Pantherhead and Enoch, were highly respected by both Indians and whites."

> "I was born on the 14th of December, 1868, and married Thomas Jones on the 6th of April, 1884. He died on the 30th July, 1888. On the 10th of May, 1892, I married again, my second husband being William Pelissier Swalwell. He got his second name by being named after the French Marshal who commanded the French Army at the time of the Crimean war in 1854. This name was popular about the time he was born. My husband was a cousin to the Postill brothers. He died on the 14th of March, 1926."[9]

Eliza Jane's rendition of her Native roots clearly indicates that Sarah, her sister, and Victor Borrie were cousins. However they did not have children but were adoptive parents to Sarah's half-brother Charlie Simpson, her nephew George Simpson III as well as George's son Clarence Simpson.

Mrs. Powley added that in 1875 there was a considerable number of Indians on the Reserve, but after this date they gradually left for other reserves until only the highly respected Chief Enoch, Mr. And Mrs. Dave McDougall and family, and Mr. And Mrs. Victor Boriot, remained.[10]

George William Junior was forty-two when he married forty-year-old Marguerite, June 24, 1919. The records reveal that Simson and Sarah were his parents and their witnesses were Simon Paul and Susanne. There is no indication that they had children and no parents are listed for Marguerite. She was however from the area, for her place of birth and residence at the time of marriage was Head of the Lake.[11] Mary Jane Lawrence recalled the days when she and her mother Katherine Louis stopped at Duck Lake Reserve to visit Maggie Simpson and a family member indicated that after his mother's death Harold Williams was taken in by Maggie Simpson of Duck Lake.[12]

By most accounts, Thomas Simpson married Eliza Jane Christian. She was better known as just "Lizette" and according to sacramental records was the daughter of just "Julien."[13] Although Christian is a very familiar name in the early history of the valley, Lizette cannot be placed on any particular family tree.

Thomas and Lizette had three children-George III, Harvey and Annie. Evidently, after Lizette's death in 1909,[14] Thomas left the area for the Chase region. He died there of typhoid fever at age thirty-one, August 20, 1912.[15] A record of baptism shows George III was born at Okanagan Mission, February, 12, 1898 and was baptized March 12, 1899 at Vernon by Reverend Hartleib.[16] His god-parents are noted as Victor and Sarah Pare (Borrie). Seemingly after Lizette's death, Victor and Sarah adopted nine-year-old George. His brother, Harvey, married Alice Struthers. She was the daughter of Thomas B. Struthers and Okanagan woman Sophie Edward. Their sister, Annie, married Alfred Sterling of Merritt but died at an early age.[17]

Herbert Simpson: *My dad was George Simpson and he married my mother, Clara Antoine, a Shuswap from Chase. My mother's mother was a Celesta. Sarah and Victor Borrie from here at Duck Lake, adopted my dad when he was real small and they adopted my brother, Clarence, when he was born. I don't know who my dad's parents were, but I think it must have been that old Simpson that owned the Eldorado Ranch long time ago, just over there on the other side of Duck Lake. I called Victor and Sarah, Grampa and Gramma.*

When we were small we weren't allowed to stay in the house when other people came to visit. It would be really cold outside and we were told to get our coats on and go outside and play. Anyway, they talked Indian and we never did learn how to speak that language. My dad, though, always spoke English. I remember when Mom and old Harriet Robins got together, though, they would have a good old time talking their language. They'd sit and talk for hours and hours. If we asked what they were talking about, they'd say it was none of our business.

I remember when my dad used to race horses. He was a jockey, you know. He raced on the ranch over there. The Eldorado Ranch. Then he'd go to Vernon and Kamloops and all over, racing his horse Maudas. They called Dad Dutchy 'cause he was pretty small. Old Tommy Gregoire, when he sees me, always says, "You look just like Dutchy." Then he tells me about Maudas and Dad.

Dad did all kinds of work. He worked on the Eldorado Ranch putting up hay, and in the orchard, but he mostly logged. He worked for Dany Miller and Steve Bata, up here at Beaver Lake. Mom always went along with Dad as the cook. She'd take lunch up to those guys in the bush. She'd walk all the way up. There was hardly no thermoses in them days so she'd take coffee in Mason jars. Take it when it was warm and she'd know how long it would take her to get there and they'd have warm coffee. Mom always wore a tam and she went to church every Sunday. It wasn't till Dad died that she quit going. I guess she just gave up.

When we were small the priest came once a month and had Mass at Gramma's house. They had an altar that stayed there and they'd fix it up for Mass. Us kids stayed for catechism after church. I remember Father Murray and Father Collins and Father Scott. One time we were at catechism and my brother Charlie [Raymond] got up and left. He said, "I had enough," and walked out. The priest didn't know what to do. He just let him go. Charlie was just little then and I guess he did have enough. He used to say, "There's just too much singing!"

At present four major families still reside at Duck Lake. They are Raymond or Charlie Simpson, Herb Simpson and his children, Ranger Robins and his family and Clara Dubrett and her large family.

Struthers

The Struthers family tie into the Simpson family through the marriage of Harvey Simpson to Alice Struthers. Sophie Edwards, the fifteen-year-old sister to Elizabeth and Julianne Edwards, married twenty-seven-year-old Thomas B. Struthers on January 27, 1903 at the military parsonage in Vernon.[18] Witnesses to the marriage were Frank Gottfriedson and Dave Cameron. Sophie's parents are noted as just Edward and Mary. Her record of baptism and marriage agree that she was born in 1889.[19] Thomas Struthers was the son of William Struthers and Jessie Dick of Ontario. Sophie and Thomas had three children-Thomas, Alice and Martha. Thomas Junior and Christine Jack had two sons, Jack and Robert. Alice married Harvey Simpson and Martha died as a girl.

Ned Louis: *Tommy Jr. was born at Siwash Creek. His mother died when he was small and he was taken in and raised by Louie Bercie at Whiteman's Creek. There was twin cabins there on that ridge. That's where Bercie lived. This way a bit was a two-story log house that someone burned down. Tommy was at that twin cabin for a while and when them guys passed away he came and lived with them other guys at this end of the field. Joe Lawrence had the beach side of that property. Sookinchute was that ol' fella that lived at Whiteman's Creek. Ol' Tommy looked after him till he died and Tommy buried him. There was another ol' couple they looked after that died of ol' age. The names escape me now.*

Tommy was late in getting his pension because he couldn't find his birth certificate. Yet, he had it with him all the time, but couldn't find out what it said. One morning I was sittin' here eating cornmeal and along come Tommy, coming back from his daily walk up to the Six-Mile flat.

He told us that nobody could read his letter, so I took it and tried to read it then gave it to Irene. She looked at it for a time till I asked her, "Are you thinkin' what I'm thinkin'." She said, "Yeah." So I studied it again and then told Tommy, "This is all written in Okanagan." So Irene and I did the best we could and I asked Tommy a few questions and it was all there. He had his certificate all the time. It was written by a priest and later I got to thinking it might have been written by Father Le Jeune 'cause he could read and write lots of languages and even started [writing] the Chinook language.

Tommy used to walk every morning. He'd go up over to those three cabins that are still up there. George Smith had the cabin on the top of the hill. Ol' Tommy B. had his cabin on the side of the hill and Dave Cameron lived on the brow of the hill. They lived close to each other up there ever since they first met. That's how Siwash Creek and Blacktown got those English names.

Tommy B. had been away one time and when he got back Dave Cameron asked him where he was and he said Siwash Creek. Quite a bit later, that little place got that name. Then the same with Blacktown. Ol' Tommy B. named it that because of the black smoke caused from them people burning pitch in the winter. Those two names stuck and were started by ol' Tommy B.

I remember when us guys were working on the Westside Road. We were camped at that camp and huntin' park, just beyond Fintry. There was I and Ben, Dad, Frank Marchand, Antoine from Penticton and ol' Tommy B. Tommy was an awful guy for listenin'; he'd ignore every thing them guys told him. They told him to build a shelter to hide in when they were blastin' them big rocks at Nahun. He didn't listen though; said he didn't need a shelter. Anyway, there was a big rock there and they set the fuse and him and Dad run over there and laid down behind that rock. A big rock about six inches through blew up in the air and came down and hit ol' Tommy on the fleshy part of his behind. He yelled and bounced around like a jack-rabbit. Guess he learned that lesson hard, 'cause before they blasted again he dug a hole under that big rock and that was their shelter. He coulda got hit in the head and killed, instead though it hit him on the other end.

At the same place, Nahun, this big steamboat was comin' in at Conard's wharf where the old man had the store and his house. The boat used to come around that point to the wharf to pick up the mail and fruit from them orchards there. This time them guys were blowin' stumps and loaded it extra heavy with powder. Just as that boat come around the point the stump blew out and sailed through the air and just barely missed the smoke stack and splashed into the water at the rear of the boat with passengers and mail. It scared the hell outa us and them guys. If that stump woulda' hit that boat it woulda' sunk it. Somebody coulda' got killed. After that, was a different story; they started blowing their horn as they come in around that point.

Yeah, all them three guys, Tommy B., Dave Cameron and George Smith stayed together up there on the flat until they separated and died of old age. George Smith was the last one left up there and they took him to Vernon to the old age home where he died. He didn't live too long though after his friends died. Tommy Jr. finally got his pension and some back pay.

Robert Struthers: *My dad told me that when his mom was going to have him, she was walking down the hill from up the flat where they lived. Her mother who lived down at Siwash Creek was walking up the hill at the same time, as she knew Sophie was close to having the baby. Sophie's mother was half way up the hill when she saw that my dad was born under that big pine tree.*

STEELE

JOE (GAZE) STEELE

MARIA & WILLIAM STEELE

MARY STEELE

ALPHONSE & VIRGINIA CHARTREND, ELIZABETH STEELE, THOMAS JONES, MARIA
IRENE, FRED & NORMAN

VIVIAN, GLORIA, IRENE & NORMAN

STEELE

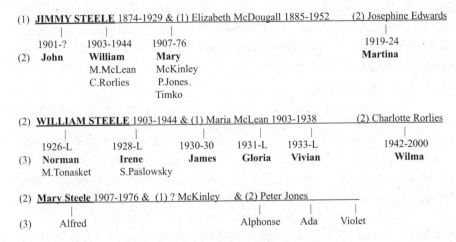

(1) **JIMMY STEELE** 1874-1929 & (1) Elizabeth McDougall 1885-1952   (2) Josephine Edwards

1901-?	1903-1944	1907-76		1919-24
(2) **John**	**William**	**Mary**		**Martina**
	M.McLean	McKinley		
	C.Rorlies	P.Jones		
		Timko		

(2) **WILLIAM STEELE** 1903-1944 & (1) Maria McLean 1903-1938   (2) Charlotte Rorlies

1926-L	1928-L	1930-30	1931-L	1933-L	1942-2000
(3) **Norman**	**Irene**	**James**	**Gloria**	**Vivian**	**Wilma**
M.Tonasket	S.Paslowsky				

(2) **Mary Steele** 1907-1976 & (1) ? McKinley   & (2) Peter Jones

(3)	Alfred		Alphonse	Ada	Violet

There are presently two versions of how the surname Steele came to be a family name of the Okanagan Band at Duck Lake. The first version is that Jimmy Steele was the son of Colonel Samuel Steele[2] of Fort Steele. The second version, told by Virginia Chartrend, aunt to William Steele, ties him in with the Steele family who founded the renowned Steele and Briggs Seed Company that is so well known in Canada. Relatives of the Company's founder R.C. Steele farmed at Hullcar, near Armstrong.[3] Neither connection has been proven, or verified, therefore leaves room here for the voice of present family.

Norman Steele: *My grandfather, Jimmy Steele, died when I was three years old. I don't know if I remember him or if I just remember seeing a picture of me with him sitting on a log by that log house at Deep Creek. In the picture though, I remember my grandfather had two white horses hooked up to the logs. He was in that picture with me. That land at Deep Creek would have been my inheritance, but after my grandfather Jimmy and grandmother Elizabeth Steele broke up, he got with Josephine Edwards and they had a daughter, Martina. She died and they said my grandfather signed that place over to Josephine. That's how she got that place. My grandfather is buried at Head of the Lake cemetery close by N'Kwala's grave.*

My dad told me that my great grandfather was Sam Steele, the Northwest Mounted Policeman from Fort Steele. He was one of those guys that abandoned his Indian family and went back to England. Indians to those Englishmen were just savages. My great grandmother, Mary, was from the Arrow Lakes and she had a sister, Ota, who lived in Incheleeum, Washington. My grandfather, James Steele, was Mary and Sam Steele's son. Jimmy Steele married my grandmother, Elizabeth McDougall, and my dad, William Steele, was born in 1903. My dad married my mother, Maria McLean. She was the daughter of Theresa Ashton. There were five of us kids born and my brother, James, died when he was a baby.

We lived on Coronation Avenue in Kelowna during the Depression. That house was still there up to only a few years ago. The last time we were there the house was gone. It had only three rooms, but we were happy there. My dad worked a trapline up at Belgo Dam. He was always away at camp. My mom was sickly. She was in the Kelowna hospital on the same floor as Gramma McDougall and your Gramma Emily. Them nurses in the hospital didn't even know that Great Gramma Theresa McDougall and Aunt Emily were mother and daughter until my mom told them.

I used to go in there with my dad and hide behind the curtains then sneak back in there to see my mom. My mom died in May 1938 and your gramma and Gramma McDougall died just two weeks apart from each other in July. I sure did love Gramma McDougall. She had lots of chickens, ducks and two milk cows, both named Bossy, at Winfield. She made her own butter and baked lots of cookies and cakes. Your gramma, Aunt Emily, was really quiet. I remember her well. What ever she was doing, she sang that song "Blue-eyed Jane."

I went to Kamloops school in 1936. There was Irene, I and Gloria. When Mom died in 1938. Tillie [Vivian] was three and a half. Dad was working on his trapline and Auntie Virginia and Uncle Happy said they would take her but for some reason they didn't and she came to Kamloops. She was still a baby and used to sleep with the nuns. They took care of her. When Mom was sick Aunt Mary would take care of her. I would stay with them when I come home from school. Mom was sickly and I remember she was one of first people to get a blood transfusion. It was a new kind of treatment for leukemia in those days. She died in my dad's arms in Kelowna hospital on January 13, 1938.

When my mom died I ran away from the school to go to the funeral. I hitch-hiked and these old people picked me up. They drove me to Gramma Teresa's, up there on O'Keefe Siding, and because they were from Winfield, they took me the rest of the way. They had Mom's wake at Gramma McDougall's. She is buried at that little cemetery at Winfield. The one up on the hill above that RV place. After the funeral, the Provincial cops came, and Dad said I had to go back and finish the year. If I didn't the cops would put him in jail. I finished that season and came back to live with my dad up at Steve Bata's, on Beaver Lake Road. My dad and I were cutting logs up there. My dad would say don't ride the saw, push and pull. I went to school from there at Ellison. I walked eight miles twice a day. I stayed with my dad till 1940 then he joined the Army and told me to stay with Gramma Steele. But he sent me to Cranbrook for one year, but I got sick and come home. That's when Father Collins took over Cranbrook. He knew all of the Okanagans. All the Terbaskets, the Allisons and the Squakins went to Cranbrook the same time. It was Father Collins who got us in there.

We used to go for walks to Fort Steele when I was there. One time they asked me if I was related to Sam Steele, but I didn't know and they never found out. The girls stayed at Kamloops until they quit. When they came back I was already in the Service.

I worked for the ranchers, Graham and Willis, in Keremeos. Me and my cousin, Alfred Jones, worked there for sixty-five dollars a month, room and board included. Those other guys, like my cousin, Alphonse, were getting only thirty dollars a month working for Tuddle at Keremeos that same time. I saved my money while I was working there. When I quit, Ernie Simpson, from Winfield came there and he and I started chasing around together and decided to join the Army. We signed up at Vernon when I was sixteen. I would have never got caught except this sergeant knew my dad and asked how I was related to Willie Steele. Like a fool I said he was my dad. Well, then they phoned the agency and said, "Don't call us, we'll call you."

After that Ernie stayed in Vernon and I caught the bus out to where Bill and Eileen Derickson were at Brewster, Washington. I was going to babysit for them while they worked in the dryer. While I was there I got two jobs. One was cooking in the restaurant and the other was working in a bakery. This lady who owned the restaurant showed me how to cook. So what I'd do was make up the cake batter at the restaurant and she'd take it and bake it in her oven at the bakery. She was real nice. She told me to stay with her. Her son came home from the Air Force and she told me to stay in the cabin she had out back. I did for a while. I worked for her, but I didn't have the freedom I wanted, so I left there and Bill Derickson signed for me to join the Army. I wanted to join the Air Force but I didn't have enough schooling. I should have told them I had Grade Nine because that is what you needed to join. In Canada, though, the education system is above the American, and I should have told them I had a higher education. I wrote to my dad and he wanted me to join the Cadets, but I signed up for the Navy and was accepted as a baker. That's what I did, and was sent out to the South Pacific.

I don't know how my dad got into the Army because he had only one kidney. He was in the Searchlight and Artillery in the Army. He got hurt and then they transferred him to logging in Scotland. He got hurt there and they sent him to Vancouver for an operation and his friend, a red-headed soldier, told me that they didn't strap him into his bed and he fell out and died. I got a bus ticket and went to stay with Lottie, my stepmother. Only Lottie [Charlotte], Aunt Mary and I and some soldiers were at his funeral.

Ned Louis: *Jimmy Steele lived at Duck Lake first. He married Elizabeth McDougall, the daughter of David and Theresa McDougall, there at Duck Lake. Then he moved to what we call Jimmy Steele Lake-a little lake up there on Goose Lake flat. He had a cabin up there and used to cut the meadow grass for feed for his cows. I don't know why he left there and came down to Deep Creek. Anyway, he bought that place and lived there for quite a while, then moved down to Whiteman's Creek. He died there.*

Ada Froehlich: *Mom told me that when she was little and lived at Duck Lake, her dad used to come down to Okanagan Landing to meet her. She would come up from Okanagan Centre or Kelowna by one of the lake boats and get off at the Landing. From there her dad would take her by horse and buggy up to Goose Lake range where he stayed. She said she would stay a while and her dad would take her back to the Landing to catch the boat home. I guess Gramma Elizabeth stayed at Duck Lake and Grampa Jimmy stayed up here at Vernon. Anyway, Mom said that her dad was putting up hay in the summer, it was really hot and felt like he was going to faint. So, he told his helper [Alec Antoine], a man from the Reserve, to go and get some water. When the man came back he saw Grampa passed out on the ground and threw the cold water in his face. Apparently what happened was the water sent him into shock and he died right there.*

The Steele surname vanishes from the Okanagan Band with Norman Steele. He now lives at Omak, Washington with his wife Millie Marchand. They had one daughter, Dee Dee, who died at aged sixteen. Through Mary Steele the paternal name reappears under the name Jones. Mary and Peter Jones had three children Alphonse, Ada and Violet.

Johnny

Julia Tonasket (Logan)
& grandson Pernell Marchand

Casimir

Tonasket Girls

John & Susan Tonasket

TONASKET

(1) **CHIEF JOSEPH TONASKET** & daughter of N'Kwala **Angeline?**
|

(2) **Baptiste**
Cecile

(2) **Tonasket & Angeline ?**
|
1871-1918/19
(3) **Johnny**
J.Logan / Dubrett

(3) **JOHNNY TONASKET** 1871-1918/19 (Choo-choo-pina) & **Julia Logan /Dubrett** 1890-1966

1912-82	1915-1929	?	?	1924-?
(4) **Casimir**	**Martin**	**Evangeline**	**Esther**	**Irene**
S.McDougall				

(4) **CASIMIR TONASKET** 1912-82 & Susan McDougall 1913-1981

L	L	L	L	1943-92	L	1947-95	1950-81	L	1951-98
(5) **Agnes**	**Eleanor**	**Evelyn**	**Gloria(Jane)**	**Carmelita**	**John**	**Willard**	**James**	**Pearl**	**Earl**

Tonasket is a surname that, according to Okanagan speakers, means "the sky is short of something."[2] Joseph Tonasket was not a Hereditary Chief, but a trustworthy individual put in charge of the south Okanagan by Chief N'Kwala. It was partly due to events in Tonasket's life, and his character, that he is remembered as Chief Tonasket. Maria Houghton Brent, James Teit, and Sister Ilma Raufer O.P. make it possible to form the following profile of Chief Tonasket. From Brent we find that after one of the Indian wars,

> "N'kwala found Tonasket an orphan. Tonasket would not go back to his own people. Old N'kwala saw good stuff in him and had him trained to be a chief. When he was old enough, Chief N'kwala married him to one of his daughters as N'kwala, though he had seventeen wives, had few sons to follow in line."[3]

After the Okanagan were divided by the boundary in 1846 Joseph Tonasket was recognized as Chief Tonasket. According to Brent, Chief N'Kwala felt the need to stay with the people of the northern portion and left Tonasket to help the people in the south. Thereafter he was recognized as Chief Tonasket by the Okanagan people of south of the border.[4] Others have information about how he gained recognition as Chief by the whites. According to James Teits' informant the story in shortened form here, went something like this.

It happened at McLaughlin Canyon just south of the American line in Okanagan territory in 1858. At that time there was unrest on both sides of the border. Some of the Okanagan were killed by miners, and in an effort to defend themselves and their land the Okanagan threatened war. Tonasket was in charge and when groups of white people came through the canyon Tonasket devised a way to stop them. He and his party of about twenty warriors built fires around a group of about one hundred and fifty whites and fired shots from behind the fires. Tonasket and some of his men rode down on the camp of the whites. The party thought they would be shot until, "Tonasket held his gun above his head and called out, 'Don't shoot, we are friends.'" He went on to say, "I am chief of all this country and I want you to recognize me by paying tribute for using and passing through this country." From that point on Tonasket accumulated many presents and was recognized by many of the whites as chief of the territory.[5]

Over the years, Chief Tonasket amassed large herds of cattle, sheep and horses. Raufer wrote that his "home ranch and wintering place was on the east side of the Okanagan River, directly across from where Oroville, Washington is today. This had been a gathering place of the Indians for horse races and games."[6] In 1884, he sold his property and moved his stock and family to Curlew, in the Kettle River region. Thereafter, he married Antoinette Somday, a widow with two children.[7]

Tonasket, Washington, south of Oroville, is named for Chief Tonasket. Said Raufer, Chief Tonasket "wanted progress in the civilization among the Indians" and "was in favour of opening the reservation, allotting lands in severalty, freer intercourse with the whites and more general adoption of their customs."[8] To make this happen he signed the Moses Agreement, and as a result of his request was given "a sawmill, gristmill, a boarding school for one hundred students, a resident doctor and one hundred dollars per year for himself."[9] According to Mourning Dove, "Shortly after the government built the school at Tonasket, Washington, it burned down. The sawmill and gristmill fell into ruin when the chief began to ignore them in favor of the beautiful Antoinette Somday."[10]

Tonasket was also much involved with Christianity through the Jesuit Order of Priests. First he donated land for a church at Schall-kees, which is now Ellisforde. It is situated between Tonasket and Oroville, Washington. Some still speak of the area as a prominent gathering place for the Okanagan. The church burned in 1910. Tonasket also desired to build a church at Curlew, for by that time he was old and handicapped. He said to the priest, "I kept away from the church these last eight years, but I couldn't help it; I am half blind and the Okanagan Church (St. Francis Regis Mission) is 50 miles distance."[11] Before the church was built, however, Tonasket went to Spokane for an eye operation. After the second operation failed he returned home to die. "The fathers received the news that the great chief had gone to his eternal reward while he was still forty-seven miles away from home."[12] Like Brent, this portion of the Tonasket family history is concluded with the inscription written on his gravestone. It reads:

> "Chief Joseph Tonasket 1822-1891. He proved himself a strong able leader, and although his was not an inherited chieftainship, he was officially recognized as Chief of the Okanogan Indians in about the year 1858. His whole life was a series of accomplishments for his people."[13]

Brent is also quite helpful with the Tonasket family relationships. However, if not for baptism records we would not know of the link between the southern and northern Tonasket family. Brent explained that Chief Tonasket's first wife, the daughter of Chief N'Kwala, was her mother and Millie Tonasket mother's aunt and the mother of Baptiste Tonasket of Republic Washington.[14]

She then added that Chief Tonasket's first wife died and was buried at Head of the Lake. She did not reveal Tonasket's wife's name or place of origin. The rest came through the baptism record of Johnny Tonasket. Father Pandosy baptized three-year-old "Jean" on February 4, 1871 at Immaculate Conception and recorded his parents as "Tonasket of the Okanagan" and "Domitille of the Grand Lake."[15] Another record names "Charles" Tonasket's parents as "Tonasket and Snemte-tkw."[16] It is not known what happened to Charles but Johnny Tonasket married Julia, the daughter of Mary Logan. They had several children, but most died very young. Johnny died about 1918. Mildred Steele, Julia's daughter, follows with her remembrances of her mother and siblings.

Millie Steele: *There were quite a few arranged marriages back in them days. My mom's marriage to Johnny Tonasket was one of those. She said she was only fifteen when they got married and for quite a while she would wrap herself tight in a blanket at night.*

My brother Martin was kicked in the chest by a milk cow and that left him with weak lungs. After that he got TB and couldn't fight it off. I only remember my brother Martin a little bit. It's like a dream now. Anyway, the time I do remember was when he tried to curl my hair. He'd put the curling iron in the coal oil lamp and when it was hot he used it to make curls. The iron was too hot and when he took it out, the hair was still on the curling iron. Boy, I cried, and he said, "I was just trying to make you look pretty." The other time I remember, Mom was covering him with white sheets.

My three sisters Evangeline, or Eva, Esther and Irene all died real close together. I think from a measles epidemic. Mom said they missed each other a lot and that's why they all died so close together.

Mom was a real good woman. She worked really hard in her lifetime. She used to go to the hop yards in Coldstream where the people picked hops. They'd finish the hops then they stayed on and would pick potatoes, carrots and turnips and stuff like that. Before they came back they would load up the wagons with vegetables and bring them back and store them in the root cellar. That way they had vegetables for the winter. When I was small all them ladies would pack up and go to Ellison, where the Kelowna Airport is now, and out to Lumby to pick potatoes. I'd stay with Aunt Annie or Aunt Rosie or Gramma Mary Logan while they were gone.

Lavina Lum: *Millie was scraggly when she was little. Her hair wasn't fixed and she used to wear women's socks. Her socks would be down past her shoes and she'd be draggin' them along behind her. Corrine's dad, Angus Oppenheimer would tease her. Oheecan. You know those Clydesdale horses! We used to go visit Aunt Julie and I'd be playin' with Millie and I'd tell my Mom, "Let's take Millie home." Mom would wash her hair and braid it like mine and we'd play and she'd sleep with me until pretty soon Aunt Julie would come and take her home. I'd get so sad.*

Millie and them lived across the creek, across the road, where ol' Brewer's barn was. There was a corral there where all the boys used to ride. That's where Julie lived. George Bessette built a house there and that house burned down. There was bushes all around there and just down below the road was a house built from boards. [The house of Julianne Logan, Julie Tonasket's grandmother]. That's where Julia was staying. She lived there part of the time, then she built that house down at Six-Mile Creek, where Eva lives now. Then, somehow, Nancy Gregoire got that property and that's where Nancy and Eva lived.

Casimir Tonasket married Susan McDougall. Susan's mother was Madeline Jack, the daughter of Pierresch and Angelique Jack. Her father, Urban, was the son of one of the first settlers of the Mission district at Kelowna. John McDougall was a Hudson's Bay employee and his wife, Melie, an Okanagan/Shuswap woman. Unfortunately, many of Casimir and Susan's sons have died in recent years leaving only a few to carry on the Tonasket name.

OLD WILLIAM

MARIA

WILLIE JOE ALBERT

WALTER

HAROLD

WILLIE WILLIAMS HOUSE

WILLIAMS

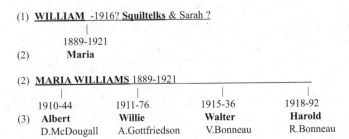

(1) **WILLIAM** -1916? **Squiltelks** & Sarah ?
     |
     1889-1921
(2) **Maria**

(2) **MARIA WILLIAMS** 1889-1921
  | | | |
 1910-44 1911-76 1915-36 1918-92
(3) **Albert** **Willie** **Walter** **Harold**
 D.McDougall A.Gottfriedson V.Bonneau R.Bonneau

Maria Williams died at thirty-two years old at Siwash Creek in 1921. She left behind her eldest, Albert, who was then ten, Willie nine, Walter five, and according to records, Harold was just two years old. Oral history remembers the boys were then raised by extended family. Albert retained his father Caprienne Saddleman's surname. Walter was adopted by Pierre and Katherine Louis which resulted in him sometimes being known as Walter Louis. Both Willie and Harold kept their mother's name. Willie went back and forth between extended family and Harold was taken in by George Simpson and his wife Maggie at Duck Lake.[2] There is some suggestion that Maggie was possibly a relative, perhaps even a sister, to Maria. After Harold was old enough Joe Abel took him from the Kamloops school and put him to work. After that, Willie and Harold "were kind of raised by their uncle Joe Abel."[3]

Although no absolute evidence can be found of Maria's heritage, Tommy Gregoire strongly suggested that she was the daughter of Sarah Simpson, the woman who left Doctor William and went to live at Duck Lake with the bachelor Victor Borrie.[4] If Tommy's suggestion is indeed correct, then it confirms oral history that Joe Abel was a close relative to the Williams' sons.

Doctor William or Old William, or say some Charlie Williams, lived at Whiteman's Creek at the time of the Royal Commission visit in 1913. In his comments made during the inquiry, he indicates he lived at Whiteman's Creek for a good deal of his life. In response to any cutoff, William said, "My irrigation ditch the roadman always fills it up when they fix the road, and this summer I was not able to raise any crop on account of it. My irrigation ditch was below the road the roadman had filled it up so that I was not able to get water this summer. I have had that ditch since thirty years ago."[5] The photograph to the left may not be the same William, however, it is included on the preceeding page only because it may be him. The photograph was taken at Shuswap Falls in 1934/35, by a school teacher who became concerned about his welfare. Apparently, he remained there after the conclusion of the salmon run and wanted the place to be his final resting place. This prompted the school teacher to call the authorities and he was returned to Whiteman's Creek.[6]

Remembering back to the war years, Tommy Gregoire told of the time when Albert enlisted for service overseas. He said Albert was concerned about his family's welfare as there was no work and he feared he could not support them. Tommy said he warned him that Indians were sent to the front lines first, but despite the warning, Albert enlisted. He was killed at age twenty-seven in WW II in Italy. Albert and Della Armstrong had four children. Della died April 7, 1969. Their son, Albert Jr., married twice and had five children. He was active on the band level, as

Councillor, then Chief from 1991-1992, and again from 1996-1998. He suffered a heart attack while gathering his cattle at Round Lake range in 1998. Maria married Lloyd Wilson and had five children. Lucy married Emery Louis and had five children. Josephine had three children.

Willie also enlisted for service in WW II but did not go overseas. On his return home he put his carpentry skills to work building homes for his family and later for others. Apparently he attained his skills while attending Kamloops Residential School. The photo included on page 218 depicts the remains of the house he built for his family on the east side of Okanagan Lake. Willie married Adeline Gottfriedsen and had three sons Dickie, Raymond and Ken. Dickie drowned in 1955. Raymond and Ken both leave descendants.

Raymond Williams: *We hardly knew our dad. It was Mom and Johnny that raised us. Johnny was pretty good to us and kept us with them most of the time. We all went to Kamloops School and I remember when Dad took us on the train to go there. I was just little, maybe about six years old. We got on the train here and I thought it was pretty good to be riding on the train with all those soldiers. When we got there we went to the dormitories and Dickie and I were split up. I was on one side and he was on the other. Some of them guys in my dormitory were a lot bigger and older than I was. I stayed there for two years the first time. But I don't remember them teaching me anything. I don't even remember having crayons or anything like that. I do remember, though, that we had to sing. Then they told us our parents were going to be there to see us sing. I went to the gym with the other kids, but I ran and sat with the other people so I could watch everything. The next day though I paid for it. That teacher, I think his name was Mr. Sands, got the strap and pounded and pounded on me. When you're little like I was, you never forget those things. I hated it there and I don't know what they did with me for those first two years. I sure didn't learn anything.*

After two years there I came back and Mom and Johnny were living at Salmon River. So I went to school there, and it was at that little school that I learned phonics. I picked it up real fast, and when I came to Six-Mile School, a year later, they moved me to Grade Three. I went there and graduated from Grade Seven, then I skipped a year and went back to Kamloops. During that year Dickie and I tried to farm across the lake. Tommy Armstrong and Angus Oppenheimer helped us to plow and plant the wheat. After it was threshed we stored the wheat by the Head of the Lake hall. We decided we would use it for seed the next spring. But our dad sold it. I don't know why he did that. Anyway, Dickie got mad and moved to Kamloops with Uncle Gus. Dickie was at Kamloops School for my graduation and drowned there in the Thompson River.

When we were small Mom took us with her down the States to thin and pick apples. I remember swimming in a pond there, and another kid from Colville was with us. I got out too far and that kid pulled me out. Then another time Dickie and I were swimming in the Similkameen River and Dickie saved me that time. Then when I got older and got a job as radio operator for the Ministry of Transport at Loran Station at Kyuquot. On the north end of Spring Island, I was out in a kayak. I was learning how to flip it over and back up. Anyway, I had flipped it and was under water when I couldn't flip it over. I knew I was in trouble and I tried kicking out of it. That was the first time I was going to pray. I said, "God if you really exist... Oh, oh, forget it... wrong choice of words." I kicked my way out of that.

My education took quite a few unexpected turns. First, I went to Kamloops School, then to Salmon River School, then on to Six-Mile until Grade Seven. After that, I went back to Kamloops for one year then tried to go to public school in town. There was my cousin Bertha, Walter's daughter, Vera and Leonard Marchand and Lloyd Wilson that caught a little bus into town. Speaking for myself, I bombed because I didn't know how to ask questions. Lloyd and I both quit and I tried to follow him down the States. But somehow I ended up in Vancouver, then decided to go back to Kamloops. It was there that I got involved in gymnastics and ball. So I thought that I should finish and come back later as a teacher. But after graduation I worked for three years on construction. Then went to Vancouver because I really wanted to be first an engineer, then, if I couldn't do that then my second choice was to be an electrician. I talked to those guys down there and they suggested that I should follow up my first choice as physical education teacher. So I went to UBC for one year. That was hard because I didn't know how to study and was on my own for the first time in my life. Vera and Leonard did okay but didn't go back after the first year. Then I told them I wanted to take up electricity. But I ended up in electronics class at King Edward Vocational School. And it was there that I got my radio operator certificate. I worked that first job at Kyuquot for two and a half years then moved onto the S.S. Stonetown weather ship at Terrace. I worked seven weeks on and five weeks off. During my time off, I ran into Dan Logan and we went down the States to thin apples. We were laid off though because the boss thought we were taking too many breaks. After that I went to Alert Bay, to the "World's Most Northerly Weather Station." I went in August of 1967 and came out in February of 1968. Something happened up there at that time and the boss told me I had to go to Toronto to headquarters. They were going to fire me for something I didn't do. So I went and stopped over at Ottawa to see Leonard. He was with the government then. We talked and I told him what I had to do. I asked him about taking my things back home for me. He said he would and I went to headquarters. At first I talked to a man who worked on the bottom floor of that building and I told him before he could fire me I would quit. And I told him to get in touch with Leonard, who worked at the House of Commons, to take my things home. I guess he didn't believe I had any connections to Leonard. Mind you who would! I had a full grown beard and was dressed in my arctic parka. I looked pretty wild. That guy didn't believe me, but then he called the big boss from upstairs. The guy came down and after hearing my story he took me upstairs and shook my hand, offered me a cigar and told me not to quit. He said, "You can have whatever job you want." So I took the Kamloops job working as radio operator at the airport.

Maria's third son, Walter, married Violet Bonneau and had one daughter, Bertha, before passing away in 1936. He was then just nineteen or twenty years old.

Harold, the youngest of Maria's children married Violet's sister, Rosie Bonneau. Their land at Siwash Creek was purchased from Rosie's sister-in-law Adeline Gottfriedson. Willie also built Harold and Rosie's house. They had a large family of ten children, nine boys and one girl.

CELINA MICHELE & GEORGE WILSON

HENRY

CELINA & GEORGE

EDDIE

ENOCH

WILSON

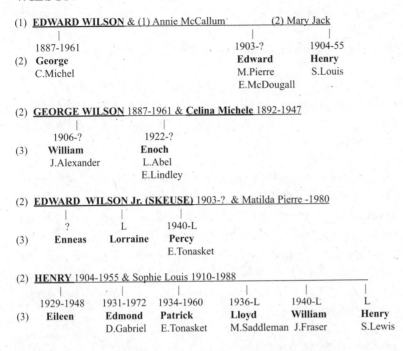

(1) **EDWARD WILSON** & (1) Annie McCallum   (2) Mary Jack

1887-1961	1903-? 1904-55
(2) **George**	**Edward** **Henry**
C.Michel	M.Pierre S.Louis
	E.McDougall

(2) **GEORGE WILSON** 1887-1961 & **Celina Michele** 1892-1947

1906-?	1922-?
(3) **William**	**Enoch**
J.Alexander	L.Abel
	E.Lindley

(2) **EDWARD WILSON Jr. (SKEUSE)** 1903-? & Matilda Pierre -1980

?	L	1940-L
(3) **Enneas**	**Lorraine**	**Percy**
		E.Tonasket

(2) **HENRY** 1904-1955 & Sophie Louis 1910-1988

1929-1948	1931-1972	1934-1960	1936-L	1940-L	L
(3) **Eileen**	**Edmond**	**Patrick**	**Lloyd**	**William**	**Henry**
	D.Gabriel	E.Tonasket	M.Saddleman	J.Fraser	S.Lewis

The Wilson family tree is formed from oral history. Some reference as to this family's origin is also noted in other sources such as sacramental records, the Indian Inquiry of 1952, and an interview conducted by Doctor Hugh Campbell-Brown of Vernon with Mrs. George Wilson before her death in 1947.

The baptism record of William Wilson of Westbank claims his parents are Ed Wilson and Marguerite[2] The record of marriage for George Wilson, nineteen, and Celina Michel, fourteen, married by Father Le Jeune on Christmas Day of 1906, reveals that George was the son of Edward Wilson and Annie.[3] Evidence given at the inquiry of 1954 gives Annie's maiden name as McCallum.

One family member indicated that he recalled being told that his grandfather went by the name of Dan Wilson and that is the reason why present Chief Dan Wilson has the same name. A thorough search of death records does not reveal a Dan Wilson living in the area. As names go, however, we have already learned that some individuals were known by various Christian names. Perhaps Dan Wilson was one of these. The following family information was collected by Doctor Campbell-Brown who attended Celina Lavina Wilson during an illness.

Celina Wilson said George was the son of a C.P.R. surveyor. His father, Edward, married two Indian women at different times. His first wife was of Thompson origin, and George was the son of that marriage. Then Wilson came down to the Okanagan and took an Okanagan woman (Mary Jack?) as his second wife. The present Wilsons on the reserve are their descendants.[4]

Ned Louis: *George Wilson's dad had a cabin up at Wilson Lake. That lake is straight across from the Cameron place, on the ridge. He homesteaded there.*

Mary Jane Lawrence: *Celina was the sister to Achtmis and Louis Michel of Westbank.*

Grace Wilson: *From what I heard, William got on the band here at Westbank because he married Julia Alexander, the daughter of the Chief, or something like that. When they got married the Chief gave them some property. That is why William is a band member, but his brother Enoch is not.*

Lawrence Wilson: *My grandfather, George Wilson, took me up to Enderby and showed me where he was born. He pointed to a place across the Shuswap River and said that is where he was born. I don't know who the parents of my grandmother were. All I remember is her name was Celina Lavina and she was a chief's daughter. I was only three when my gramma died. It's like a dream. She was there at the house and some women were fixing her up. Johnny Lawrence came with his truck and they put her in there. I don't know where they took her. It's like a dream. I remember Annie Logan was holding me. She had on buckskin gloves with fringes all the way up her arms. My gramma had a dress on that was made of buckskin.*

Ol' George worked as a fireman on one of those boats that ran on the lake. He said he didn't like it though. He wanted to get back in the mountains all the time. I don't remember the name of that boat. Course, he quit his job and went to the mountains. He was hunting all his life and logging and things like that.

Ol' George and Celina lived down Tommy Armstrong's place there for a long time, until they kicked them off the Reserve. Then he built that place up there above Whiteman's Creek. Willie Marchand and them guys were doing the fencing up there one time and said half that house was on the Reserve and the other half was off the Reserve. He said that's what you call a "half-breed" house!

The day ol' George died he was talking like you and me here and he went to have a drink of water. After that he went and sat on his bed and that was it. He keeled over! I threw a blanket over him and ran about three, four miles down the hill to Tommy Armstrong's place. Tommy was alive then and I told him what happened. I had quite a time to talk 'cause I had no wind by the time I got there. That's a long way to run when you're young! Tommy said, "We'll go to Johnny Alexis' place." So we did and ol' Johnny said, "Well, we'll go tell the police." We went to town and told the cops and they asked me a lot of questions and they just about throwed me in jail. Ol' Johnny got mad and said, "Gee, give him a chance; he's only a kid, can't you see?" They said, "Okay, we'll let him go but don't let him go no place." – Just like I was under suspicion of something! So we went back up there and they come with the ambulance and took him to town. They found out he had a tumour in his brain. That's what caused his heart attack. He went so fast.

You know he was happy, walkin' around there. He was goin' to get wood. I told him, well, I was goin' down to the Reserve. I used to go down Albert Saddleman's all the time, you know. I go down there and play all day then go home.

I was about fourteen when ol' George died. Then I went down and stayed at Armstrong's for about three years, before I ended up down the States. I come back to Six-Mile and worked for that sheep man Bill Palmer up there above Six-Mile for three years. Then I worked at Hoover's Sawmill. They had some trouble with the boys drinkin' until I started drinkin' and run into their gas pump. I come down there on Monday mornin' to get gas. He said, "You can't have any gas. You broke the pump! You broke the pump!" I run into it when I was drunk on that Friday night, I guess. That's what they tol' me anyway.

Eddie Wilson married Matilda Pierre, August 21, 1922. Eddie later married Elsie McDougall. Their wedding at Six-Mile Creek was a big celebration that included many band members. Henry Wilson was born in 1904 and married Sophie Louis September 21, 1925.

Lloyd Wilson: *My dad and Johnny Alexis were best friends. They worked together logging and they built that little dam and the irrigation ditch that ran on the sidehill down to where the Alexis' had those vegetable gardens. Before that my day had a trapline back in towards Pinaus Lake. When he walked out he put his traps in a tree and left them there. Other than that, he logged with Johnny Alexis, up there above Siwash Creek, and helped Johnny and them others build the little dam above our house. Then they flumed the water alongside the hill where it was too steep to ditch it. Then ditched it down to the Alexis'. My brother Ed and Johnny, and his boys, all worked on that ditch. That was quite a feat for them guys in those days. They didn't have any instruments or anything. That was my dad's engineering. He was a perfectionist, a real task master, and sometimes I guess you could call him a frustrated engineer.*

My dad worked with Johnny up at Cougar Camp. Johnny had a logging show up there for Simpson. My brother Ed worked up there too with my dad. They worked for a logger named Tommy Williamson. He was a contractor for Simpson. Other guys will remember Williamson too. Quite a few guys worked for him.

When I was real small we lived across the lake. My dad traded his properties here at Six-Mile with Louie Marchand, but that house was too far away from school. I was staying with my grampa, Pierre Louis, and Gramma Katherine and going to school from there. I remember one spring when I was about seven years old, about 1943 or 1944, I ran away from school when the ice was breaking up in the spring. I was lonesome for my mother. She was at the house across the lake. I walked all the way from Six-Mile to about Hoover's sawmill and I was going to cross over on the ice. I hit this crack in the ice and it was about six feet wide. I was going to jump across, but I remember I was looking at it and I was trying to get up the guts to jump, but chickened out and walked back south until I was across from Wilfred Bonneau's place before I could get across. So I guess they figured they better get a place on that side by the school. But that time they didn't send me back. So I wasted that year and the following year they sent me to Kamloops.

My sister Eileen was the oldest. She was still a teenager when she died. She had polio, and was weak, then got TB, but died of pneumonia. She spent some time at Coquleetza. We were living at Siwash Creek when she died. That time I ran away, I came over there and was scared to go inside. I got her attention and got her to come out. Of course, she went in and stole me some bread and peanut butter and brought it out so I could eat. Finally, they caught on she wasn't eating all that herself.

My dad had TB too, and he went quite a few times to Coquleetza. Every time he'd get a start on something, to get a business going for himself, he'd get TB and wind up back at Coquleetza for two or three more years. I remember he started a business. He had pure-bred stock. That was quite a thing around here. He made a deal with a guy they called Smally who lived in town and supplied my dad with papered stock. He was starting to raise them out here. He had quite a few at Six-Mile. He was just getting well enough to pay everything off and he got TB again and went back to the coast. Soon as Smally heard that he was sick, he came right out and seized everything. After that he was worse off than ever. My dad would just disappear and we'd have to survive one way or another.

My earlier years, when Mom and Dad would go apple picking, I stayed with my grampa. Just him and I all alone at home. Everybody else was gone. When I was old enough I went with my mom and dad to Oroville to pick apples; whole families went. They worked seven days a week. They logged here in the spring and went to the States in the fall. Dad was a night watchman at Laraby's and Mom and us boys picked apples. All our wages were pooled together and that's how we made it through the following winter. Apple harvest was big business for those people down there. They sent buses to Vanderhoof and brought bus-loads of people to Oroville at picking time. They would drive them back home after apple harvest was over. That was before the Mexicans started coming in.

Dad had cows across the lake and even when we moved to Six-Mile he still kept some across the lake. When we moved, he traded some cows to Harold Williams for that house at Siwash Creek. The house had four rooms and he built the lean-to kitchen onto it.

My mother worked hard all her life. I remember, when I was a kid and my dad must have been at Coquleetza. I don't know where Pat and Ed were, maybe in Kamloops school. My mom and I cut wood on that flat above the house at Siwash Creek. We'd go up there with just an axe, a crosscut saw and a sledge hammer and a wedge. Mom would pick out the small fir, the ones that had the least limbs and she'd cut them down, cut them up in four foot lengths and I'd limb, split and stack them. We worked all week and Basaraba would come from town to pick up a load. So we got a full load; five cords in one week. I remember we caught a truck to town and Mom bought groceries. I don't know how we got home. We did that all winter. That is how we survived. No one else was there. Dad and Eileen were probably at Coquleetza and William, if he was there, was probably at Grampa and Gramma's.

Mom taught us the difference between right and wrong. Sometimes she'd have to back up her word with a switch. I remember one time William and I went to Whiteman's Creek. We knew we couldn't stay away too long, but we did and we knew we were going to get a whippin'. We saw the old stove outside and stuck the lids down in our pants. We came to the door and Mom got her switch. Clang! She just looked funny and suddenly figured out what we were doing and started to laugh. That was the end of that, we didn't get a whippin'. She laughed and laughed. Sometimes she got over protective. But I guess she was the hub for everybody around her. That's where home was for everybody. Even if you had your own home, that was still home. You always knew you were welcome.

In 1945, they sent me, Ed and Pat to Kamloops school. You know a funny thing happened to me then. You know I used to have comic books and just look at the pictures. I couldn't read. And I was on the truck heading to Kamloops, and all of a sudden, I could read. I don't know, I guess when I was going to school for that little bit of time and learned my ABC's, I guess it got through 'cause all of a sudden I could read. So when I got to Kamloops, I hadn't even finished Grade One, they asked me what grade I was in and I said I was in Grade Two. They said you can't be in Grade Two, you're too young. I said, sure I'm in Grade Two. So they tested me and put me in Grade Two.

After that year they never sent me back. My mother took one look at me and starting crying 'cause I was so skinny. There are pictures of me when I went up there. I was nice and chubby, but when I came back I was skinny as a rail. Then, there was no school for three years. They didn't have a teacher, I guess. Then after the fourth year Sister Patrica came. If I have any good memories of the Catholic religion it is my memories of her. She took me from Grade Three to Grade Nine in two years. Then I went back to Kamloops because you couldn't go to high school in town. Indians weren't allowed. I finished Grade Nine and Ten there, and after that year they started allowing us to go to town. Leonard Marchand and I were the first to go to school in town. We boarded in town and we went for Grade Eleven and Twelve. But, when we got to the school they took one look at us, and because we were Indians, stuck us in Industrial Arts. They trained you not to own a business, but to run the tractor for the guys that had the business. I skipped school a lot. I'd get to the school and get off the bus and go down to the pool hall. I'd spend all day there. But I got through Grade Eleven and was recommended to Grade Twelve. I left in the second semester of Grade Twelve and went to the States.

My dad died in '55. We were at home around Christmas. He'd been working up until that time at Laraby's as night watchman. We were all working in the same place. William and I picked apples until it was over. Mom was packing. We came back and were all at home. It was Sunday morning and the snow was about a foot deep on the roof. My dad told me to go shovel the roof off. I can't remember what it was, but I had to go to Six-Mile, so I told him, I'll shovel the roof off when I get back. I came back in not too long and he'd been up there and shovelled it off. He was impatient. When something had to be done he wanted it down now. He got pneumonia. So it was the usual, the inferior Indian deal. He went to town to the doctor's office. Doctor Salow had his office across the street from Nolan's Drug Store. One side of his office was street level and for white people. You turned and went down the stairs and that's where the Indians went. We'd have to wait until he was finished with the white people before he'd have time for us. That's the way it was. That day I went with my dad in the pickup he had bought from that years work down the States. He was pretty sick. We went in, went down the stairs, and sat down until the doctor finally came down. He grunted and asked my dad "What's wrong with you?" and handed him some sulfur tablets. That was the standard treatment for Indians. They gave you sulfur tablets. He said, take them and sent us home. I brought my dad back in the next morning by ambulance and he died a couple hours later in the hospital. He died of pneumonia. We buried him at Head of the Lake cemetery.

PROFILES

Tim Alexis is the son of Johnny and Ella Cameron Alexis. Tim married Mabel Louis, the daughter of Ned and Irene Louis. Their seven children were raised on the family farm south of Siwash Creek. Tim retired from Riverside Forest Products in 1999, but keeps busy with his ranch and with the band council. Hank Alexis is Tim's brother and very handy with a guitar.

Victor Antoine the son of Alex Antoine and Mary Abel, is a fluent speaker of the Okanagan language. He was raised by his grandparents Jimmy Antoine and Mariette Gregoire. Victor has been called upon to teach the Okanagan language at public schools and on-reserve. He was also active in band affairs in the mid-seventies when the Indian Affairs office was put under pressure to give control back to the Okanagan Band. He married Wendy Eckert and has three children and three grandchildren.

Hilda Belanger and **Louie Fred** are children of Mary Abel and Edward Fred. Their enthusiastic and valuable contribution of community photos and their mother's community death journal makes this book explode with profiles as well as provide the means for confirmation of death dates. Hilda and her husband, Marcel Belanger, had three children. Marcel Jr. was tragically killed by a drunk driver in 1995. Louie also has several children. While Hilda lives at the home estate at Blacktown on Okanagan Lake. Louie lives on the home place at Bradley Creek.

Gladys Bonneau (nee Simla) born 1922, is the daughter of Alex and Rosie Simla. Gladys grew up at Rope Ranch and after she married, moved across the lake with her husband Wilfred Bonneau. Later, they moved to Six-Mile Creek. Gladys is a fluent Okanagan speaker and takes a keen interest in preserving the language.

Riley Brewer was born April 29, 1921. He is the son of past Chief Ernest Brewer and Emily Jacko. He attended the Kamloops Indian Residential School and later the Six-Mile Creek School. He is a fluent speaker of the Okanagan language. Riley married Sally Louis March 4, 1940. They make their home at Salmon River.

Lucy Brett (nee Cameron) married George Brett June 21, 1947. They have five children and several grandchildren, as well as one great grandchild. Lucy attended school first at Six Mile Creek and the brick school at Polson Park and at Vancouver. She worked at the Anderson Ranch and the Vernon Jubilee Hospital, cooking and cleaning. Lucy and George remain in Vernon.

William Brewer, born 1926, is a brother to Riley. He is also a fluent Okanagan speaker. He married school teacher Peggy Greene and has five children. Peggy is the last school teacher who taught at Six-Mile Creek School. She presently serves the Inkamuplux Elders' Society as President and has been a willing volunteer at various functions with the Roman Catholic Church and in the community.

Clara Dubrett was born January 13, 1933. She married Abraham Dubrett September 8, 1952. After their marriage, Clara and Abraham moved to Duck Lake where they raised a large family. Clara is a fluent Okanagan speaker and takes a keen interest in the preservation of the language. She was raised by her mother, Ella Antoine, and stepfather, Charlie Lezard, at Six-Mile Creek/ Blacktown area. When her mother died, Clara and her brothers, Basil and Austa, took care of the younger children. Clara remembers the days when local women acted as midwives and women worked in the local Chinese gardens. She too, remains a valued member of the Inkamuplux Elder's Society.

Mary Ann Eli is the daughter of Maggie Bessette and Peter Jones. She was raised at Penticton and went to school at Kamloops Indian Residential School. She is a fluent speaker and has acted as interpreter in band affairs. She was employed as telephone operator in her early years. Mary married Alex Eli, the son of Antoine Eli and Mary Shwartz of Westbank, and had four children. Her many memories about certain ancestors are valuable to this project.

Zena Eli is a specialized source of family history at Westbank. Her research of family lines and history has served to sort family names and kinship lines for use in this book. She is the granddaughter of Alex and Helene Marchand, and the daughter of Marjorie Marchand and Lloyd Eli. Zena has conducted extensive research in the Marchand and Louis family lines. Her contribution to this project is greatly appreciated.

Edward Fred was born December 2, 1921, at Chapperon Lake. He was a fluent Okanagan speaker and shared much of his knowledge of traditional and transitional life for purposes here. After the death of his father, he and his sisters were brought to Six-Mile Creek by his grandmother Achtmis Michele and step grandfather Johnny Andrew. Edward attended Six-Mile Creek School and served as driver mechanic in WW II. He died of cancer in 1999. Edward and Mary Abel had two children, Hilda and Louie.

Edna Gregoire, daughter of Edith Harris and Christie Parker, was born August 30, 1923. She married David Gregoire in 1944 and made their home at O'Keefe Siding on Highway 97. Edna was honoured with the Mother of the Year Award in 1993. Edna is also a loyal member of the Roman Catholic Church. Edna says she picked up the language from her husband David. Edna is a member of the Inkamuplux Elders' Society and enjoys getting out in the community. Her husband Dave died in 1995.

Tommy Gregoire is the son of Millie Paul of Penticton and Francois Gregoire. He lived to be close to one hundred years old. His knowledge of place and people names as well as general knowledge of band affairs and political processes made him a valuable mentor in different situations. He was also sought after for his knowledge of the Okanagan language. Tommy passed away in 1999. He and his wife Mary Cameron had several children.

Rosie Jack was born to parents Alice Gregoire and Pierre Jack. She is a fluent Okanagan speaker. She never had children. She and her nephew, Terry Jack, live at Six-Mile Creek on the home ranch. Rosie's memories are helpful to any project because of her cultural knowledge and experience. Terry, too, is one of the youngest speakers of the Okanagan language.

Eva Lawrence is a good example of an Okanagan student who learned to speak English at the Six-Mile Day School. Her stories are comparable to others who learned in the same way. She is the daughter of Johnny Oppenheimer and Edith Nicholas, but was raised by her mother's cousin Nancy Gregoire and Nancy's mother Sqwnim-te-nalqs. Her stories of growing up in hard times are told with care and humour. She married Okanagan Band member William Lawrence, and they have six children. Their eldest son, David, is an RCMP Constable and currently works on the Okanagan Reserve at Vernon.

Mary Jane Lawrence (nee Louis) born 1919, is a sister to Ned and Ben Louis. Mary Jane continues to reside at Whiteman's Creek where she and her husband Joe Lawrence raised a large family. Mary Jane is active in the Roman Catholic Church. Her knowledge of social history, family lineage and traditional place and people names continue to be of value to this work.

Carol Louie married John Louie the son of William and Esther Louie. At present they live at Irish Creek, across the way from John's family. Carol's memories of her maternal grandmother, Theresa Ashton, help to form a more extensive family history from the view of the more contemporary voice.

Esther Louie is a prime example of a traditional women in transition. She married William Louie at the tender age of thirteen and came to Head of the Lake from her home in Summerland. Esther and William had several children. William died in 1997, and Esther now resides at Gateby Care Facility in Vernon. She is now in her eighties. Esther graciously participated in the writing and compilation of the Louie family history. Esther died in February of 2002.

Ned Louis was born in 1912 to Catherine (nee Haynes) and Pierre Louis. He was raised partly across the lake and still resides at Six-Mile Creek. He is a fluent Okanagan speaker. It has been his dream to see the traditional places preserved with signage. He is a past band councillor and travelled extensively, driving his father Chief Pierre Louis to meetings and gatherings of the North American Indian Brotherhood and related events. One major highlight in his life is travelling to Europe and to Fort Smith in the Yukon for the Pope's visit. Ned's participation in the compilation of this book is highly valued. Ned married Irene, nee McDougall, and has thirteen children. Irene passed away in 1992. Ned passed away in October 2002.

Rose Louis was born April 29, 1915. She is the only remaining child of Emma McDonald and Frank Gottfriedson/Gottfriedsen. Rose married Ben Louis June 26, 1933. Rose and Ben made their permanent home at Six-Mile Creek and had fifteen children. Though not a fluent speaker, Rose understands the basics of the Okanagan language. She attended both the Anglican Residential School at Lytton and the Roman Catholic Residential School at Kamloops. Throughout her life she was active in the Homemaker's Club, the North American Indian Brotherhood, Inkamuplux Elders' Society and other interest groups. Ben Louis died in 1995, but not before leaving many stories and place names on record.

Lavina Lum (nee McDougall) was born in a tent in 1916, at Okanagan Landing. She was raised by her uncle Billy Swalwell and his wife Annie, nee Dubrett, in the area around Deep Creek. Lavina's biological parents are Theresa Adamson and Ned McDougall, two mixed-blood descendants of Okanagan origin. Lavina's many stories are important as she reveals details and locations of the past era. Being that her first language is Okanagan her words and nuances provide a human element possibly omitted if written in proper English grammar. Lavina is one of the first women who left to seek life outside the Reserve system. She now resides in Omak, Washington.

Corinne Marchand's (nee Oppenheimer) roots lead back to Marcus Washington on her paternal side and to Okanagan grandparents Charlie Edwards and Theresa Ashton of the Okanagan Reserve. Corinne's life experiences speak clearly of a child growing up during the time of the Residential and Day School years as well as a young woman who underwent the transition from the Okanagan language to English. She is a fluent Okanagan speaker who draws on her traditional roots and lifestyle from her aunt, Lavina Lum. Her constant support towards this project is a valued component that is greatly appreciated. She presently lives at Round Lake. She married Carey Marchand and has a large family.

Jenny Marchand is a sister to Riley and William Brewer. She was born April 2, 1918 and married Louie Marchand January 27, 1936. Jenny's first language is Okanagan. She learned English while attending Kamloops Indian Residential School. Jenny lives at Coyote Creek ranch near Irish Creek. She has a good understanding of sites and places, as she remained directly involved with family Elders. Jenny passed away in January 2002.

Leonard Marchand is the son of Joseph Marchand and Agnes Robinson. He was one of the first Okanagan students from this area to graduate from high school and further his education at the post-secondary level. His education led him into the agricultural field then into the Senate of Canada. He has just published a book entitled *Breaking Trail* which includes his family history as well as his professional life in the Senate. Leonard's enthusiasm and encouragement has helped toward the completion of this book.

Louisa Isaac, John, Ralph, Michael and **Arthur Marchand** are children of Alex and Helene Marchand. Other than John and Ralph the siblings live in the Salmon River/Round Lake community. John lives at Irish Creek and Ralph at Six-Mile Creek. Louisa, John and Arthur regularly attend the Inkamuplux weekly luncheons at Six-Mile Creek. Louisa makes it known that she is a willing participant in the annual Sadie's Walk for diabetes. She and her wheelchair can be seen trucking along Westside Road on their way to Parker Cove on Good Friday. She married Dick Isaac and has several sons. John married Marguerite Bessette and has three sons. John's story can be seen in the military section while Ralph speaks of his younger years and his relationship with people of other reserves and with his father, Alex. Michael is soft spoken and speaks of his involvement with the Reserve community. He has quite a collection of photographs taken himself at the weekly luncheons. Arthur is a good storyteller and remains youthful-looking like his father Alex.

Marguerite Marchand is the daughter of Rosie Duprett and George Bessette. When Marguerite was just an infant her mother Rosie died and she was then raised by her maternal aunt Annie and her husband, Billy Swalwell. She lives with her husband John at Irish Creek. They have three children. Marguerite is a fluent speaker of the Okanagan language and enjoys being a grandmother. She takes keen interest in the Inkamupalux Elders' Society.

Peter Marchand was born July 1, 1923 at Six-Mile Creek. He is the son of Victoria Marchand and Joe Abel, but his stories involving his grandparents, Frank and Christine Marchand, are a fitting contribution to this book. He spent a number of years at Coquleetza Tuberculosis Sanitarium when he was a young man. Pete is a fluent speaker and a valuable source of early school days' experience and reserve life at Six-Mile Creek where he still resides. Pete is a thoughtful and kind man. He has two sons, Gordon and Bert.

Rosie Marchand was born to parents Mary Abel and Charlie Bessette. She speaks fluent Okanagan and is the epitome of an Okanagan woman who stresses the importance of preserving Okanagan culture through language. Rosie attended school first at Six-Mile Creek then at Irish Creek. She married Ralph, the son of Frank Marchand and Susan Nicholas. After her children came of age Rosie returned to classes at Okanagan College. It is obvious that her children and grandchildren are her greatest joy.

David Parker was born February 28, 1915 to Cecelia McDougall and Charlie Parker. He was a fluent Okanagan speaker and teacher of the language. In past years he has shared his knowledge of the language with the Six-Mile Creek pre-school and on most occasions with local band members. He was an active member of the Friendship Centre, Aboriginal Disability Association and Alcoholic Anonymous. David's contribution to this book lends vital information to his family lineage as well as the white community outside the Reserve. He passed away on his birthday February 28, 2000. He leaves five children.

Isaac Parker is a brother to Edna Gregoire. He lives at Oroville, Washington. As acting keeper of the Harris and Parker records, he is an important source of family lineage and stories. Isaac offered the photograph of his grandmother Christine O'Keefe Harris. Also of importance is the birth, death and marriage records that Isaac holds. His co-operation in this project has verified family claims to their past history as well provides a window to the past.

Shirley Paul is the daughter of Mary Paul. She teaches the Okanagan language at Sn-c-ca-malatn Kindergarten and Day Care at Blacktown. She considers herself fortunate to remember her grandmother Catherine and appreciates the teachings of her mother Mary. I am grateful to her contributions of family history and photographs have proved valuable. Shirley has three children and lives at Head of the Lake.

Ranger Robins is the son of Johnny Robins and Harriet, nee McDougall. Ranger is a real storyteller. His detailed reflections included in the Robins' history highlights the life of his father Johnny. Ranger is a band member at Duck Lake, a fluent Okanagan speaker and a dedicated father of three children. He presently works at SIR homes at Winfield.

Herb Simpson also represents life at Duck Lake. Although he could not help with his family roots his story of early life at Duck Lake exemplifies a small community's struggle to exist within the wider world. Herb has spent most of his life working in the fruit, logging and construction industries around Winfield. Herb grew up at the time when the Okanagan language was shunned by outside institutions and therefore learned only to speak English. His father is George Simpson and his mother Clara Antoine from the Chase area.

Jon Spotted Eagle was born Jack Bonneau after his great grandfather of the same name. He is a valued genealogist who specializes in Okanagan heritage. His parents are Adeline, nee Gottfriedsen, and Johnny Bonneau.

Mildred Steele is the daughter of Joe Marchand and Julia Dubrett (Logan). Millie married Norman Steele and now lives at Omak, Washington. Anyone that knows Millie appreciates her good sense of humour and lively stories. She presently works as part of a team of fluent speakers at Omak, Washington, translating, writing and thus preserving the language. She is also known and appreciated for her wonderful voice. Her rendition of "Amazing Grace" presented in the Okanagan language is reminiscent of the early years when hymns were a large part of the Oblate presence.

Norman Steele was born to William Steele and Maria McLean. Like Millie, Norman has the gift for contemporary storytelling. His stories of his time in the US Navy and his lifetime adventures are told with humour. making all his stories lively. He prides himself on the great love and care he has for his grand and great grandchildren. Many of his stories are centered around "his kids" and their adventures.

Tom Tronson is the son of Harry and Ida Tronson. Tom is a prime example of a mixed-blood individual who grew up in the white community. His memory of school days and family history is valuable in this context. He worked all his life in the logging industry. He now lives at Westbank with his wife Edith (nee McDougall.) They have several children.

Raymond Williams, born December 15, 1935 is the son of Willie Williams and Adeline Gottfriedson. Raymond attended Kamloops Indian Residential School at Kamloops as well as the Day School at Six-Mile Creek and later public school in Vernon. Still later he attended the University of British Columbia and Technical School. His story is included in the education chapter and in the Williams family history. He now lives at Head of the Lake with his daughter and three grandsons and continues his education at Pathfinders School at Six-Mile Creek.

Perry Joe Williams is the son of Susan Joe. Perry spent many years with his grandmother, Mary Louise Alexander and her husband Speed Powers. He speaks the language well and his educational skills in research have benefited many. Perry currently lives at Penticton.

Rosie Williams and **Violet Marchand** are daughters of Jimmy and Sarah Bonneau. Rosie married Harold Williams and has numerous children. Violet first married Walter Williams and after he died married Willie Marchand. She, too, has a large family. Both speak fluent Okanagan and live in the Six-Mile/Siwash Creek area.

Lawrence Wilson is the grandson of George Wilson and Celina Michele. He was raised by his grandparents on the fringe of the Reserve at Whiteman's Creek. His parents are Enoch Wilson and Ida Abel, the daughter of Donald Abel. Lawrence never married and lives at Westbank.

Lloyd Wilson is the son of Sophie (nee Louis) and Henry Wilson. He married Maria Saddleman and has five children. Lloyd was involved with band administration and affairs during the last two decades. He recalls the details of life with his father Henry in the Wilson family history. More research needs to done to complete this family's history.

Martin Wilson is a fluent Okanagan speaker who has been called upon quite often to settle matters of language and expression. His willingness to participate in language projects on a casual basis is greatly appreciated. In many ways Martin is a traditional man. He lives by the teachings of his grandparents, Narcisse Pierre and Therese. His one regret is that he never had children to pass down the stories told to him by his Elders. Martin remains a bachelor and lives at Six-Mile Creek/Blacktown area.

BIBLIOGRAPHY

Family trees and history are made up of various records and are seen in the bibliography as:

Public Archives of Canada (PAC)

Provincial Archives of British Columbia, Provincial Board of Health, Division of Vital Statistics on Microfilm (PABC Marriage Reel #) (PABC Death Reel #)

Department of Indian Affairs Census of Okanagan Indians (DIA 1920-46)

Fr. J.M Baudre of the Order of Mary Immaculate Census of Okanagan Indians, 1877 (Baudre 1877)

Oblate of the Order of Mary Immaculate Archives Nelson, Kamloops and Vancouver (Roman Catholic Church Records)

Okanagan Historical Society Report (OHS)

Okanagan Indian Band Cemetery List (OKIB Cemetery List)

OKANAGAN HISTORY

1. Teit, James. 1918, *Mythology of the Thompson Indians, Memoirs of the American Museum of Natural History,* Whole Series, Vol.12, Part 2, *Publications of the Jesup North Pacific Expedition*, Vol.8, Part 2, New York, pp.199-416

2. Baker, James. 1990, "Archaeological Research Concerning the Origins of the Okanagan People," *Okanagan Sources*, Theytus Books, Penticton, p.10.

3. Armstrong, Derickson, Maracle & Young-Ing. 1993/94, *We Get Our Living Like Milk From the Land*, Theytus Books, Penticton, p.10.

4. Teit. 1927, p.267.

5. Brent, Maria Houghton. 1966, "Indian Lore," *Okanagan Historical Society Report 20*, p.112.

6. Todd, John. *Trading Experiences on the Thompson River 1841-1843, Journal by John Todd*, Legislative Library of Victoria.

7. Brent, Maria Houghton. 1966, p.108.

8. Mourning Dove. 1990, *MOURNING DOVE: A Salishan Autobiography*, Ed. Jay Miller, University of Nebraska Press.

9. Ibid., p.51.

10. Ibid., p.35.

11. Armstrong, Derickson, Maracle & Young-Ing, 1993/94, *We Get Our Living Like Milk From the Land*, p.27.

12. Webber, Jean. 1993, "Fur Trading Posts in the Okanagan and Similkameen," *OHS 57*, pp.6-33.

13. Buckland, F.M. 1926, "The Hudson's Bay Brigade Trail," *OHS 1*, p.13.

14. Ross, Alexander. 1956, *The Fur Hunters of the Far West*, Ed. K.A. Spalding, University of Oklahoma Press, Norman, p.330.

15. Thomson, Duane. 1985, "A History of the Okanagan," University of British Columbia, PhD thesis, p.116.

16. Ibid., 1978, "Opportunity Lost: A History of Okanagan Indian Reserves in the Colonial Period," *OHS*, pp.45-46

17. Carstens, Peter. 1991, *The Queen's People: A Study of Hegemony, Coercion, and Accommodation among the Okanagan of Canada*, University of Toronto Press, pp.55-66, 89-102

18. Barman, Jean. 1991, *THE WEST BEYOND THE WEST: A History of British Columbia*, University of Toronto Press, p.152.

Early Church Photos

Gathering One	Mary Abel Collection
Gathering Two	Mary Abel Collection
Funeral St. Ben	Mary Abel Collection
St. Benedicts	Mary Abel Collection
St. Theresa's	Shirley Louis
St. Theresa's	Shirley Louis
Father Le Jeune	Julia Tonasket Collection
Corpus Christi	Mary Jane Lawrence Collection

EARLY CHURCH

1. Ross, D. A. 1960, "St. Joseph's Jesuit Mission in the Okanagan," *OHS 24*, pp.59-61.

2. Buckland, F.M. 1926, "Some Noteable Men In the Okanagan," *OHS 1*, p.15.

3. Buckland, Frank. 1926, *Ogopogo's Vigil*, p.27.

4. Ibid., 1926, p.26.

5. Ned Louis, Interview, 1998.

6. Thomson, Duane. 1990, "The Missionaries," *Okanagan Sources*, Theytus Books, Penticton, p.126.

7. Ibid., 1990, p.125.

8. Ibid., 1990, p.122.

9. Kowrach, Edward J. 1991, *Mie. Charles Pandosy OMI: A Missionary of the Northwest*, YE Galleon Press, Fairfield, Washington, p.123.

10. Thomson. 1990, p137.

11. Ibid., p.129.

12. Ibid., p.130.

13. Ibid., p.131.

14. Ibid., p.138.

15. Cronin, Kay. 1960, *A Cross in the Wilderness*, Mitchell Press, p.170.

16. Ibid., p.169.

17. Ibid., p.171.

18. Ibid., p.177.

19. *Vernon News*, 9 July 1891.

20. *Vernon News*, 1 November 1894.

21. John Veillette and Gary White. 1977, *Early Indian Village Churches*, University of British Columbia Press, Vancouver, p.113.

22. Ned Louis, Interview, 1998.

23. Veillette and White. 1977.

Education Photos

School Photo 1	Mary Jane Lawrence
School Photo 2	Mary Jane Lawrence
School Photo 3	Mary Jane Lawrence
School Photo 4	Mary Jane Lawrence
School Photo	Corinne Marchand

1. Thomson, Duane. 1985, "A History of the Okanagan," PhD Thesis, University of British Columbia, p.97.

2. Ibid., 1985, pp.97-98.

3. Ibid., p.98.

4. Ibid., p.97.

5. Ibid., p.98.

6. *Kamloops Inland Sentinel*, 23 July 1887.

7. Thomson. 1985, p.107.

8. *Vernon News*, 1920.

Military Photos

WW#I

Billy Brewer	Josephine Logan Collection
Tronson	Josephine Logan Collection
Charlie Parker	Sarah Parker Collection
George McLean	Lavina Lum
Manuel Bercier	OKIB Photo File-not numbered
Harry Parker	Sarah Parker
Charlie Edwards	Josephine Logan Collection
Willie Lawrence	OKIB Photo File-not munbered
Johnny Harris	OKIB Photo File-not numbered
Harry Tronson	Tom Tronson
Charlie Simpson	Pete Simpson

Tommy Armstrong	Mary Abel Collection
WW#II	
Edward Fred	Corinne Marchand
John Marchand	John Marchand
Riley Brewer	Riley Brewer
Norman Steele	Norman Steele / Alice Miller
Bill Steele	Gloria Seitsma
David Parker	David Parker
Angus Oppenheimer	Raymond Williams / Corinne Marchand
Albert Saddleman	Josephine Saddleman
Joseph Fraser	Lavina Lum
Johnny Shuttleworth	Raymond Williams
Willie Williams	Raymond Williams
Stanley Mitchell	Raymond Williams
Florence Harris	Terry Harris
Winifred Harris	OKIB Photo File-not numbered
Wilbur Harris	Terry Harris
Ernest Simpson	Herb Simpson
Clarence Simpson	Herb Simpson
Bert Simpson	Thomas Simpson / Gail McAllister
Group	Mary Abel Collection

PELKAMULOX / N'KWALA

1. Teit, James. 1927, *The Salishan Tribes of the Western Plateaus*, Ed. Franz Boaz, Annual Report, Bureau of American Anthology, Smithsonian Institute, Washington, pp.264-270.

Abel Photos

Mary Terese	Louie Fred
Komasket	OKIB Photo File F3-19
Madeline	OKIB Photo File-not numbered
Group Photo	Mary Abel Collection / Hilda Belanger
Mary	Mary Abel Collection
Pete	Peter Marchand

ABEL / KOMASKET

1. Family tree: Abel Death Journal, DIA 1877, DIA 1920-1946, PABC Death Reel #: Donald 81 1969 B13301, Moses 53 1974 B13334.
2. Roman Catholic Church Records.
3. Edward Fred, David Parker, Tommy Gregoire.
4. "Royal Commission on Indian Affairs for the Province of B.C. Proceedings," 4 volumes. Victoria: 1916 and Evidence of the Royal Commission's Meetings, transcribed ver batim 1913.
5. Carstens, Peter. 1991, *The Queen's People. A study of Hegemony, Coercion and Accommodation among the Okanagan People of Canada*, University of Toronto Press, p.71.
6. Ibid., p.71.
7. Roman Catholic Church Records.
8. DIA 1920-46.
9. Lawrence Wilson, grandson of Donald Abel.
10. David Parker, Martin Wilson, Clara Dubrett.
11. Carstens. 1991, p.292.
12. *Vernon News*, 4 October 1937.

Alexander Photos

Margaret	Lavina Lum
Basil	Lavina Lum

Mary Ann	Margaret Marchand / Corinne Marchand
Louie	Margaret Marchand / Corinne Marchand
Theresa	Lavina Lum
William	Lavina Lum
Harriet	Lavina Lum
Mary Louise	Lavina Lum
Alexander Place	Shirley Louis

ALEXANDER

1. Family tree: Abel Death Journal, DIA 1877, Baudre 1877, DIA 1920-46, Lavina Lum, John Spotted Eagle, PABC Death Reel #: Johnny 17 1926 B13360, Louisa 86 1925 B13360, Basil 75 1950 B13377, Domatilda 80 1960 B13250, Harry 8, 1925 B13360, Mary 0 1926 B13360, Daniel 70 1969 B13295.
2. Baudre 1877.
3. Roman Catholic Church Records.
4. *Vernon News*, 3 September 1908.

Alexis / Cameron Photos

Kwitasket	Greater Vernon Museum and Archives
John	OKIB Photo File F-14-9
Elizabeth	Julia Tonasket Collection
Ella	Peter Simpson
Mary	Julia Tonasket Collection
Annie	Lavina Lum
Ella and Children	Thomas Simpson and Gail McAllister

ALEXIS / CAMERON

1. Family tree: Abel Death Journal, Alexis Family, DIA 1920-46. PABC Death Reel #: Alex Alexine 80, 1921 B13359, John Lawrence 58 1961 B13251, Herbert 32 1962 B13256, Baby 0 1936 B13357, Jesse 0 1940 B13375, David Cameron 76 1953 B13218.
2. Armstrong, Derickson, Maracle & Young-Ing. 1993/94, *We Get Our Living Like Milk From the Land*, Theytus Books, Penticton, p.2.
3. PABC Marriage Reel #B11384.
4. DIA 1920-46 / Baudre 1877 / DIA Census 1877.
5. See Q'sapi, p.159.
6. PABC Reel #B11384.
7. PABC Reel #B11384.

Antoine / Barnes / Powers Photos

Sam & Rosie	OKIB Photo File F 15-11
Rosie & Family	OKIB Photo File F-30-19
Dennis	Mary Abel Collection
Dennis Emily and children	Rose Caldwell / Wilfred Barnes

ANTIONE / BARNES / POWERS

1. Family tree: Abel Death Journal, DIA 1920-46, PABC Death Reel #: Dennis 48 1963 B13262, Rosie 55 1934 B13362, Louisa 13 1931 B13362.
2. PABC Marriage Reel #B13888.
3. Pat Lean with Sigurd Teit. 1995, *Teit Times*, Nicola Valley Archives Association, Merritt, BC., p.37.
4. *Vernon News*, January 1916.
5. Edward Fred, Interview 1998.
6. PABC Death Reel #B13362.
7. DIA 1920-46.
8. DIA 1920-46.
9. *Vernon News*, 20 October 1938.
10. DIA Census 1920-46.

Bessette Photos

Bessette Family	Peter Simpson
Mary Helene	Mary Eli
George	OKIB Photo FileF-9-5
Steve	Raymond Williams
Tarzan	Mary Eli
George	Kathy Jones
Willie	Josephine Logan Collection
Marguerite	Edna Gregoire
Mary	Edna Gregoire
Mickey	Mary Eli
Christine	Julia Tonasket Collection
Harry	Mary Eli
Johnny	Mary Eli
Charlie, Adeline, Florence	Julia Tonasket Collection

BESSETTE

1. Family tree: Abel Death Journal, DIA 1920-46, Marguerite Marchand, PABC Death Reel #: Christine 22, 1951 B13377, George 77 1968 B13294, Marie Helene 58 1941 B13173, Peter 78 1933 B13362, Rosie 39 1932 B13362.
2. Roman Catholic Church Records.
3. *Grassroots of Lumby 1877-1927*. 1979, Lumby Historians, pp.10-11.
4. DIA 1920-46.
5. PABC Marriage Reel #B13888.

Bonneau Photos

Jimmy	Lavina Lum
Edward Ella & Virginia	Okanagan Elders Society/Laura Miller
Bonneau Family	Raymond Williams
Jimmy with horse	Bertha Phelan
Jimmy and Sarah	Bertha Phelan
Bonneau House	Shirley Louis

BONNEAU

1. Family tree: Abel Death Journal, DIA 1920-46, PABC Jack 66 1930 B13310, Edward 58 1971 B13315, Harriet 10 1924 B13360, Margaret 60 1933 B13362, Manuel 23 1932 B13365, Benjamin 5 1941 B13375, Bernice 1 1944 B13375, Mary Magdalen 1 1944 B13375, Manuel John 7 1945 B13376, Douglas 0 1951 B13377, Hubert 0 1941 B13377, Faustine 0 1933 B13377, Ella 54 1968 B13294, Jimmy 80 1971 B13310, Winifred 0 1944 B13375.
2. DIA 1920-46.
3. DIA 1920-46.
4. DIA 1920-46.
5. *Vernon News*, 1930, September.

Brewer Photos

Jennie	Jennie Marchand
Christine	Jennie Marchand
Billy and Millie	Jennie Marchand
Ernest and Family	Jennie Marchand
Emma	OKIB Photo File F-9-8
Maurice	OKIB Photo File F-8-18
Charlie	OKIB Photo File F-17-1

BREWER

1. Family tree: Abel Death Journal, DIA 1920-46, Jenny Marchand, Geraldine Schroeder, PABC Death Reel #: Christine 60 1929, Amy (Emily) 47 1936 B13363, Ernest 82 1976 B13356, Billy 2 1920 B13359, Bercier 7 1931

B13362, Gordon 3 1936 B13363.
2. Roman Catholic Church Records.
3. *Vernon News*, January 1905.
4. John Spotted Eagle, Interview 1999.
5. Taped 1967, Interviewer unidentified.
6. Clara Dubrett, Martin Wilson, Edward Fred.

Fred / Michele / Andrew Photos

Therese Qualtier	Mary Jane Lawrence
Alphonse Louie	OKIB Photo File F-12-2
Johnny Pants	Lavina Lum
Katherine Louis	Rose Louis
Edward Fred	Corinne Marchand
Elizabeth Fred	OKIB Photo File-not numbered
Lena Fred	OKIB Photo File F-11-8
Johnny and Maggie Victor	Mary Abel Collection
Louie Victor	OKIB Photo File-not numbered
William Victor	Lavina Lum

FRED / ANDREW / QUALTIER / VICTOR

1. Family Tree: Abel Death Journal, PABC Death Reel #: Jimmy Fred ? B13363, Charlie Andrew 4 1928 B13361, Mary Andrew B13363, Johnny Andrew 64 1939 B13374, Sophie Andrew 4 1923 B13361. QUALTIER Alphonse Louie 65 1958 B13238, Francis 47 1939 B13374, Joseph 28 1963 B13260, Mary 98 1958 B13238, Pierre 23 1930 B13361, William 68 1928 B13361, Johnny 23 1919 B13359, Allen Edwards 80 1955 B13377, Big Louie 72 1920 B13359.
2. PABC Marriage Reel #B13888.
3. PABC Marriage Reel #B13888.
4. Millie Jack, Interview 1999.
5. PABC Reel #B133359.
6. PABC Reel #B133360.
7. PABC Marriage Reel #B13890.
8. PABC Reel #B13360.

Gottfriedson/Gottfriedsen Photos

Frank	Rose Louis
Clarence	Rose Louis
Josephine	Rose Louis
George	Cathy Gottfriedsen
Gus	En'owkin Center
Rose Louis	Rose Louis
Teddy	Rose Louis
Adeline	Raymond Williams
Angeline	Raymond Williams
John	Rose Louis
Jane	Rose Louis
Clement	Riley Brewer
Spider Ranch	Raymond Williams

GOTTFRIEDSON / GOTTFRIEDSEN

1. Family tree: Abel Death Journal, Rose Louis Family Bible, PABC Death, November 69 1941 B13172, Frank 86 1950 B13377, George 54 1966 B13279, Richard 3 1930 B13361, Clarence 21 1930 B13361, Newman 1 1930 B13361, Violet 14 1939 B13374, Teddy 29 1946 B13376.
2. Roman Catholic Church Records, Rose Louis.
3. "Okanagan Place Names," 1948, *OHS 12*. p.205.

4. PABC Marriage Reel #B11387.

5. PABC Marriage Reel #B11387.

6. PABC Marriage Reel #B11386.

7. PABC Marriage Reel #B11386.

8. Roman Catholic Church Records, Rose Louis.

Gregoire Photos

Harriet & grandchildren	Josephine Logan Collection
Francois	Edna Gregoire
Alice & Celestine	Rosie Jack
Tommy	Mary Abel Collection
Felix	OKIB Photo File F-14-2
David	Edna Gregoire
Mary Anne	Rosie Jack
Pete	Mary Abel Collection
Louisa	OKIB Photo File-not numbered
Lewis wedding	Mary Abel Collection

GREGOIRE

1. Family tree: Abel Death Journal, DIA 1920-46, PABC Death Reel #: Felix 62 1961 B13251, Hermon 70 1945 B13376, Nancy 89 1963 B13262, Harriet B13376, Lizzie 69 1967 B13286, Josephine 91 1968 B13290, Mary 68 1972 B13322, Johnny 20 1925 B13362, Sadie 17 1956 B13377, Tommy 6 1951 B13377, Lizzie 47 1944 B13378, William Lewis 57 1935, Celestine 75 B13347, Louie Lewis 84 1975 B13339 Mary Ann Joseph 83 1940 B13374, Jimmy Joseph 99 1940 B13375.

2. *Shuswap Chronicles Volume Two*, 1989, North Shuswap Historical Society, Celista, BC., p.5.

3. Mary Gregoire, daughter of David and Edna Gregoire.

4. DIA 1920-46.

5. DIA 1920-46.

6. *Vernon News*, 9 September 1915.

7. PABC Birth 93 09 998 624.

8. PABC Reel #B13375.

9. PABC Reel #B13374.

10. DIA Census 1920-46.

11. David Gregoire Family.

12. Michael Marchand, son of Alex and Helene Marchand.

Harris Photos

Isaac	OKIB Photo File-not numbered
Christine	Isaac Parker
Harry	Eileen Giuliani
Johnny	OKIB Photo File-not numbered
Edith	Edna Gregoire
Harris Children	Lavina Lum
Florence	Terry Harris
Wilbur	Terry Harris

HARRIS

1. Family tree: DIA 1920-46, Edith Parker Death Journal, Edna Gregoire, PABC Reel #: Christine 19 1933 B13362, Evelyn 12 1923 B13360, Harry 78 1975 B13340, Isaac 59 1930 B13361, Isabelle 13 1933 B13362, Leslie 9 1924 B13360, Lillian 0 1924 B13360.

2. *Vernon News*, 26 May 1916.

3. Roman Catholic Church Records.

4. PABC Marriage Form #44491.

5. *Vernon News*, 20 April 1905.

6. Eileen Giuliani. Correspondence, Vancouver, BC.
7. PABC Marriage Registration Form #1090-09-544-797. Not filmed.
8. "Kenny Mclean," 1976, *OHS 40*, p.33.
9. Webber, Jean. 1993, "Hudson's Bay Trading Posts in the Okanagan and Similkameen" *OHS 57*, pp.28-29.
10. *Vernon News*, 25 May 1933.
11. *Vernon News*, 1 June 1933.
12. *Vernon News*, 29 September 1930.
13. Roman Catholic Church Records.
14. *Vernon News*, 19 January 1922.

Isaac / Simla Photos

Arcelle & Dick	OKIB Photo File F-8-20
Alex	OKIB Photo File-not numbered
Rosie	Rick Oppenheimer
Dick	Peter Marchand
Martha	Lavina Lum
Gladys & Dorothy	Raymond Williams
Raymond	Riley Brewer
Hazel, Rosie, Violet	Gladys Bonneau

ISAAC / SIMLA

1. Family tree: Abel Death Journal, Gladys Bonneau, DIA 1920-46, PABC Death Reel #: Nancy Isaac 74 1948 B13376, Johnny Isaac 80 1950 B13377, Alexander Simla 88 1959 B13241, Rose Simla 72 1962 B13256, Mary Isaac 65 1919 B13359, Alec 2 1926 B13360.
2. PABC #B13377.
3. Calculation from death date.
4. *Vernon News*, November 1918.
5. Carstens. 1991, p.135.
6. Gladys Bonneau 1999.
7. PABC Marriage Reel # 13888
8. "Frank Richter," 1961, *OHS 25*, pp.78-101.
10. Barman, Jean. 1996, "Lost Okanagan: In Search of the First Settlers Families," *OHS 60*, p.12.
11. Ibid., p.12.

Jack / Jim Photos

Pirreche & Angelique	Edna Gregoire
Madeline	OKIB Photo File F-3-6
Pierre	Rosie Jack
Christine	Rosie Jack
Narcisse	Lavina Lum
Onn	OKIB Photo File F4-15
Frank	Rosie Jack
Phillip	Rosie Jack
Lizzie	OKIB Photo File F4-15
Ethel	OKIB Photo File F4-15
Rosie	Edna Gregoire
Andy	Rosie Jack
Angie	Rosie Jack

JACK / JIM

1. Family tree: Abel Death Journal, DIA 1920-46, Rosie Jack, PABC Death Reel #: Pierre 100 1971 B13309, Joseph 1 1924 B13360, August 33 1949 B13362, Ten Dollar Jack 89 1934 B13362, Pirreche 89 1934 B13362, Angeline 16 1946, B13376, Johnny 11 1949 B13376, Casimir 14 1949 B13376, Phillip 19 1946 B13376, Andy 22 1951 B13377, Narcisse 71 1951 B13377, Jenny 18 1918 B13359.

2. Ned Louis, Interview 1998.
3. "Royal Commission on Indian Affairs for the Province of B.C. Proceedings," 1913, Victoria.
4. DIA 1920-46.
5. PABC Marriage Reel #B13888.
6. Sawicki, Dorothy. 1971, "Pierre Jack," *OHS 35*. pp.140-1.
7. Rosie Jack, Interview 1998.
8. Mourning Dove. 1990.
9. Ned Louis, Interview 1998.
10. *Vernon News*, 28 September 1895.
11. *Vernon News*, 3 September 1896.
12. *Vernon News*, 14 April 1898.
13. Carstens. 1991, p.119.
14. *Vernon News*, November 1918.

Jacko Photos

Louie	OKIB Photo File F-6-13
Emily Jacko & Family	Jennie Marchand
Millie Michel	Shirley Louis
Jacko Cabin	Shirley Louis

JACKO

1. Family tree: Abel Death Journal, Jenny Brewer, Head of the Lake Cemetery List, PABC Death Reel #: Johnny Jacko 60 1946 B13375, Louis Jacko 76 1938 B13374.
2. Balf, Mary. 1978, *Why that Name? Place Names of Kamloops District*, p.3. (*History of Kamloops*, p.129, repeats naming of creek.)
3. Jackson, John C. 1995, *Children of the Fur Trade: Forgotten Metis of the Pacific Northwest*, Mountain Press Publishing Company, Missoula, Montana, p.35.
4. Ibid., p.36.
5. Ibid., p.37.
6. Ibid., p.37.
7. Ibid., p.254.
8. Edward Fred's funeral brought Sapelle's granddaughter, Millie, to the place where she was raised so many years ago. I first noticed her offering prayers at the graveside. As it happened I noticed her again outside the graveyard gesturing toward the Gregoire place below the community hall. Something about her told me that her presence there held more than what was obvious. I quickly approached her-introduced myself and asked how she knew Edward. She informed me, with an easy smile, that she was related to Edward on his father's side. Then she went on to say that her grandfather Amap Jacko was buried in the same cemetery. I didn't know exactly who she was. Yet because she is a fairly tiny women and the granddaughter of Sapelle, I was reminded of Riley Brewer's reference to her. After making our way through the large crowd into the hall we continued our conversation. Millie was Sapelle's granddaughter and was raised at the Jacko place in the Round Lake area by her grandmother and step-grandfather, Amap. Both she and her sister Hilda considered the Brewer family their siblings and she was hoping to see them again. Only William Brewer was present in the hall and I immediately brought him to her. Their reunion was thoroughly touching. They chatted like long lost friends. Unfortunately she could not get to see Jenny, but stopped at Riley's on her way back to Kamloops. Millie died in 2001.

Joe Williams Photos

Millie	Mary Abel Collection
Pierre Joe Williams	OKIB Photo File F-12-7
Edward	Corinne Marchand
Susan	OKIB Photo File-not numbered
Helene	Corinne Marchand
George	Julia Tonasket Collection
Louie	Mary Abel Collection

JOE WILLIAMS

1. Family tree: Abel Death Journal, PABC Death Reel #: Joe Williams 70 1926 B13360, Edward Joseph Williams 65 1968 B13291, Millie 89 1955 B13377.

2. Ruby, Robert H. and Brown, John A. 1970, *The Spokane Indians: Children of the Sun*, University of Oklahoma Press. p.89.

3. Buckland, Frank. 1950, "PEON" *OHS 14*. p.35.

4. Ibid., 1950, p.37.

5. Kelowna Museum and Archives.

6. Buckland. 1950, p.41.

7. Roman Catholic Church Records of the Pion Family at Immaculate Conception Mission. 1860 Julia Pion "de la tribe des Couteaux" acted as god-parent. Julia's parents were Joseph Laroque and Stuwix woman Sukomelelks, the daughter of Chief N'Kwala. 1861 son of Gedeon and Esther Pion was baptized. Gedeon and Bazil Pion acted as godparents to other children the same day. March 1862, Joseph the son of Basile Pion and Josephine Pheneli was baptized. In May of the same year Basile Pion died and was buried at the Immaculate Conception cemetery. April 1863, Jean, the son of Gedeon Peon and Esther was baptized. In the same record Esther is noted as an "Okanagan du lac Nicolas." January 1864, Gedeon, the major son of Louis Pion from "Canada" and Josephine Pheneli, "de la riviere rouge," married Esther, the daughter of "Silritza de lac Nicolas." On June 3, 1865, Julia Pion died and was buried in Immaculate Conception cemetery. By August 1865 William Pion, the son of Louis Pion and Spokane woman Marie, married Marie Stlakem, the widow of fur trader Francois Duchequet. May 1866, a daughter, Rosalie, was born to William and Marie Pion.

Kalamalka / Nicholas / Antione / Vernon Photos

Koostemeena	Greater Vernon Museum and Archives
Sqwnimtexnalqs	Greater Vernon Museum and Archives
Alex	OKIB Photo File-not numbered
Gilbert	Mary Abel Collection
Harry	OKIB Photo File-not numbered
Jimmy	OKIB Photo File F-3-8
Baptiste Nicholas	Mary Abel Collection

KALAMALKA / ANTIONE / NICHOLAS / VERNON

1. Family tree: Roman Catholic Church Records, Nelson BC. PABC Death Reel #: ANTIONE James 78 1970 B13303, Christine 0 1920 B13359, Mabel 0 1922 B13360, Edward 2 1927 B13361, Mary Louise 41 1933 B13362, Lucy 29 1955 B13377, Francis 18 B13359. NICHOLAS Francis 16 1941 B13375, Isabel 39 1961 B13350, Joe 35 1933 B13362, Joe 2 1933 B13363, Johnny 2 1924 B13360, Mary 48 1949 B13376, Amelia 46 1960 B13246.

2. Buckland, Frank. 1950, "PEON" *OHS 14*, pp.35-43.

3. Ned Louis, Interview 1999.

4. Pearson, Anne. 1986, *An Early History of Coldstream and Lavington*, Wayside Press, Vernon, BC, p.4.

5. Cronin, Kay. 1960, *A Cross in the Wilderness*, Mitchell Press, pp.132-134.

6. The pronunciation of this surname is very close to Hwistesmetxe'qen-the son of Pelkamulox III. See page 56.

7. Roman Catholic Church Records.

8. PABC Reel #B13359.

9. Roman Catholic Church Records.

10. Jimmie Antione to Indian Agent A. Megraw, "Statement of Jimmie Antione in reference to history of the Antione Estate, Given October 31, 1919."

11. Roman Catholic Church Records.

12. Ormsby, Margaret. 1990, *Coldstream Nulli Secundu. A History of the Corporation of the District of Coldstream*, Freisen Printers, Altona, Manitoba., p.4.

13. Ibid., p.22.

14. Roman Catholic Church Records.

15. *Vernon News*, February 1902.

16. PABC Reel #B13359.

17. DIA 1920-46.

18. *Vernon News*, 1 April 1903.

19. *Vernon News*, 25 January 1906.
20. *Vernon News*, 12 May 1979.

Lawrence Photos

Susan	Lynn Phelan
Joe, Susan, Henry	Mary Jane Lawrence
Harriet & Willie	OKIB Photo File F-4-20
Agnes	Lavina Lum
Helene & Sarah	Judy Marchand
Andrew Thomas	OKIB Photo File F-3-13

LAWRENCE
1. Family tree: Baudre 1877, Abel Death Journal, DIA 1920-46, Mary Jane Lawrence, PABC Death Reel #: Lena 95 1967 B13287, Christine 2 1934 B13362, Hugh 13 1933 B13362, Mary Ann 68 1939 B13374, Mary 6 1934 B13362, William 59 1952 B13263, Jennifer 3 1963 B13263, John Henry 1955 B13361, Joseph Leslie 2 1928 B13361.
2. Baudre 1877.
3. PABC Marriage Reel #B13888.
4. DIA 1920-46

Logan / Duprett / Swalwell / Edwards Photos

Logan Family	Josephine Logan Collection
Mary Logan	Shirley Paul
Alex	OKIB Photo File F-17-1
Baptiste	Julia Tonasket Collection
Abraham	Julia Tonasket Collection
Josephine & Family	OKIB Photo File F-10-4
Josephine	OKIB Photo File F-20-17
Charlie	Josephine Logan Collection
William Swalwell	Julia Tonasket Collection
Annie	Julia Tonasket Collection
Christine	Greater Vernon Museum and Archives

LOGAN / DUBRETT / SWALWELL / EDWARDS
1. Family tree: Abel Death Journal, DIA 1920-46, Jenny Marchand, Millie Steele, PABC Death Reel #: Alexander Logan (Alex Dubrett) 27 1926 B13360, Baptiste Logan 51 1920 B13359, Julienne 72 1930 B13361, Pierre 89 1957 B13232, Annie 69 1934 B13377, James 68 1951 B13377, SWALWELL William P. Swalwell 1926 B13129, EDWARDS Charlie 49 1947 B13370.
2. Teit, James A and Frank Boaz. 1975, *The Salishan Tribes of the Western Plateaus*, The Shorey Book Store, Seattle, Washington, pp.264-5.
3. Peggy Brewer, Interview 1998.
4. Balf, Mary. 1978, *Why that Name? Place Names of Kamloops District*, Kamloops Museum and Archives.
5. de Pfyffer, Robert L. 1990, "Okanagan Indians Non-Registered. The Reason Why," *OHS 54*. p.82.
6. "Okanagan Place Names," 1939, *OHS 8*, p.40.
8. PABC Marriage Reel #B13888.
9. Josephine unveils monument 1960s.
10. PABC Marriage Reel #B13888.
11. PABC Marriage Reel #B13888.

Louie / Lamprow / Tronson Photos

Agnes	OKIB Photo File F-9-7
Celina	OKIB Photo File F-9-7
Manuel	OKIB Photo File F-8-14
Alex	Julia Tonasket Collection
William Esther Andrew	Esther Louie
Tronson Group	OKIB Photo File F4-19

LOUIE / LAMPROW / TRONSON

1. Family tree: Abel Death Journal, DIA 1920-46, James and Esther Louie, PABC Death Reel #: Alexander 18 1950 B13377, Alex 59 1950 B13262, Richard Louie B13378, Susan Gasto 20 1933, B13362, Marie Therese Louie 0 1930 B13361, Charlie William 0 1937 B13363, TRONSON George 66 1939 B13165, Harry 13 1895 B13110, Louisa 91 1965 B13270.

2. Interview, Pierre Louis to Douglas Ross. Greater Vernon Museum and Archives, 1958.

3. de Pfyffer, Robert L. 1990, "Okanagan Indians Non-Registered. The Reason Why," *OHS 54*, pp.77-91.

4. Ned Louis, Interview 1999.

5. de Pfyffer. 1990, p.82.

6. DIA 1920-46.

7. Louie Family.

8. DIA 1920-46.

9. Roman Catholic Church Records.

10. Roman Catholic Church Records.

11. PABC Death Reel #B13110.

12. Oram, Edna. 1985, *The History of Vernon 1867-1937*, Wayside Press, Vernon, BC., pp.57-58.

15. Tom Tronson / Peggy Brewer.

16. PABC Marriage Reel #B13888.

17. PABC Marriage Reel #B13888.

Louis Photos

Terese Qualtier	Mary Jane Lawrence
Katherine	Rose Louis
Mary Anne	Lavina Lum
Pierre	Lavina Lum
Queen's Visit	Rose Louis
Alex	Lavina Lum
Pierre & Family	Rose Louis
Alex's Family	Judy Marchand
Steve Marchand	Julia Tonasket Collection

LOUIS

1. Family tree: Abel Death Journal, DIA 1920-46, OKIB Cemetery list, Mary Jane Lawrence, Ned Louis, Colville Confederated Tribes, Nespelem, Washington, PABC Death Reel #: Pierre 82, 1968 B13289, Ella Louis 18 1930 B13361.

2. Shirley Leon and Zena Eli, 1999.

3. Sequin, Jacques J. "The Marchand Story," Unpublished.

4. Chance, David H. 1986, *People of the Falls*, Kettle Falls Historical Center, Inc., p.47, 107.

5. Ned Louis, Interview 1999.

6. "In the matter of the Indian Act being Chapter 149 of the Revised Statutes of Canada 1952 (Part 2)," Greater Vernon Museum and Archives.

7. Ned Louis.

8. Ibid., p.72.

9. Ibid., p.73.

10. Ibid., p.70.

11. Ibid., p.73.

12. Ibid., p.74.

13. Ibid., p.94

14. Ibid., p.74.

15. Ibid., p.75.

16. Ibid., p.74.

17. Ibid., p.89.

18. Ibid., p.90.

19. Zena Eli.

20. George and Celina Wilson were married December 25, 1906.

Marchand Photos

Joachim	Pete Marchand
Christine and Frank	Pete Marchand
Louie	Pete Marchand
Joe	Lavina Lum
Victoria	Dora Louie
Charlie	Mary Abel Collection
Willie	Corinne Marchand
Sarah	Lavina Lum
Pete	Pete Marchand
Louie	Jenny Marchand

MARCHAND

1. Family tree: Abel Death Journal, DIA 1920-1946, PABC Death Reel #: Christina 91 1961 B13254, Frank 97 1967 B13285, Ernest James 4 1936 B13363, Mary Ann 96 1957 B13235, Louie 88 1947 B13376, Joseph 72 1973 B13326.

2. Seguin, Jacques J. "The Marchand Story," Unpublished.

Michel Photos

Buckskin Susan	OKIB Photo File F-11-1

MICHEL

1. Family tree: Abel Death Journal, DIA 1920-46, PABC Death Reel #: Pierre 50 1918 B13359, Susan Michel 85 1940 B13374.

2. PABC Death Reel #B13359.

3. *Vernon News*, November 1918.

Oppenheimer Photos

Johnny	Peter Marchand
Edith & Children	Corinne Marchand
Ernest	Eleanor Oppenheimer
Angus	Corinne Marchand
Angus Wedding	Corinne Marchand
Eva	Shirley Paul
Ernest and Dorothy's children	Rick Oppenheimer
Ernest and Dorothy's children	Rick Oppenheimer
Corrine	Josephine Logan Collection

OPPENHEIMER

1. Family tree: Abel Death Journal, DIA 1920-46, Eva Lawrence, PABC Death Reel #: Angus 60 1976 B13356, John 0 1949 B13376, John Louie 88 1969 B13296, Marcus 7 1925 B13363, Phyllis 7 1934 B13377, Irene E. Oppenheimer 2 1920 B13359, David 0 1961 B13359.

2. Mildred Leon Smith, Interview 1998.

3. Taped 1967. Interviewer unidentified.

4. Charlie Quintasket lives at Omak, Washington.

5. *Stevens County Historical Society*. Colville, Washington. No date or page number.

6. Mourning Dove. 1990, p.179.

7. Ibid., p.4.

8. Ibid., Appendix p.196.

9. Ibid., p.5.

Parker Photos

Joseph	Sarah Parker
Annie Joseph	Edna Gregoire
Charlie	Sarah Parker
Louie Christie	OKIB Photo File F-3-13
Harry	Sarah Parker
Mary Louise	OKIB Photo File F-3-8
George	Edna Gregoire
Edna	Edna Gregoire
Caroline	Edna Gregoire
Bertha	Edna Gregoire
Rosie	Edna Gregoire

PARKER

1. Family tree: Abel Death Journal, DIA 1920-46, Edith Parker Journal, Edna Gregoire, PABC Death Reel #: Joe 71 1939 B13374, Annie Joseph 74 1953 B13377, Charles Matthew 83 1957 B13231, Sadie 13 1937 B13363, Rosie 15 1943 B13375, Joe 21 1943 B13375.
2. DIA 1920-46.
3. PABC Marriage Reel #B13888.
4. PABC Marriage Reel #B13888.

Paul Photos

Catherine	Shirley Paul
Michele & Sophie Jack	Shirley Paul
Peter	OKIB Photo File-not numbered
Mary	Mary Abel Collection
Semo Paul	OKIB Photo File F13-16
Paul House	Shirley Paul
Paul Group	Shirley Paul

PAUL

1. Family tree: Shirley Paul, PABC Death Reel # Luke Paul 69 1934 B13362.
2. Shirley Paul.
3. DIA 1920-46.
4. From James Christie to Frank Pedley. 1909, Deputy Superintendent General, Indian Affairs. Ottawa, Canada.

Pierre Photos

Anne (Onn)	OKIB Photo File-not numbered
Narcisse & Terese	Raymond Williams / Martin Wilson
Pierre House	Shirley Louis
Matilda	Evelyn Wilson Collection
Elizabeth	Mary Abel Collection
Henry	Mary Abel Collection

PIERRE

1. Family tree: Abel Death Journal, DIA 1920-46, Martin Wilson, PABC Death Reel #: death, Elizabeth 70 1975 B13342, Henry 64 1972 B13316, Joe 54 1933 B13363, Narcisse 91 1937 B13232, Theresa 79 1938 B13238, Angus 62 1974 B13330.
2. David Parker, Martin Wilson.
3. DIA 1920-46.
4. DIA 1920-46.
5. de Pfyffer, Robert. 1990, p.86.
6. Clara Dubrett.

Robins Photos

Johnny	OKIB Photo File-not numbered
Harriet	Ranger Robins
Roy	Ranger Robins
Emery	Edna Louis
Tommy and Josephine	Edna Louis
Irene	Edna Louis
Della	Josephine Saddleman

ROBINS / ARMSTRONG

1. Family tree: Abel Death Journal, Delphine Armstrong, PABC Death Reel #: Johnny 64 1971 B13308, Harriet 67 1974 B13338, William 18 1962 B13257.
2. Cox, Doug. 1981, "Charlie Armstrong," *OHS 45*, pp.97-99.
3. Ibid., p.97.

Shuttleworth / Smith Photos

Lord Shuttleworth	Greater Vernon Museum & Archives
George & Charlotte	Theresa Bonneau
George Smith	Thomas Simpson / Gail McAllister Kamloops
Francis and Susan	Isabelle Burgemaster
Maria	Isabelle Burgemaster
Norman	Isabelle Burgemaster
Reggie	Shirley Paul
Mary	Theresa Bonneau
Johnny	Lavina Lum
Isabelle	Isabelle Burgemaster

SHUTTLEWORTH / SMITH

1. Family tree: Abel Death Journal, DIA 1920-46, Canada Census 1881, 1891, PABC Death Reel #: Reginald 69 1966 B13277, Richard 60 1976 B13349, Rosie 13 1961 B13336, Charles 80 1965 B13274, Charlotte 81 1957 B13234, George 15 1927 B13361, George 104 13240, Henry 69 1968 B13289, Johnny 56 1974 B13331, Josephine 83 1950 B13206, Mary 24 1945 B13376.
2. PABC Marriage Reel B13888. Form #772. A later addition changed Joe's marital status from bachelor to widower.
3. Names of Joe's parents were added later.
4. Names of Ann's parents were added later.
5. PABC Marriage Reel #B13888.
6. Sismey, Eric. 1971, "Shuttleworths of Okanagan Falls," *OHS 35*, pp.136-137.
7. Ibid., p.136.
8. *Vernon News*, 2 August 1956.

Simpson / Borrie / Struthers Photos

G.W.Simpson	Peter Simpson
Eliza Jane Swalwell	Thomas Simpson / Gail McAllister
Sarah Borrie	Peter Simpson
Charlie Simpson	Peter Simpson
Annie & George	Peter Simpson
George	Herb Simpson
Clara	Herb Simpson
Thomas B. Struthers	Thomas Simpson / Gail McAllister
Martha and Alice	Thomas Simpson / Gail McAllister

SIMPSON / BORRIE / STRUTHERS

1. Family tree: Canada Census 1881-1891, DIA 1920-46, Herb Simpson, Peter Simpson, Gail McAllister, PABC Reel

#: George Simpson 59 1930 B13140, George Simpson 54 1952 B13377, Eliza Jane Swalwell 75 1944 B13182, Mary Lillian 36 1966 B13278, Clara 65 1968 B13289, Thomas 31 1912 B13112, Eliza Simpson 30 1909 B13111.

2. Buckland, Frank. 1927, "Settlement at L'Anse au Sable," *OHS 2*, p.16.

3. Haughton spelling Houghton.

4. Powley. 1958, *History of Winfield*, p.16.

5. Ibid., p.16.

6. Ibid., p.16.

7. Tutt. 1959, *The History of the Ellison District 1858-1958*, Ellison Centennial Committee, Kelowna Printing Company, p.12.

8. *Vernon News*, 27 February 1902.

9. Swalwell, Jane. 1939, "Girlhood Days in Okanagan," *OHS 8*, p.40.

10. Powley. 1958, p.15.

11. PABC Marriage Reel #B13888.

12. Rosie Williams 2000.

13. Roman Catholic Church Records.

14. *Vernon News*, 1 July 1909.

15. PABC Death Reel #B13112.

16. Roman Catholic Church Records.

17. Gail McAllister, granddaughter of Thomas Simpson and Elizabeth Christian.

18. PABC Marriage Reel #B11387.

19. Roman Catholic Church Records.

Steele Photos

Joseph	Herb Simpson
Maria & Jimmy	Gloria Seitsma
Mary	Ada Froehlich
Steele Family	Gloria Seitsma
Steele Family	Shirley Louis

STEELE

1. Family tree: Abel Death Journal Canada Census 1891, DIA 1920-46, PABC Death Reel #: William 40 1944 B13163, Martina 4 1924 B13378, William James Steele 2 1930 B13140, Joseph 53 1971 B13311, Elizabeth 66 1952 B13377.

2. The Old West. 1977, *The Canadians*, Time Life Books, Alexandria, Virginia.

3. 1936. *OHS 6*, p.14.

Tonasket Photos

Johnny	OKIB Photo File-not numbered
Julia & grandson	Barbara Marchand Collection
Casimir	OKIB Photo File-not numbered
Tonasket girls and friends	Isabelle Burgemaster
Susan and John	Isabelle Burgemaster

TONASKET

1. Family tree: Maria Brent, PABC Death Reel #: Martin 14 1929 B13361, Julia 81 1966 B13279.

2. Martin Wilson, Dave Parker, Clara Dubrett.

3. Brent. 1966, p.111.

4. Ibid., p.112.

5. Teit, James A. and Frank Boaz. 1975, pp.264-5.

6. Raufer, Ilma. 1966, *Black Robes and Indians on the Last Frontier*, Statesman-Examiner Publishing, Colville, Washington, p.115.

7. Raufer. p.115.

8. Ibid., p.115.

9. Ibid., p.74.

10. Mourning Dove. 1990, p.120.
11. Raufer. 1966, p.116.
12. Ibid., p.116.
13. Brent.1966, p.112.
14. Ibid., p.112.
15. Roman Catholic Church Records.
16. Roman Catholic Church Records.

Williams Photos

Old William	Lucy McCormick
Maria	Rosie Williams
Willie / Joe Abel / Albert	Mary Abel Collection
Walter	Bertha Phelan
Harold	Bertha Phelan
Willie's Home	Shirley Louis

WILLIAMS

1. Family tree: Abel Death Journal, Head of the Lake Cemetery List, PABC Death Reel #: Maria 32 1921, B13359, Walter Williams (Louis) 1926.
2. Rosie Williams 2000.
3. Edward Fred 1998.
4. Tommy Gregoire 1999.
5. Royal Commission into Indian Affairs, Okanagan Agency 1913, p.15.
6. Lucy McCormick,Vernon, BC.

Wilson Photos

Celina & George	Lawrence Wilson
Henry	Mary Abel Collection
Celina & George	OKIB Photo File-not numbered
Eddie	Mary Abel Collection
Enoch	Ranger Robins

WILSON

1. Family tree: Abel Death Journal, PABC Death Reel #: Eileen 18 1948 B13376, Indian Act Inquiry 1952. Greater Vernon Museum and Archives.
2. Roman Catholic Church Records.
3. PABC Marriage Reel #B13888.
4. Hugh Campbell Brown. Greater Vernon Museum and Archives.

Qsapi	q'əsapíʔ	long ago	6
Okanagan	ukanaqín	bringing something to top or head of	10
Inkampulux	nk'mápəlks	head of Okanagan Lake	10
Chaptilk	captíkʷɬ	legends	10
N'kwala	n'kʷalaʔ	Chiefs' name	10
Secwepemc	síxʷapmx	Shuswap Tribe	13
Nespelem	nəspíləm	Southern Okanagan tribe Washington State	14
Sinquilten	sənc'əq'íltən	to make ammunition	14
Inkameep	nk'míp	bottom of lake system	14
Similkameen	sməlqmíx	Smilkameen Valley	15
atklokem	aksƛ'uk'əm	Winfield	15
atchlutus	acɬuc'us	Peninsula going across Oyama	15
Smitkan	smítqn	Man's name	15
Nkakukum	nqixʷlxəm	Sucker Creek	16
	ncəqaqiwləm	Okanagan Landing	16
Kalamalka	kəlmaxka	name of Lake	16

Nahun	nahun	look back over whole valley	16
Snoheokeuten	sníxwxʷiewtən	Short's Creek	16
Twakaweeten	tqʔʷaqʔʷaqíntn	Sugar Loaf Mountain	16
N'klanum	nqʷəɫínəm	Birch all the way from the lake	16
Pukkapeeksasun	pəqpqísaʔxən	White rock	16
Nkuxpeena	nc'əc'q'ɫapína?k	patch of fir trees	16
spuxmlees	cp'əp'λ'əmíʔs	end of bush	16
Inuxskeetuk	nˁaʔstqʷítaʔkʷ	little spring water coming out	17
Sntootun	sənλ'uxuxtan	Six Mile Creek area	17
Komasket	qʔʷumasq'ət	horn/antler in the sky	17
Kailpth	x̌əx̌áyt	holy thorns	17
Isinsoolouw	n'səsulaʔxʷ	Dry Creek	17
Neehoot	níxʷt	Deep Creek	17
Inkulteekun	tqəltíkn	top of hill	18
axseeptcn	sp'íp'c'ən	Rope Ranch	18
Inskepulch	n'ɫkapəlks	bush or swamp at end of lake	18
Intuklukaloo	n'λ'uλ'uk'ˁalʔxʷ	mud hole	18
Inswakeetlup	sxʷəxʷankíɫaʔp	thorns	18

SnMarceltn	sənMarcəltn	where Marcel lives	18
Intaseequawitsp	n'k'ək'síta'kʷ	dirty lake	18
Snkulkan	sənqaltkan	reach the top	18
Snhoolow	sənluxʷəla'xʷ	hollow	18
axtswin	sc'uwín	Bony fish	18
Inteeteex	ntítyix	they are fat	18
Sookin	sk'əqín	A draw on top /trail between Falkland and Chase	18
aklookameena	akɬxʷəxʷmína'	Fish lake	18
Neskonlith		Shuswap Reserve	18
N'Wha quisten	n'xʷaqʷa'stən F.M. Buckland	a stone for scraping and shaping weapons	19
Kelowna	ki'láwna' F.M.Buckland	Grizzly bear	19
So-remt	sur'imt	little snail shell	19
Qual-ulkh	kululalqʷ	tree burned by lightening	19
squilx	squalix	Reserve near Chase	23
Spapowcheen	spəpawcín	His voice echo's across the land	25

npoohkmen	npuxmən	Buffalo horn	25
Tonasket	kətunasq'ət	The sky is short of something	29
Kwolila	kᶦʷlila	Shuswap Chief	56
Wohollesicle		Okanagan Chief	56
Pelkamulox	p'əlk'mulaʔxʷ	Turning earth/ Okanagan Chief	56
Chilkposmen	cilkspusəm	Five hearts/ Okanagan Chief	56
Chwail	cwayɬx	Okanagan chief	56
Qway-um-qin	qʷaymqin	wealthy head	59
sqwr'han	skʷər'xan	crane	59
Squil-thil-kən		Man's name	59
Kr-lat-wmkren	OMI	Man's name	59
sorprenalks	sapxənálqs	something dress	59
Shumick	sumíx	animal spirit	60
komasket	qʾʷumasq'ət	Horn or antler in the sky	63
Sn-c-ca-mala?tn	səncəcmalaʔtn	where the children are	63
Qum-peetsa	k'əmpíc'aʔ	Woman's name	65
kamskasoulat	OMI	Man's name	65
Keslawistsa	OMI	Woman's name	65

Cepoulsalay	OMI	Woman's name	65
Tatupa	tʼatʼúpaʔ	great grandparent	66
Sneena	snínaʔ	owl	67
Sqwt-palqs	skʷətpalks	Woman's name	68
Kwitkweetasket	qʷayqʷaytasqʼət	Man's name	71
Wscumnelqs		Woman's name	78
Senklip	sənkʼlíp	coyote	78
Qwunlpitsa	qʷənɬpícʼaʔ	tattered blanket	78
Klekampitsa	kɬkʼəmpícʼaʔ	evening shadows	78
hapa	hˤápa	grampa	82
Qwithumlukn		Man's name	82
Chchookin		man's name	83
Sowlowat		Man's name	89
Skukeela		Man's name	89
Qwilchana	qʷuilcna	Nicola Valley	96
Inceaqwelps	nyirʼqʼʷ ïlps	twisted neck	93
Agnes	achtmis	Woman's name	95
Sqwnwtxnalqs	skʷənmtxənálqs	dress changes colour	98

Incowsoolah	snqʷʼasúlaʔxʷ	come in, I'm making pancakes	98
Sinklahootn			99
atmin	ʕaʕtmín	yellow bell	104
tetwit	tətwit	boy	104
hehotum	xixuʔtem	girl	104
Newslasket	DIA/ OMI	Woman's surname	109
Ahoolah	DIA	Chief's name	109
Chevely	DIA	Chief's name	109
Arlchelqua	OMI	Woman's surname	113
Sumleah	sʔumlaʔxʷ	Man's name	117
Sitpeetsa	sətpícʼaʔ	Woman's	117
Tchlopa	cʼlʼupa	old man	117
Kemitiken	DIA/ Carstons	Chief's name	123
Sappel	OMI		128
Amap		Man's name	128
Sukomelelks	James Teit	Woman's name	253
Stlakem	OMI	Woman's surname	253
Skmkeest	skəmxíst	bear	132
Kikinee	kikni	fish	133
Whychoochin	way cuncín	I already told you	133

Krenamalkra/	OMI	Man's name	138
Kalamalka	kəlmaxka	place name	138
Shamelitk	OMI	Woman's name	135
Cohastimene	DIA/ Victor	Man's name	135
Kwentek/ Kuintkou/ Kuintlou	qʷintkʷ	teal color	135
Clemah	DIA/OMI	Chief's name	136
K'lnkamuplux	nk'ək'mapəlks	head of small lake	136
Houstrashemreiken	OMI	Man's name	137
Chianwt	ciy-anút	Man's name	137
Skwe-t-nalkrs		Woman's name	137
Horolsiken	OMI		137
Stelkia	xʷistalk'iyaʔ	Surname/ Osoyoos/ Oliver	138
Spallumcheen		Shuswap area	138
Ahoolah	DIA	Woman's surname	138
Koiatumkan		Man's name	143
Tslakan / Logan	sƛ'akan	Man's name	147
Chista	c'ísta	Man's nick name	147
Baptiste	pachise	Man's name	147

Sqwilpelks		Woman's name	150
Umtoosoola	Douglas Ross	Man's name	155
Simlimtitach	DIA	Woman's surname	155
Twohympt		Woman's name	155
Shuyalsht	DIA (súʔyalst)	Woman's surname	156
Xcooscasa		Hair on the chest	158
Kinkinahwa	kənkanaxwa	Salmon Chief	163
Impaweecan	np'əp'aʔxʷíkən	light on the back	163
Klapilkan	klˤapílxkən	put something on horns	163
husem	sxʷusəm	soap berries	168
Klasakee/ Hlakay	Peter Carstens	Pierre Michel	175
Quintasket	tqʷíntasq'ət	touching the sky	177
Inkameep	nk'míp	Place name	177
En-hwx-kwas-t'nun	nxʷaqʷaʔstən	place name	178
Pah-tah-heet-sa	ˤax̌əx̌píc'aʔ	Woman's name	178
Sqee-elks	sqʷayalqs	blue dress	179
Koweseetsa	kʷəsíc'aʔ	singe hair off groundhog	181
Qweemkin	kʷʼíymqín	frost on top of mountain	181

Squalkin	sqalxən	Man's name	181
Katamintim	k'aʔtmíntəm	get close	181
Anyes		Woman's name	182
Skitikiilɔw	scaqəqulaʔxʷ	Man's name set on ground	183
skishislahw	sk'əsíslaʔxʷ	man's name sticks on ground	183
Sylhimpt	clx̌imtkʷ	Woman's name	184
Phillip	pleep	Man's name	184
Inclimclapish	nɬəmɬəmils	Man's name / kind hearted	184
Camstoochulst	xˤamcusəlst	breeze from the heart	184
Tsalipa	c'aˤlípa	solid or pine pitch stump	184
Tskaskooskin	c'kaskusxən	big toes	184
Arcut	DIA(aqat)	Woman's name	187
Supee	Sophie	Woman's name	187
Sasapeen	Josephine	Woman's name	188
Snsnkanult		Man's name	189

MARQUIS

Marquis Book Printing Inc.

Québec, Canada
2008